DARDISTAN

IN

1866, 1886 AND 1893

BEING

AN ACCOUNT OF THE HISTORY, RELIGIONS, CUSTOMS, LEGENDS, FABLES AND SONGS OF GILGIT, CHILAS, KANDIA (GABRIAL), DASIN, CHITRAL, HUNSA, NAGYR AND OTHER PARTS OF THE HINDUKUSH

AS ALSO A SUPPLEMENT TO THE SECOND EDITION OF

THE HUNZA AND NAGYR HANDBOOK

AND AN EPITOME OF

PART III. OF THE AUTHOR'S "THE LANGUAGES AND RACES OF DARDISTAN

DARDISTAN

IN

1866, 1886 AND 1893

BEING

AN ACCOUNT OF THE HISTORY, RELIGIONS, CUSTOMS, LEGENDS, FABLES AND SONGS OF GILGIT, CHILAS, KANDIA (GABRIAL), DASIN, CHITRAL, HUNSA, NAGYR AND OTHER PARTS OF THE HINDUKUSH

AS ALSO A SUPPLEMENT TO THE SECOND EDITION OF

THE HUNZA AND NAGYR HANDBOOK

AND AN EPITOME OF

PART III. OF THE AUTHOR'S "THE LANGUAGES AND RACES OF DARDISTAN

G. W. LEITNER

(WITH APPENDICES ON RECENT EVENTS,

A MAP AND NUMEROUS ILLUSTRATIONS.)

GYAN

Published by

GYAN

Gyan Publishing House
5, Ansari Road
Daryaganj, New Delhi-110002
Phone: 011-47034999, 9811692060
E-mail: books@gyanbooks.com

Distribution Network
gyanbooks.com
India, USA, Canada, UK, Australia, France

ISBN : 978-81-212-3293-7 (PB)
First Published, 1890

2nd Impression 2020

Printed at: Gyan Press, Delhi.

Dardistan in 1866, 1886 and 1893
Author: G. W. Leitner

DARDISTAN IN 1866, 1886 AND 1893

BEING

An Account of the History, Religions, Customs, Legends, Fables, and Songs of Gilgit, Chilás, Kandiá (Gabriál), Yasin, Chitrál, Hunza, Nagyr and other Parts of the Hindukush,

AS ALSO A SUPPLEMENT TO THE SECOND EDITION OF

THE HUNZA AND NAGYR HANDBOOK

(*printed by the Government of India in 1889*),

AND AN EPITOME OF

PART III. OF THE AUTHOR'S "THE LANGUAGES AND RACES OF DARDISTAN."

BY

G. W. LEITNER, M.A., PH.D., LL.D., D.O.L., ETC.,
OF THE MIDDLE TEMPLE, BARRISTER-AT-LAW,
DEPUTED BY THE PANJAB GOVERNMENT IN 1866 ON A MISSION OF LINGUISTIC ENQUIRY TO KASHMIR AND CHILÁS,
LATE ON SPECIAL DUTY WITH THE GOVERNMENT OF INDIA IN THE FOREIGN DEPARTMENT.

(*WITH APPENDICES ON RECENT EVENTS, A MAP, AND NUMEROUS ILLUSTRATIONS.*)

TEXT AND APPENDICES 254 PAGES.

PUBLISHING DEPARTMENT:
ORIENTAL UNIVERSITY INSTITUTE, WOKING.
ENGLAND.

CONTENTS.

LIST OF ILLUSTRATIONS.

Illustrations in the Text.

Illustrations in the Appendices.

A NOTE ON CLASSICAL ALLUSIONS TO THE DARDS AND TO GREEK INFLUENCE ON INDIA.

THE DARDS.

Herodotus (III. 102-105) is the first author who refers to the country of the Dards, placing it on the frontier of Kashmir and in the vicinity of Afghanistan. "Other Indians are those who reside on the frontiers of the town 'Kaspatyros' and the Paktyan country; they dwell to the north of the other Indians and live like the Baktrians; they are also the most warlike of the Indians and are sent for the gold," etc. Then follows the legend of the gold-digging ants (which has been shown to have been the name of a tribe of Tibetans by Schiern), and on which, as an important side-issue, consult Strabo, Arrian, Dio Chrysostomus, Flavius Philostratus the elder, Clemens Alexandrinus, Ælian, Harpokration, Themistius Euphrades, Heliodorus of Emesa, Joannes Tzetzes, the Pseudo-Kallisthenes and the scholiast to the Antigone of Sophocles* — and among Romans, the poems of Propertius, the geography of Pomponius Mela, the natural history of the elder Pliny and the collections of Julius Solinus.† The Mahabharata also mentions the tribute of the ant-gold "paipilika" brought by the nations of the north to one of the Pandu sons, king Yudhisthira.

In another place Herodotus [IV. 13-27] again mentions the town of Kaspatyros and the Paktyan country. This is where he refers to the anxiety of Darius to ascertain the flow of the Indus into the sea. He accordingly sent Skylax with vessels. "They started from the town of Κασπάτυρος and the Πακτυική χώρη towards the east to the sea." I take this to be the point where the Indus river makes a sudden bend, and for the first time actually does lie between Kashmir and Pakhtu-land (for this, although long unknown, must be the country alluded to),‡ in other words, below the Makpon-i-Shang-Rong, and at Bunji, where the Indus becomes navigable.§ The Paktyes are also mentioned as one of the races that followed Xerxes in his invasion of Hellas (Herod. VII. 67-85). Like our own geographers till 1866, Herodotus thought that the Indus from that point flowed duly from north to south, and India being, according to his system of geography, the most easterly country, the flow of the Indus was accordingly described as being easterly. I, in 1866, and Hayward in 1870, described its flow from that point to be due west for a considerable distance (about one hundred miles). (The PAKTYES are, of course, the Afghans, called Patans, or more properly PAKHTUS, the very same Greek word). "Kaspatyros" is evidently a mis-spelling for "Kaspapyros," the form in which the name occurs in one of the most acccurate codes of

* Strabo II. I., XV. I.—Arrian de Exped. Alex. V. 4 Indica c. 5.—Dio-Chrysos. Orat. XXXV.—Philostrat. de vitâ Apollon. Tyan. VI. I.—Clem. Alex. Paed, II. 12.—Aelian de Nat. An. XV. 14.—Harpokrat, s. v. χρυσοχοεῖν, Themist. Orat. XXVII.—Heliodor. X. 26.—Tzetz. Chil. XII. 330-340.—Pseudo Kallisth. II. 29.—Schol. ad Sophocl. Antig., v. 1,025.

† Propert. Eleg. III. 13.—Pomp. Mel. III. 7.—Plin. H. N. XI. 36, XXXIII. 21.—Solin, c. 30.

‡ Indeed, there *is* no other country between Kaspatyros and the Paktyan country excepting Dardistan.

§ This is the Bunji of recent Chilás fights (1893).

Herodotus which belonged to Archbishop Sancroft (the Codex Sancrostianus) and which is now preserved at Emmanuel College, Cambridge. Stephanus Byzantianus (A. V.) also ascribes this spelling to Hekatœus of Miletus.*

Now Kaspapyros or Kaspapuros is evidently *Kashmir* or "*Kasyapapura*," the town of *Kasyapa*, the founder of Kashmir, and to the present day one may talk indifferently of the town of Kashmir, or of the country of *Kashmir*, when mentioning that name, so that there is no necessity to seek for the *town* of Srinagar when discussing the term Kaspatyrus, or, if corrected, Kaspapuros, of Herodotus.

Herodotus, although he thus mentions the people (of the Dards) as one neighbouring (πλησιοχῶροι) on Kashmir and residing between Kashmir and Afghanistan, and also refers to the invasions which (from time immemorial it may be supposed, and certainly within our own times) this people have made against Tibet for the purpose of devastating the gold-fields of the so-called ants, does not use the name of "Dard" in the above quotations, but Strabo and the elder Pliny, who repeat the legend, mention the very name of that people as *Derdæ* or *Dardæ*, vide Strabo XV., ἐν Δέρδαις ἔθνει μεγάλῳ τῶν προσεώων καὶ ὀρεινῶν Ἰνδῶν. Pliny, in his Natural History, XI. 36, refers to "*in regione Septentrionalium Indorum, qui Dardæ vacantur.*" Both Pliny and Strabo refer to Megasthenes as their authority in Chapter VI., 22. Pliny again speaks of "*Fertilissimi sunt auri Dardæ.*" The Dards have still settlements in Tibet where they are called Brokhpa (see page 60 of text). The Dards are the "Darada" of the Sanscrit writers. The "Darada" and the "Himavanta" were the regions to which Buddha sent his missionaries, and the Dards are finally the "Dards, an independent people which plundered Dras in the last year, has its home in the mountains three or four days' journey distant, and talks the *Pakhtu* or DARADI language. Those, whom they take prisoners in these raids, they sell as slaves" (as they do still). (Voyage par Mir Izzetulla in 1812 in Klaproth's Magasin Asiatique, II., 3-5.) (The above arrangement of quotations is due to Schiern.)†

INFLUENCE OF GREECE ON ASIA IN GENERAL AND INDIA IN PARTICULAR.

The most important contribution to this question, however, is Plutarch's *Speech* on Alexander's fortune and virtue (περὶ Ἀλεξάνδρου τύχης καὶ ἀρετῆς), the keynote to which may be found in the passage which contains the assertion that he Κατέσπειρε τὴν Ἀσίαν ἑλληνικοῖς τέλεσι, but the whole speech refers to that marvellous influence.

That this influence was at any rate believed in, may be also gathered from a passage in Aelian, in which he speaks of the Indians and Persian kings singing Homer in their own tongues. I owe the communication of this passage to Sir Edward Fry, Q.C., which runs as follows: Ὅτι Ἰνδοὶ τῇ παρὰ σφίσιν ἐπιχωριά φωνῇ τά Ὁμήρου μεταγράψαντες ᾄδουσιν οὐ μόνοι, ἀλλὰ

* General A. Cunningham very kindly sent me the quotation last year. It runs as follows: Κασπάπυρος πόλις Γανδαρική, Σκυθῶν ἀκτή.

† Who refers to my "Results of a Tour in Dardistan, Kashmir, Little Tibet, Ladak, etc., in 1867-70," and other papers in his pamphlet on the origin of that legend.

καὶ οἱ Περσῶν βασιλεῖς εἴ τι χρὴ πιστεύειν τοῖς ὑπὲρ τούτων ἱστοροῦσι.—Aeliani Variæ Historiæ, Lib. XII., Cap. 48. [I find from a note in my edition that Dio Chrysostom tells the same story of the Indians in his 53rd Oration.—E. F.]

I trust to be able to show, if permitted to do so, in a future note (1) that the Aryan dialects of Dardistan are, at least, contemporaneous with Sanskrit, (2) that the Khajuná is a remnant of a prehistoric language, (3) that certain sculptors followed on Alexander's invasion and taught the natives of India to execute what I first termed "Græco-Buddhistic" sculptures, a term which specifies a distinct period in history and in the history of Art. G. W. LEITNER.

P.S. in 1893.—The above, which appeared in "the Calcutta Review" of January 1878, was also reprinted in the *Asiatic Quarterly Review* of April 1893 with reference to Mr. J. W. McCrindle's recent work on "Ancient India: Its Invasion by Alexander the Great," in which he omits to draw attention to the importance of Plutarch's *Speech* on the civilizing results of Alexander's invasion, and makes no mention whatever of the traces which Greek art has left on the Buddhistic sculptures of the Panjab.

He only just mentions Plutarch's speech on page 13 of his otherwise excellent work, published by Messrs. Constable of 14 Parliament Street, London. As that speech, which is divided into two parts, is, however, of the utmost importance in showing what were believed to be in Plutarch's days the results of Alexander's mission, I think it necessary to quote some of the most prominent passages from it relating to the subject under inquiry. I also propose to show in a monograph on the græco-buddhistic sculptures, now at the Woking Museum, which I brought from beyond the Panjab frontier, that Alexander introduced not only Greek Art but also Greek mythology into India. I will specially refer to the "Pallas Athene," "the rape of Ganymede," and "the Centaur" in my collection, leaving such sculptures as "Olympian games," "Greek soldiers accompanying Buddhist processions," "the Buddhist Parthenon," [if not also Silanion's "Sappho with the lyre,"]—all executed by Indian artists—to tell their own tale as to the corroborations in sculpture of passages in ancient Greek and Roman writers relating to the genial assimilation of Eastern with Western culture which the Great Conqueror of the Two Continents, "the possessor of two horns," the "Zu'l-Qarnein" (Al-Asghar) of the Arabs, endeavoured to bring about.

The following passages from Plutarch's Speech may, I hope, be read with interest. The author endeavours to answer his question as to whether Alexander owed his success "to his fortune or to his virtue" by showing that he was almost solely indebted to his good qualities:

"The discipline of Alexander . . . oh marvellous philosophy, through which the Indians worship the Greek gods."

"When Alexander had recivilized Asia, they read Homer and the children of the Persians . . . sang the tragedies of Euripides and Sophocles." "Socrates was condemned in Athens because he introduced foreign Gods . . . but, through Alexander, Bactria and the Caucasus worshipped the

Greek Gods." "Few among us, as yet, read the laws of Plato, but myriads of men use, and have used, those of Alexander, the vanquished deeming themselves more fortunate than those who had escaped his arms, for the latter had no one who saved them from the miseries of life, whilst the conqueror had forced the conquered to live happily."

"Plato only wrote one form of Government and not a single man followed it because it was too severe, whereas Alexander founded more than 70 cities among barbarous nations and permeating Asia with Hellenic Institutions. . ." Plutarch makes the conquered say that if they had not been subdued "Egypt would not have had Alexandria nor India Bucephalia," that "Alexander made no distinction between Greek and Barbarian, but considered the virtuous only among either as Greek and the vicious as Barbarian" and that he by "intermarriages and the adaptation of customs and dresses sought to found that union which he considered himself as sent from heaven to bring about as the arbitrator and the reformer of the universe." "Thus do the wise unite Asia and Europe." "By the adoption of (Asiatic) dress, the minds were conciliated." Alexander desired that "One common justice should administer the Republic of the Universe."

"He disseminated Greece and diffused throughout the world justice and peace." Alexander himself announces to the Greeks, "Through me you will know them (the Indians) and they will know you, but I must yet strike coins and stamp the bronze of the barbarians with Greek impressions." The fulfilment of this statement is attested by the Bactrian coins. I submit that he who left his mark on metal did so also on sculpture, as I have endeavoured to show since 1870 when I first called my finds "græco-buddhistic," a term which has, at last, been adopted after much opposition, as descriptive of a period in History and in the history of Art and Religion.

[The above quotations are all from the 1st Part of Plutarch's oration; the second is reserved for the proposed monograph.]

G. W. Leitner.

For "Divisions of the Dard Race" and the countries which they occupy see page 58.

FIRST GROUP OF DARDS, ETC., TAKEN IN 1866.

GHULÁM MUHAMMAD, OF GILGIT (A SHIAH MUHAMMADAN). GHARIB SHAH AND FRIEND, BOTH OF CHILÁS (SUNNI MUHAMMADANS). MIRZA BEG, OF ASTOR (SUNNI). KÁZIM, FROM SKARDO (LITTLE TIBET) (SHIAH). MALEK AND BATSHU, (KALÁSHA AND BASHGALI KAFIRS) (SUBJECTS OF CHITRÁL).

LEGENDS, SONGS, AND CUSTOMS OF DARDISTAN,*

(GILGIT, YASIN, HUNZA, NAGYR, CHITRÁL, &C., AND KAFIRISTAN).

I. DARDU LEGENDS, *in Shiná* (the language, with dialectic modifications, of Gilgit, Astor, Guraiz, Chilás, Hódur, Dareyl, Tangír, etc., and the language of historical songs in Hunza and Nagyr).

(Committed to writing for the first time in 1866,
By DR. G. W. LEITNER,
from the dictation of Dards. This race has no written character of its own.)

A.—DEMONS = YATSH [1] (YUECCI ?).

DEMONS are of a gigantic size, and have only *one eye, which is on the forehead.* They used to rule over the mountains and oppose the cultivation of the soil by man. They often dragged people away into their recesses. Since the adoption of the Muhammadan religion, the demons have relinquished their possessions, and only occasionally trouble the believers.

They do not walk by day, but confine themselves to promenading at night. A spot is shown near Astor, at a village called Bulent, where five large mounds are pointed out which have somewhat the shape of huge baskets. Their existence is explained as follows. A Zemindar (cultivator) at Grukōt, a village farther on, on the Kashmir road, had, with great trouble, sifted his grain for storing, and had put it into baskets and sacks. He then went away. The demons came—five in number—carrying huge leather

* "Dardistan," or the country of the Daradas of Hindu mythology, embraces, in the narrowest sense of the term, the Shiná-speaking countries (Gilgit, &c.); in a wider sense, Hunza, Nagyr, Yasin, and Chitrál; and in the widest, also parts of Kafiristan. (See my "Dardistan," part III.)

[1] "Yatsh" means "bad" in Kashmiri.

sacks, into which they put the grain. They then went to a place which is still pointed out and called "*Gué* Gutumé Yatsheyn gau boki," or "The place of the demons' loads at the hollow"—Gué being the Shiná name for the present village of Grukōt. There they brought up a huge flat stone—which is still shown—and made it into a kind of pan, "tawa," for the preparation of bread. But the morning dawned and obliged them to disappear; they converted the sacks and their contents into earthen mounds, which have the shape of baskets and are still shown.

1.—The Wedding of Demons.

A Shikari (sportsman) was once hunting in the hills. He had taken provisions with him for five days. On the sixth day he found himself without any food. Excited and fatigued by his fruitless expedition, he wandered into the deepest mountain recesses, careless whither he went as long as he could find water to assuage his thirst, and a few wild berries to allay his hunger. Even that search was unsuccessful, and, tired and hungry, he endeavoured to compose himself to sleep. Even that comfort was denied him, and, nearly maddened with the situation, he again arose and looked around him. It was the first or second hour of night, and, at a short distance, he descried a large fire blazing a most cheerful welcome to the hungry, and now chilled, wanderer. He approached it quietly, hoping to meet some other sportsman who might provide him with food. Coming near the fire, he saw a very large and curious assembly of giants, eating, drinking, and singing. In great terror, he wanted to make his way back, when one of the assembly, who had a squint in his eye, got up for the purpose of fetching water for the others. He overtook him, and asked him whether he was a "child of man." Half dead with terror, he could scarcely answer that he was, when the demon invited him to join them at the meeting, which was described to be a wedding party. The Shikari replied: "You are a demon, and will destroy me"; on which the spirit took an oath, *by the sun and the moon*, that he certainly would not do so. He then hid him under a bush and went back with the water. He had scarcely returned when a plant was torn out of the ground and a small aperture was made, into which the giants managed to throw all their property, and, gradually making themselves thinner and thinner, themselves vanished into the ground through it. Our sportsman was then taken by the hand by the friendly demon, and, before he knew how, he himself glided through the hole and found himself in a huge apartment, which was splendidly illuminated. He was placed in a corner where he could not be observed. He received some food, and gazed in mute astonishment on the assembled spirits. At last, he saw the mother of the bride taking her daughter's head into her lap and weeping bitterly at the prospect of her departure into another household. Unable to control her grief, and in compliance with an old Shîn custom, she began the singing of the evening by launching into the following strains:

SONG OF THE MOTHER.

ORIGINAL:—

Ajjeyn Biráni![2] *mey palise, shikk sanéy,*
(Thy) mother's Biráni! my little darling, ornaments will wear,
Inne Buldar Bútshe angai tapp bey hani,
(Whilst) here at Buldar Bútshe the heavens dark will become;
Nágeri Phall Tshátshe Kani mirâni in,
The Nagari (of race) Phall Tshátshe of Khans the prince will come,
Têyn Mîrkân málose tshê gûm bagéy,
Thy Mirkan father-from new corn will be distributed.
Sátti Yabeo wey bo! Shadú Malik bojum thêum.
Seven rivers' water be! Shadu Malik a going will make,
Tey Mirkann malo Tshe gi bage.
Thy Mirkann, father, now ghee will distribute.

TRANSLATION:—

"Oh, Biráni, thy mother's own; thou, little darling, wilt wear ornaments, whilst to me, who will remain here at Buldar Butshe, the heavens will appear dark. The prince of Lords of Phall Tshatshe race is coming from Nagyr; and Mirkann, thy father, now distributes corn (as an act of welcome). Be (as fruitful and pleasant) as the water of *seven rivers*, for Shadu Malik (the prince) is determined to start, and now thy father Mirkann is distributing ghee (as a compliment to the departing guest)."

---

[2] The father's name was Mir Khan. The daughter's name was Birani. The bridegroom's name was Shadu Malik of Nagyr, of Phall Tshatshe race, and the place of the wedding was Buldar Butshe.

The Shikari began to enjoy the scene and would have liked to have stayed, but his squinting friend told him now that he could not be allowed to remain any longer. So he got up, but before again vanishing through the above-mentioned aperture into the human world, he took a good look at the demons. To his astonishment he beheld on the shoulders of one a shawl which he had safely left at home. Another held his gun; a third was eating out of his own dishes; one had his many-coloured stockings on, and another disported himself in pidjamas (drawers) which he only ventured to put on, on great occasions. He also saw many of the things that had excited his admiration among the property of his neighbours in his native village, being most familiarly used by the demons. He scarcely could be got to move away, but his friendly guide took hold of him and brought him again to the place where he had first met him. On taking leave he gave him three loaves of bread. As his village was far off, he consumed two of the loaves on the road. On reaching home, he found his father, who had been getting rather anxious at his prolonged absence. To him he told all that had happened, and showed him the remaining loaf, of which the old man ate half. His mother, a good housewife, took the remaining half and threw it into a large granary, where, as it was the season of Sharó (autumn), a sufficient store of flour had been placed for the use of the family during the winter. Strange to say, that half-loaf brought luck, for demons mean it sometimes kindly to the children of men, and only hurt them when they consider themselves offended. The granary remained always full, and the people of the village rejoiced with the family, for they were liked and were good people.

It also should be told that as soon as the Shikari came home he looked after his costly shawl, dishes, and clothes, but he found all in its proper place and perfectly uninjured. On inquiring amongst his neighbours he also found that they too had not lost anything. He was much astonished at all this, till an old woman who had a great reputation for wisdom, told him that this was the custom of demons, and that they invariably borrowed the property of mankind for their weddings, and as invariably restored it. On occasions of rejoicings amongst them they felt kindly towards mankind.

Thus ends one of the prettiest tales that I have heard.

2.—The Demon's Present of Coals is Turned into Gold.

Something similar to what has just been related, is said to have happened at Doyur, on the road from Gilgit to Nagyr. A man of the name of Phûko had a son named Laskirr, who, one day going out to fetch water was caught by a Yatsh, who tore up a plant (" reeds " ?) " phuru " and entered with the lad into the fissure which was thereby created. He brought him to a large palace in which a number of goblins, male and female, were diverting themselves. He there saw all the valuables of the inhabitants of his village. A wedding was being celebrated and the mother sang :—

Gúm bagé déy, Buduléy Khatúni.
Gúm bagé déy, huhá huhá ! !
Gí bagé déy, Buduléy Khatúnise.
Gí bagé déy, huhá huhá ! !
Motz bagé déy, Buduléy Khatúni.
Motz bagé déy, huhá huhá ! !
Mô bagé déy, huhá huhá ! ! &c., &c.

Translation :—

Corn is being distributed, daughter of Budul.
Corn is being distributed, hurrah ! hurrah ! (*Chorus.*)
Ghee is being distributed, &c. (*Chorus.*)
Meat is being distributed, &c. (*Chorus.*)
Wine is being distributed, &c., &c. (*Chorus.*)

On his departure, the demon gave him a sackful of coals, and conducted him through the aperture made by the tearing up of the reed, towards his village. The moment the demon had left, the boy emptied the sack of the coals and went home, when he told his father what had happened. In the emptied sack they found a small bit of coal, which, as soon as they touched it, became a gold coin, very much to the regret of the boy's father, who would have liked his son to have brought home the whole sackful.

B.—"Barai," "Peris," "Fairies."

They are handsome, in contradistinction to the Yatsh or Demons, and stronger; they have a beautiful castle on the top of the Nanga Parbat or Dyarmul (so called from being inaccessible). This castle is made of crystal, and the people fancy they can see it. They call it "Shell-batte-kōt" or "Castle of Glass-stone."

1.—The Sportsman and the Castle of the Fairies.

Once a sportsman ventured up the Nanga Parbat. To his surprise he found no difficulty, and venturing farther and farther, he at last reached the top. There he saw a beautiful castle made of glass, and pushing one of the doors he entered it, and found himself in a most magnificent apartment. Through it he saw an open space that appeared to be the garden of the castle, but there was in it only one tree of excessive height, and which was entirely composed of pearls and corals. The delighted sportsman filled his sack in which he carried his corn, and left the place, hoping to enrich himself by the sale of the pearls. As he was going out of the door he saw an innumerable crowd of serpents following him. In his agitation he shouldered the sack and attempted to run, when a pearl fell out. It was eagerly swallowed by a serpent which immediately disappeared. The sportsman, glad to get rid of his pursuers at any price, threw pearl after pearl to them, and in every case it had the desired effect. At last, only one serpent remained, but for her (a fairy in that shape?) he found no pearl; and urged on by fear, he hastened to his village, Tarsing, which is at the very foot of the Nanga Parbat. On entering his house, he found it in great agitation; bread was being distributed to the poor as they do at funerals, for his family had given him up as lost. The serpent still followed and stopped at the door. In despair, the man threw the corn-sack at her, when lo! a pearl glided out. It was eagerly swallowed by the serpent, which immediately disappeared. However, the man was not the same being as before. He was ill for days, and in about a fortnight after the events narrated, died, for fairies never forgive a man who has surprised their secrets.

2.—The Fairy who Punished her Human Lover.

It is not believed in Astor that fairies ever marry human beings, but in Gilgit there is a legend to that effect. A famous sportsman, Kibá Lorí, who never returned empty-handed from any excursion, kept company with a fairy to whom he was deeply attached. Once in the hot weather the fairy said to him not to go out shooting during "the seven days of the summer," "Caniculars," which are called "Bardá," and are supposed to be the hottest days in Dardistan. "I am," said she, "obliged to leave you for that period, and, mind, you do not follow me." The sportsman promised obedience and the fairy vanished, saying that he would certainly die if he attempted to follow her. Our love-intoxicated Nimrod, however, could not endure her absence. On the fourth day he shouldered his gun and went out with the hope of meeting her. Crossing a range, he came upon a plain, where he saw an immense gathering of game of all sorts and his beloved fairy milking a "Kill" (markhor) and gathering the milk into a silver vessel. The noise which Kibá Lorí made caused the animal to start and to strike out with his legs, which upset the silver vessel. The fairy looked up, and to her anger beheld the disobedient lover. She went up to him and, after reproaching him, struck him in the face. But she had scarcely done so when despair mastered her heart, and she cried out in the deepest anguish that "he now must die within four days." "However," she said, "do shoot one of these animals, so that people may not say that you have returned empty-handed." The poor man returned crestfallen to his home, lay down, and died on the fourth day.

C.—Dayall = Wizards and Witches.

The gift of second sight, or rather the intercourse with fairies, is confined to a few families in which it is hereditary. The wizard is made to inhale the fumes of a fire which is lit with the wood of the *tshilí*[3] (Panjabi = Padam), a kind

[3] Elsewhere called *tshi.*

of fir-wood which gives much smoke. Into the fire the milk of a white sheep or goat is poured. The wizard inhales the smoke till he apparently becomes insensible. He is then taken on the lap of one of the spectators, who sings a song which restores him to his senses. In the meanwhile, a goat is slaughtered, and the moment the fortune-teller jumps up, its bleeding neck is presented to him, which he sucks as long as a drop remains. The assembled musicians then strike up a great noise, and the wizard rushes about in the circle which is formed round him and talks unintelligibly. The fairy then appears at some distance and sings, which, however, only the wizard hears. He then communicates her sayings in a song to one of the musicians, who explains its meaning to the people. The wizard is called upon to foretell events and to give advice in cases of illness, etc. The people believe that in ancient times these Dayalls invariably spoke correctly, but that now scarcely one saying in a hundred turns out to be true. Wizards do not now make a livelihood by their talent, which is considered its own reward.

There are few legends so exquisite as the one which chronicles the origin, or rather the rise, of Gilgit. The traditions regarding Alexander the Great, which Vigne and others have imagined to exist among the people of Dardistan, are unknown to, at any rate, the Shiná race, excepting in so far as any Munshi accompanying the Maharajah's troops may, perhaps, accidentally have referred to them in conversation with a Shîn. Any such information would have been derived frôm the Sikandarnama of Nizámi, and would, therefore, possess no original value. There exist nò ruins, as far as I have gone, to point to an occupation of Dardistan by the soldiers of Alexander. The following legend, however, which not only lives in the memories of all the Shîn people, whether they be Chilasis, Astoris, Gilgitis, or Brokhpá (the latter, as I discovered, living actually side by side with the Baltis in Little Tibet), but which also an annual festival commemorates, is not devoid of interest from either a historical or a purely literary point of view.

D.—Historical Legend of the Origin of Gilgit.

"Once upon a time there lived a race at Gilgit, whose origin is uncertain. Whether they sprang from the soil, or had immigrated from a distant region, is doubtful; so much is believed, that they were Gayupí = spontaneous, aborigines, unknown. Over them ruled a monarch who was a descendant of the evil spirits, the Yatsh, that terrorized over the world. His name was Shiribadatt, and he resided at a castle, in front of which there was a course for the performance of the manly game of Polo. (See my Hunza Nagyr Handbook.) His tastes were capricious, and in every one of his actions his fiendish origin could be discerned. The natives bore his rule with resignation, for what could they effect against a monarch at whose command even magic aids were placed? However, the country was rendered fertile, and round the capital bloomed attractive gardens.

"The heavens, or rather the virtuous Peris, at last grew tired of his tyranny, for he had crowned his iniquities by indulging in a propensity for cannibalism. This taste had been developed by an accident. One day his cook brought him some mutton broth, the like of which he had never tasted. After much inquiry as to the nature of the food on which the sheep had been brought up, it was eventually traced to an old woman, its first owner. She stated that her child and the sheep were born on the same day, and losing the former, she had consoled herself by suckling the latter. This was a revelation to the tyrant. He had discovered the secret of the palatability of the broth, and was determined to have a never-ending supply of it. So he ordered that his kitchen should be regularly provided with children of tender age, whose flesh, when converted into broth, would remind him of the exquisite dish he had once so much relished. This cruel order was carried out. The people of the country were dismayed at such a state of things, and sought slightly to improve it by sacrificing, in the first place, all orphans and children of neighbouring tribes! The tyrant, however, was insatiable, and soon was his cruelty felt by many families at Gilgit, who were compelled to give up their children to slaughter.

"Relief came at last. At the top of the mountain. Ko, which it takes a day to ascend, and which overlooks the village of Doyur, below Gilgit, on the side of the river, appeared three figures. They looked like men, but much more strong and handsome. In their arms they carried bows and arrows, and turning their eyes in the direction of Doyur, they perceived innumerable flocks of sheep and cattle grazing on a prairie between that village and the foot of the mountain. The strangers were fairies, and had come (perhaps from Nagyr ?) to this region with the view of ridding Gilgit of the monster that ruled over it. However, this intention was confined to the two elder ones. The three strangers were brothers, and none of them had been born at the same time. It was their intention to make Azru Shemsher, the youngest, Rajah of Gilgit, and, in order to achieve their purpose, they hit upon the following plan.

"On the already-noticed plain, which is called Didingé, a sportive calf was gamboling towards and away from its mother. It was the pride of its owner, and its brilliant red colour could be seen from a distance. 'Let us see who is the best marksman,' exclaimed the eldest, and saying this, he shot an arrow in the direction of the calf, but missed his aim. The second brother also tried to hit it, but also failed. At last, Azru Shemsher, who took a deep interest in the sport, shot his arrow, which pierced the poor animal from side to side and killed it. The brothers, whilst descending, congratulated Azru on his sportsmanship, and on arriving at the spot where the calf was lying, proceeded to cut its throat, and to take out from its body *the titbits, namely the kidneys and the liver*.

"They then roasted these delicacies, and invited Azru to partake of them first. He respectfully declined, on the ground of his youth; but they urged him to do so, 'in order,' they said, 'to reward you for such an excellent shot.' Scarcely had the meat touched the lips of Azru, than the brothers got up, and vanishing into the air, called out, 'Brother! you have touched impure food, which Peris never should eat, and we have made use of your ignorance of this law, because we want to make you a human being,[*] who shall rule over Gilgit ; remain therefore at Doyur.'

"Azru in deep grief at the separation, cried, 'Why remain at Doyur, unless it be to grind corn ?' 'Then,' said the brothers, 'go to Gilgit.' 'Why,' was the reply, 'go to Gilgit, unless it be to work in the gardens ?' 'No, no,' was the last and consoling rejoinder ; 'you will assuredly become the king of this country, and deliver it from its merciless oppressor.'

"No more was heard of the departing fairies, and Azru remained by himself, endeavouring to gather consolation from the great mission which had been bestowed on him. A villager met him, and, struck by his appearance, offered him shelter in his house. Next morning he went on the roof of his host's house, and calling out to him to come up, pointed to the Ko mountain, on which, he said, he plainly discerned a wild goat. The incredulous villager began to fear he had harboured a maniac, if no worse character ; but Azru shot off his arrow, and accompanied by the villager (who had assembled some friends for protection, as he was afraid his young guest might be an associate of robbers, and lead him into a trap), went in the direction of the mountain. There, to be sure, at the very spot that had been pointed out, though many miles distant, was lying the wild goat, with Azru's arrow transfixing its body. The astonished peasants at once hailed him as their leader, but he exacted an oath of secrecy from them, for he had come to deliver them from their tyrant, and would keep his incognito till such time as his plans for the destruction of the monster were matured.

"He then took leave of the hospitable people of Doyur, and went to Gilgit. On reaching the place, which is scarcely four miles distant from Doyur, he amused himself by prowling about in the gardens adjoining the royal residence. There he met one of the female companions of Shiribadatt's daughter (*goli* in Hill Punjabi, *Shadróy* in Gilgiti) fetching water for the princess, a lady both

[*] Eating meat was the process of *incarnation*.

remarkably handsome, and of a sweet disposition. The companion rushed back, and told the young lady to look from over the ramparts of the castle at a wonderfully handsome young man whom she had just met. The princess placed herself in a spot from which she could observe any one approaching the fort. Her maid then returned, and induced Azru to come with her on the Polo ground, the "Shavaran," in front of the castle; the princess was smitten with his beauty and at once fell in love with him. She then sent word to the young prince to come and see her. When he was admitted into her presence, he for a long time denied being anything else than a common labourer. At last, he confessed to being a fairy's child, and the overjoyed princess offered him her heart and hand. It may be mentioned here that the tyrant Shiribadatt had a wonderful horse, which could cross a mile at every jump, and which its rider had accustomed to jump both into and out of the fort, over its walls. So regular were the leaps which that famous animal could take, that he invariably alighted at a distance of a mile from the fort and at the same place.

"On that very day on which the princess had admitted young Azru into the fort, King Shiribadatt was out hunting, of which he was desperately fond, and to which he used sometimes to devote a week or two at a time. We must now return to Azru, whom we left conversing with the princess. Azru remained silent when the lady confessed her love. Urged to declare his sentiments, he said that he would not marry her unless she bound herself to him by the most stringent oath; this she did, and *they became in the sight of God as if they were wedded man and wife.*[5] He then announced that he had come to destroy her father, and asked her to kill him herself. This she refused; but as she had sworn to aid him in every way she could, he finally induced her to promise that she would ask her father *where his soul was.* 'Refuse food,' said Azru, 'for three or four days, and your father, who is devotedly fond

[5] The story of the famous horse, the love-making between Azru and the Princess, the manner of their marriage and other incidents connected with the expulsion of the tyrant deserve attention.

of you will ask for the reason of your strange conduct; then say, " Father, you are often staying away from me for several days at a time, and I am getting distressed lest something should happen to you; do reassure me by letting me know where your soul is, and let me feel certain that your life is safe." ' This the princess promised to do, and when her father returned refused food for several days. The anxious Shiribadatt made inquiries, to which she replied by making the already-named request. The tyrant was for a few moments thrown into mute astonishment, and finally refused compliance with her preposterous demand. The love-smitten lady went on starving herself, till at last her father, fearful for his daughter's life, told her not to fret herself about him, as *his soul was [of snow ?] in the snows,* and that he could only perish by fire. The princess communicated this information to her lover. Azru went back to Doyur and the villages around, and assembled his faithful peasants. Them he asked to take twigs of the fir-tree or *tshi,* bind them together and light them—then to proceed in a body with the torches to the castle in a circle, keep close together, and surround it on every side. He then went and dug out a very deep hole, as deep as a well, in the place where Shiribadatt's horse used to alight, and covered it with green boughs. The next day he received information that the torches (*talên* in Gilgiti and *Lome* in Astori) were ready. He at once ordered the villagers gradually to draw near the fort in the manner which he had already indicated.

" King Shiribadatt was then sitting in his castle; near him his treacherous daughter, who was so soon to lose her parent. All at once he exclaimed, ' I feel very close; go out, dearest, and see what has happened.' The girl went out, and saw torches approaching from a distance; but fancying it to be something connected with the plans of her husband, she went back, and said it was nothing. The torches came nearer and nearer, and the tyrant became exceedingly restless. ' Air, air,' he cried, ' I feel very, very ill; do see, daughter, what is the matter.' The dutiful lady went, and returned with the same answer as before. At last, the torch-bearers had fairly surrounded the fort, and Shiribadatt, with a presentiment of impending danger, rushed out of the room, saying 'that he felt he was dying.' He then ran to the stables and mounted his favourite charger, and with one blow of the whip made him jump over the wall of the castle. Faithful to its habit, the noble animal alighted at the same place, but alas! only to find itself engulfed in a treacherous pit. Before the king had time to extricate himself, the villagers had run up with their torches. 'Throw them upon him,' cried Azru. With one accord all the blazing wood was thrown upon Shiribadatt, who miserably perished. Azru was then most enthusiastically proclaimed king, celebrated his nuptials with the fair traitor, *and, as sole tribute, exacted the offering of one sheep, instead of that of a human child, annually from every one of the natives.*[6] This custom has prevailed down to the present day, and the people of Shîn, wherever they be, celebrate their delivery from the rule of a monster, and the inauguration of a more humane government, in the month preceding the beginning of winter—a month which they call Dawakió or Daykió—after the full moon is over and the new moon has set in. The day of this national celebration is called 'nôs tshilí,' 'the feast of firs.' The day generally follows four or five days after the meat provision for the winter has been laid in to dry. A few days of rejoicing precede the special festivity, which takes place at night. Then all the men of the villages go forth, having torches in their hands, which, at the sound of music, they swing round their heads, and throw in the direction of Gilgit, if they are at any distance from that place; whilst the people of Gilgit throw them indifferently about the plain in which that town, if town it may be called, is situated. When the throwing away of the brands is over, every man

[6] Possibly this legend is one of the causes of the unfounded reputation of cannibalism which was given by Kashmiris and others to the Dards before 1866, and of which one Dardu tribe accuses another, with which, even if it should reside in a neighbouring valley, it may have no intercourse. I refer elsewhere to the custom of drinking a portion of the blood of an enemy, to which my two Kafirs confessed.—("Dardistan," Part III.)

returns to his house, where a curious custom is observed. He finds the door locked. The wife then asks: 'Where have you been all night? I won't let you come in now.' Then her husband entreats her and says, 'I have brought you property, and children, and happiness, and everything you desire.' Then, after some further parley, the door is opened, and the husband walks in. He is, however, stopped by a beam which goes across the room, whilst all the females of the family rush into an inner apartment to the eldest lady of the place. The man then assumes sulkiness and refuses to advance, when the repenting wife launches into the following song:—

ORIGINAL :—

Mù tútè shábilès, wó rajó tolyá.
I of thee glad am, oh Rajah's presented with tolahs!
Mù tútè shábilès, wó ashpa panu.
I of thee glad am, oh steed's rider.
Mù tùtè shábilès, wó tumák ginu.
I of thee glad am, oh gun-wearer. [Evidently a modern interpolation.]
Mú tútè shábilès, wó kangár ginu.
I of thee glad am, oh sword-wearer.
Mú tútè shábilès, wó tshapàn banu.
I of thee glad am, oh mantle-wearer.
Mú tútè shábilès, shá mul dè ginum.
I of thee glad am, pleasure's price giving I will buy.
Mú tútè shábilès, wó gúmy tshíno.
I of thee glad am, oh corn-heap!
Shábilès shá mul de ginum.
Rejoicing pleasure's price giving I will buy.
Mú tútè shábilès, wó gïëy loto.
I of thee glad am, oh ghée-ball.
Shábilès sha mul de ginum.
Rejoicing pleasure's price giving I will buy.

TRANSLATION :—

Thou hast made me glad! thou favourite of the Rajah!
Thou hast rejoiced me, oh bold horseman!
I am pleased with thee who so well usest gun and sword!
Thou hast delighted me, oh thou who art invested with a mantle of honour!
Oh great happiness! I will buy it all by giving pleasure's price.
Oh thou [nourishment to us] a heap of corn and a store of ghee!
Delighted will I buy it all by giving pleasure's price!

"Then the husband relents and steps over the partition beam. They all sit down, dine together, and thus end the festivities of the 'Nôs.' The little domestic scene is not observed at Gilgit; but it is thought to be an essential element in the celebration of the day by people whose ancestors may have been retainers of the Gilgit Raja Azru Shemsher, and by whom they may have been dismissed to their homes with costly presents.

"The song itself is, however, well known at Gilgit.

"When Azru had safely ascended the throne, he ordered the tyrant's palace to be levelled to the ground. The willing peasants, manufacturing spades of iron, 'Killi,' flocked to accomplish a grateful task, and sang whilst demolishing his castle:

ORIGINAL:—

Kúro tēyto Shiri-ga-Badàt djē kurò
[I am] hard said Shiri and Badatt![1] why hard?
Demm Singēy Khotò kúro
Dem Sing's Khotó [is] hard
Na tshumáre kille tēy ráke phala thēm
[With] this iron spade thy palace level I do
Tshakē! túto Shatshò Malika Demm Singēy
Behold! thou Shatshó Malika Dem Singh's
Khotò kurò na tshumare killēyi
Khotó hard; [with] this iron spade
Tēy rake-ga phalatēm, tshakē
Thy palace very I level, behold!

TRANSLATION:—

"'My nature is of a hard metal,' said Shiri and Badatt. 'Why hard? I Khoto, the son of the peasant Dem Singh, am alone hardy; with this iron spade I raze to the ground thy kingly house. Behold now, although thou art of race accursed, of Shatsho Malika, I, Dem Singh's son, am of hard metal; for with this iron spade I level thy very palace; look out! look out!'"

During the Nauroz [evidently because it is not a national festival] and the Eed, none of these national Shîn songs are sung. Eggs are dyed in different colours and people go about amusing themselves by trying which eggs are hardest by striking the end of one against the end of another. The possessor of the hard egg wins the broken one. The women, however, amuse themselves on those days by tying ropes to trees and swinging themselves about on them.

[1] Elsewhere called "Shiribadatt" in one name.

BUJONI=RIDDLES, PROVERBS AND FABLES.

A. RIDDLES.

THE NAVEL.

1. *Tishkóreya ushkúrey halól.*

"The perpendicular mountain's sparrow's nest.
The body's sparrow's hole."

A STICK.

2. *Méy sazik héyn, súreo peréyn, bás darre*
my sister is at day [*she*] walks, at night door
*pató; búja.**
behind; listen!

"Now listen! My sister walks in the day-time and at night stands behind the door." As "Sas" "Sazik" also means a stick, ordinarily called "Kunali" in Astori, the riddle means: "I have a stick which assists me in walking by day and which I put behind the door at night."

3. The Gilgitis say "méy káke tré pay; dashtea"= my brother has three feet; explain now. This means a man's two legs and a stick.

A RADISH.

4. *Astóri mió dádo dimm dáwa-lók; dáyn sarpa-lók, buja.*
My grandfather's body [is] in Hades; his beard [is in] this world, [now] explain!

This riddle is explained by "radish" whose body is in the earth and whose sprouts, compared to a beard, are above the ground. Remarkable above all, however, is that the unknown future state, referred to in this riddle, should be called, whether blessed or cursed, "Dawalók" [the place of Gods] by these nominal Muhammadans. This world is called "Sarpalók,"=the world of serpents. "Sarpe" is also the name for man. "Lók" is "place," but the name by itself is not at present understood by the Shins.

* Words inviting attention, such as "listen," "explain," etc., etc., are generally put at the end of riddles.

A HOOKA.

5. *G. méy* DADI *shishédji agár, lúpenu*
my father's mother on her head fire is burning.

The top of the Hooka is the *dadi's* or grandmother's head.

A SWORD.

6. *Tutâng gotéjo rúi nikai*

"Darkness from the house the female demon is coming out," viz., "out of the dark sheath the beautiful, but destructive, steel issues." It is remarkable that the female Yatsh should be called "Rûi."

RED PEPPER.

7. *Lólo bakuró shé tshá lá há—búja !*

In the red sheep's pen white young ones many are—attend !

This refers to the Redpepper husk in which there are many white seeds.

B. PROVERBS.

DOTAGE.

To an old man people say :

8. *Tú djarro mbto shûdung* { "You are old and have
thou and old brains delivered, { got rid of your senses."

Old women are very much dreaded and are accused of creating mischief wherever they go.

DUTIES TO THE AGED.

9. (*G.**) *Djuwanie keneru digasus, djarvelo betshumus*
In youth's time I gave, in old age I demand

"When young I gave away, now that I am old you should support me."

A BURNT CHILD, ETC., ETC.

10. *Ek damm agáru dáddo dugúni shang thé !*

Once in fire you have been burnt, a second time take care !

EVIL COMMUNICATIONS, ETC., ETC.

11. *Ek khatsh látshek bilo búdo donate she.*

One bad sheep if there be, to the whole flock is an insult =One rotten sheep spoils the whole flock.

12. *Ek khatsho manújo budote sha=one* bad man is to *all* an insult.

* The abbreviations "G." and "A." stand respectively for "in the Gilgiti dialect" and "in the Astori dialect."

ADVICE TO KEEP GOOD COMPANY.

13. A. *Mishto manújo—katshi béyto, to mishto sitshé*
Katsho manujo—katshi béyto, to katsho sitshe

When you [who are bad ?] are sitting near a good man you learn good things.

When you [who are bad ?] are sitting near a bad man you learn bad things.

This proverb is not very intelligible, if literally translated.

DIMMI CON CHI TU PRATTICHI, ETC., ETC.

14. *Tús máte rá : mey shughulo ró hun, mas tute rám : tu ko hanu* = " Tell me : my friend is such and such a one, I will tell you who *you* are."

DISAPPOINTMENT.

15. *Sháharè kóru gé shing shém thé—konu tshiní tey tshiní téyanú.*

" Into the city he went horns to place (acquire), but ears he cut thus he did. He went to acquire horns and got his ears cut off."

HOW TO TREAT AN ENEMY.

Dî dé, putsh kàh = " give the daughter and eat the son," is a Gilgit proverb with regard to how one ought to treat an enemy. The recommendation given is : " marry your daughter to your foe and then kill him," [by which you get a male's head which is more valuable than that of a female.] The Dards have sometimes acted on this maxim in order to lull the suspicions of their Kashmir enemies.*

C. FABLES.

THE WOMAN AND THE HEN.

16. *Eyk tshéekeyn kokói ek asíllı ; sése sóni thúl* (*hané*) *déli ; setshéy-se kokóïte zanmá láo wîi ; tulé dù déy*
(food, grain) eggs two giving
thé ; sè ékenu lang bilí ; kokói dêr páy, múy.
does ; this one rid got ; the hen's stomach bursting, died.

MORAL.—*Anésey maní aní haní* = the meaning of this is this :

Láo arém thé ápejo lang biló.
Much to gain the little lost becomes.

* Not very many years ago the Albanian robbers in attacking shepherds used to consider themselves victorious if they had robbed more sheep than they had lost men.

Translation.

A woman had a hen; it used to lay one golden egg; the woman thought that if she gave much food it would lay two eggs; but she lost even the one, for the hen died, its stomach bursting.

MORAL.—People often lose the little they have by aspiring to more.

17. THE SPARROW AND THE MOUNTAIN.

"A sparrow who tried to kick the mountain himself toppled over."

Shunítur-se tshíshe—sáti pájja dem thé náre gó.
The sparrow with the mountain kicked fall went.

18. THE BAT SUPPORTING THE FIRMAMENT.

The bat is in the habit of sleeping on its back. It is believed to be very proud. It is supposed to say as it lies down and stretches its legs towards heaven, "This I do so that when the heavens fall down I may be able to support them."

Tilteò ráte súto—to pey húnte angái—warì
A bat at night sleeping its legs upwards heaven—ward
theun; angái wáti—to pêy—gì sanarem theun.
does; the heavens when falling with my feet uphold I will.

19. "NEVER WALK BEHIND A HORSE OR BEFORE A KING" as you will get kicked in either case.

ashpe patanì nè bó; rajó mutshanì nè bó.
horse behind not walk; raja in front not walk.

20. UNION IS STRENGTH.

"A kettle cannot balance itself on one stone; on three, however, it does."

Ey pútsh! èk gutur-yá dêh nè quriyein; tré gútúrey á*
Oh son! one stone on a kettle not stops; three stones on
dek quréyn.
a kettle stop.

The Gilgitis instead of "ya" = "upon" say "dja."

"Gutur" is, I believe, used for a stone [ordinarily "bàtt"] only in the above proverb.

* "Tré" = "three" is pronounced like "tshé."

21. THE FROG IN A DILEMMA.

"If I speak, the water will rush against my mouth, and if I keep silent I will die bursting with rage."

This was said by a frog who was in the water and angry at something that occurred. If he croaked, he would be drowned by the water rushing down his throat, and if he did not croak he would burst with suppressed rage. This saying is often referred to by women when they are angry with their husbands, who may, perhaps, beat them if they say anything. A frog is called "manok."

Tós thèm—to áze—jya wéy bojé ; né them*
Voice I do—if mouth in water will come ; not do,
to py muos.
then bursting I will die.

22. THE FOX AND THE UNIVERSE.

When a man threatens a lot of people with impossible menaces, the reply often is "Don't act like the fox 'Lóyn' who was carried away by the water." A fox one day fell into a river : as he swept past the shore he cried out, "The water is carrying off the universe." The people on the banks of the river said, "We can only see a fox whom the river is drifting down."

23. THE FOX AND THE POMEGRANATE.

Lóyn danù né utshàtte somm tshàmm
The fox the pomegranate not reached on account sour,
thù : tshùrko hanú.
spitting, sour it is.

"The fox wanted to eat pomegranates : as he could not reach them, he went to a distance and *biting his lips* [as "tshàmm" was explained by an Astori although Gilgitis call it "tshappé,"] spat on the ground, saying, they are too sour." I venture to consider the conduct of this fox more cunning than the one of "sour grapes" memory. His biting his lips and, in consequence, spitting on the ground, would make his disappointed face really look as if he had tasted something sour.

* Ae = (*Gilgiti*) mouth ; aru = in the mouth ; ázeju = against the mouth. Aze = (*Astori*) mouth ; ázeru = in the mouth ; azeju = against the mouth.

SONGS.

THE GILGIT QUEEN AND THE MOGULS.

1. GILGITI SONG.

Once upon a time a Mogul army came down and surrounded the fort of Gilgit. At that time Gilgit was governed by a woman, Mirzéy Juwāri* by name. She was the widow of a Rajah supposed to have been of Balti descent. The Lady seeing herself surrounded by enemies sang:

I. Mirzéy Juwārí = Oh [daughter of] Mirza, Juwāri!
Shakeréy piál; darú = [Thou art a] sugar cup; in the
Dunyá sang taréye = world [thy] light has shone

II. Abi Khānn† djālo = Abi Khān [my son] was born
Lamâyi tey! latshār tāro = [I thy mother] am thy sacrifice; the morning star
Nikāto = has risen

The meaning of this, according to my Gilgiti informant, is: Juwāri laments that "I, the daughter of a brave King, am only a woman, a cup of pleasures, exposed to dangers from any one who wishes to sip from it. To my misfortune, my prominent position has brought me enemies. Oh, my dear son, for whom I would sacrifice myself, I have sacrificed you! Instead of preserving the Government for you, the morning-star which shines on its destruction has now risen on you."

SONG OF DEFIANCE.

2. GILGITI WAR SONG.

In ancient times there was a war between the Rajahs of Hunza and Nagyr. Muko and Báko were their respective Wazeers. Muko was killed and Báko sang:

Gilgiti.

Ala, mardāney, Báko-se: má shos they!
Múko-se: má shos they!
Báko-ga dīn sajjéy
Múko mayáro they

* [Her father was a Mirza and she was, therefore, called Mirzéy.]
† Khān is pronounced Khann for the sake of the metre.

English.

Hurrah! warriors, Bako [says]: *I* will do well
Muko [also says] *I* will do well
And Bako turned out to be the lion
[Whilst] Muko was [its prey], a [mere] Markhōr [the wild "snake-eating" goat]

LAMENT FOR THE ABSENT WARRIOR BY HIS MOTHER.

3. ANOTHER GILGITI WAR SONG.

Biyashtëyn náng Kashíru
A Paradise [is the lot of whoever is struck by] the bullet of Kashiru?
Góu nélli, áje Sahibe Khann*
He has gone, my child, mother of Sahibe Khann [to the wars].
Suregga karé wey jill bey?
And the sun when coming will it shining become?
(When will his return cause the sun again to shine for me?)
Mutshútshul shong putéye
Of Mutshutshul† the ravine he has conquered
Híyokto bijéy, lamayi
Yet my soul is in fear, oh my beloved child, [literally: oh my sacrifice]
Ardàm Dolója yujéy
To snatch [conquer] Doloja‡ is [yet necessary = has yet to be done].

Translation.

"The bullet of Kashiru sends many to Paradise. He has gone to the wars, oh my child and mother of Sahib Khan! Will the sun ever shine for me by his returning? It is true that he has taken by assault the ravine of Mutshutshul, but yet, oh beloved child, my soul is in fear for his fate, as the danger has *not* passed, since the village Doloja yet remains to be conquered."

* Term of familiarity used in calling a daughter.

† Mutshutshul is a narrow pass leading from Gakutsh to Yassen.

‡ Doloja is a village ahead of Mutshutshul.

4. THE SHIN SHAMMI SHAH.

OLD NATIONAL SHINA SONG.

Shammi Shah Shaîtingêy mítojo.
Shammi Shah Shaíting, from his courtyard.

Djálle	*tshâye*	*dûloe*	*dên.*
The green fields'	birds	promenade	they give.
Nyé	*tziréye*	*tshayote*	*kóy bijéy.*
They (near)	twitter	birds	who fears ?*
Tómi tom		*shiudóke*	*dên*
From tree to tree		a whistle	they give.
Alldátey	*pótskeyn*	*mítojo.*	
Alldát's	grandson's	from the courtyard.	
Djalle	*tshaye*	*dûloe*	*dên.*
The green fields	birds	promenade	give.
Nyé	*tziréye*	*tshayote*	*kóy bijey.*
They	twitter	birds	who fears ?*
Tomi tom ; ,		*shiudôke*	*den.*
From tree to tree ; :		a whistling	they give.

Shammi Shah Shaíthing was one of the founders of the Shín rule. His wife, although she sees her husband surrounded by women anxious to gain his good graces, rests secure in the knowledge of his affections belonging to her and of her being the mother of his children. She, therefore, ridicules the pretensions of her rivals, who, she fancies, will, at the utmost, only have a temporary success. In the above still preserved song she says, with a serene confidence, not shared by *Indian* wives

Translation.

" In the very courtyard of Shammi Sha Shaíting.

" The little birds of the field flutter gaily about.

" Hear how they twitter ; yet, who would fear little birds,

" That fly from tree to tree giving [instead of lasting love] a gay whistle ?

" In the very courtyards of Alldat's grandson these birds flutter gaily about, yet who would fear them ?

" Hear how they twitter, etc., etc., etc.

* [To fear is construed with the Dative.]

5. A WOMAN'S SONG (GILGITI).

[THE DESERTED WIFE AND THE FAITHLESS HUSBAND.]

The Wife:

Mey kukúri Patan gayta béyto djék tòn?
My kukuri Pathán going he sat what am I to do?
Pípi batzísse garáo dên; múso tshúsh.
Aunt! from the family he absence has given; I cocoon.
Gá sikkìm qatì bring báleo dês;
And coloured silk spinning animal bind do = could.
Mió dudélo tshût biló!
My milk-sweet late has become!

The Husband:

*Anì Azari rey**
That Azari, [is] a Deodar cedar [?]
Rajóy, nà sómmo? anì Azareo rôk bilôs.
Kingly, is it not so [my] love! That Azari illness I have.
Anì Wazíreyn shuyi gas-mall, na sommo!
This Wazír's child princess, not [so] love?
Bálli dapúјo gí bem; anì pâr
Then from my waist (girdle) taking I'll sit; this beyond
tshísheyn
the mountains.
Súri war tshîsheyn djondjì† tzáe bijôte.
Sun this side's mountain birch tree (?) to you both.
Somm tshinèm; anù shëò qoáreyn kinì — ga
Alike I love; This white hawk black and
Tshikki‡ méy begà beìh; balli pashéjo
fragrant bag mine being sit; Then on my turban
gi beyim.
wearing I will sit.

* More probably "rey" is the pine called the Picea Webbiana.

† Part II., page 16, gives the following for "Birch." "Birch? = Djônjî (the white bark of which is used for paper) in Kashmîr where it is called the book-tree "Burus kull" lit: Burus = the book; kúll = plant, tree."

‡ "Tshikkí" is a black fragrant matter said to be gathered under the

Translation of " A Woman's Song."

The deserted wife sings :—My Pathan! oh kukúri, far away from me has he made a home; but, aunt, what am I to do. since he has left his own! The silk that I have been weaving during his absence would be sufficient to bind all the animals of the field. Oh, how my darling is delaying his return!

The faithless husband sings :—[My new love] Azari is like a royal Deodar; is it not so, my love? for Azari I am sick with desire. She is a Wazeer's princess; is it not so, my love? Let me put you in my waist. The sun on yonder mountain, and the tree on this nigh mountain, ye both I love dearly. I will recline when this white hawk and her black fragrant tresses become mine; encircling with them my head I will recline [in happiness.]

6. THE JILTED LOVER'S DREAM.

[IN THE ASTORI DIALECT.]

*Tshunni nazdik mulayi.**
(Oh) Little delicate [maid] woman.
Barêyo báro, na.†
The husband old is, [is he not?]
Hapótok thyayé gé.
With a bear done it going, [you have " been and gone and done it."]
Sómmi rátijo Sómmi shakejo Mey nish
In the sleep of night The sleep from the arm. My sleep
harayé gé. Mashàq phirì phùt
awake has gone. Turning round again opening hastily
talósto Méy laktéy píribann tshîtsho häun. Datshîno
I saw. My darling waistband variegated was. Right

wing-pits of the hawk; " djónji " is, to me, an unknown tree, but I conjecture it to be the birch tree. " Gas " is a princess and " mal " is added for euphony.

* [" Mulayi " for woman is not very respectful; women are generally addressed as " kaki " sister, or " dhì " daughter.]

† *Na?* is it? is it not so? *na* seems generally to be a mere exclamation.

nata-jó aina giní, Tshakéoje wazze. Nu kabbo
hand-from mirror taking, Looking she came. This left
hata-jó surmá giní. Paléoje wazze.
hand-from antimony taking, Applying she came.

The above describes the dream of a lover whose sweetheart has married one older than herself; he says:

Translation.

"That dear delicate little woman has a frightful old husband.

"Thou hast married a bear! In the dead of night, resting on my arm,

"My sleep became like waking. Hastily I turned and with a quick glance saw

"That my darling's waistband shone with many colours.

"That she advanced towards me holding in her right a mirror into which she looked,

"That she came near me applying with her left the antimony to her eyes."

7. MODERN ASTORI SONG.

This Song was composed by Rajah Bahadur Khan, now at Astōr, who fell in love with the daughter of the Rajah of Hunza to whom he was affianced. When the war between Kashmir and Hunza broke out, the Astoris and Hunzas were in different camps; Rajah Bahadur Khan, son of Rajah Shakul Khan, of the Shíah persuasion,* thus laments his misfortunes:

Lotshûko sabäin kēn nimâz thé duwá
Early in morning's time [usual] prayers done supplication
them Qabûl thé, Rahîma Garìbëy duwa
I make Accept, oh merciful [God] of the poor the prayer.
Dòn makî—yeen dim
[her] teeth [are] of fish bone = like ivory, [her] body
puru—yeen tshamûye tshîké hane me armán
[like a] reed† [her] hair musk is. My longing
tûte hane Bulbûl shakàr.
to you is [Oh] nightingale sweet!

* The people of Astor are mostly Sunnis, and the Gilgitis mostly Shiahs; the Chilásis are all Sunnis.

† A reed which grows in the Gilgit country of white or red colour

Chorus falls in with "*hai, hai, armân bulbûl*" = "oh, oh, the longing [for the] nightingale!"*

Translation.

After having discharged my usual religious duties in the early morning, I offer a prayer which, oh thou merciful God, accept from thy humble worshipper. [Then, thinking of his beloved.] Her teeth are as white as ivory, her body as graceful as a reed, her hair is like musk. My whole longing is towards you, oh sweet nightingale.

Chorus: Alas, how absorbing this longing for the nightingale.

8. GURAIZI SONGS.

This district used to be under Ahmad Shah of Skardo, and has since its conquest by Ghulab Singh come permanently under the Maharajah of Kashmîr. Its possession used to be the apple of discord between the Nawäbs of Astor and the Rajahs of Skardo. It appears never to have had a real Government of its own. The fertility of its valleys always invited invasion. Yet the people are of Shîná origin and appear much more manly than the other subjects of Kashmîr. Their loyalty to that power is not much to be relied upon, but it is probable that with the great intermixture which has taken place between them and the Kashmîri Mussulmans for many years past, they will become equally demoralized. The old territory of Guraiz used in former days to extend up to Kuyam or Bandipur on the Wular Lake. The women are reputed to be very chaste, and Colonel Gardiner told me that the handsomest women in Kashmìr came from that district. To me, however, they appeared to be tolerably plain, although rather innocent-looking, which may render them attractive, especially after one has seen the handsome, but sensual-looking, women of Kashmir. The people of Guraiz are certainly very dirty, but they are not so plain as the Chilásis. At Guraiz three languages are spoken: Kashmîri, Guraizi (a corruption of a Shiná dialect), and Pan-

* It is rather unusual to find the nightingale representing the beloved. She is generally "the rose" and the lover "the nightingale"

jabi—the latter on account of its occupation by the Maharajah's officials. I found some difficulty in getting a number of them together from the different villages which compose the district of Guraiz, the Arcadia of Kashmir, but I gave them food and money, and after I got them into a good humour they sang :

GURAIZI HUNTING SONG.

Guraizi.		*English.*
Pere, tshaké, gazàri meyaru Beyond, look! a fine stag.	=	Look beyond! what a fine stag!
Chorus. *Pére, tshaké, djôk maar âke dey.*	=	Chorus. Look beyond! how gracefully he struts.
Beyond, look! how he struts!		
Pére, tshaké, bhapûri bay bâro Beyond, look! shawl wool 12 loads.	=	Look beyond! he bears twelve loads of wool.
Chorus. *Pére, tshaké, djôk maar-âke dey.*	=	Chorus. Look beyond! how gracefully he struts.
Beyond, look! how he does strut!		
Pére, tshaké, dòni shilélu Beyond, look! [his] teeth are of crystal [glass]	=	Look beyond! his very teeth are of crystal.
Chorus. *Pére, tshaké, djôk maarâke dey.*	=	Chorus. Look beyond! how gracefully he struts.

This is apparently a hunting song, but seems also to be applied to singing the praises of a favourite.

There is another song, which was evidently given with great gusto, in praise of Sheir Shah Ali Shah, Rajah of Skardo.* That Rajah, who is said to have temporarily conquered Chitrál, which the Chilasis call Tshatshál,† made a road of steps up the Atsho mountain which overlooks Bûnji, the most distant point reached before 1866 by

* Possibly Ali Sher Khan, also called Ali Shah, the father of Ahmed Shah, the successful and popular Rajah of Skardo in the Sikh days—or else the great Ali Sher Khan, the founder of the race or caste of the Makpon Rajahs of Skardo. He built a great stone aqueduct from the Satpur stream which also banked up a quantity of useful soil against inundations.

† Murad was, I believe, the first Skardo Rajah who conquered Gilgit, Nagyr, Hunza and Chitrál. He built a bridge near the Chitrál fort. Traces of invasion from Little Tibet exist in Dardistan. A number of historical events, occurring at different periods, seem to be mixed up in this song.

travellers or the Great Trigonometrical Survey. From the Atsho mountain Vigne returned, "the suspicious Rajah of Gilgit suddenly giving orders for burning the bridge over the Indus." It is, however, more probable that his Astori companions fabricated the story in order to prevent him from entering an unfriendly territory in which Mr. Vigne's life might have been in danger, for had he reached Bûnji he might have known that the Indus never was spanned by a bridge at that or any neighbouring point. The miserable Kashmîri coolies and boatmen who were forced to go up-country with the troops in 1866 were, some of them, employed, in rowing people across, and that is how I got over the Indus at Bûnji ; however to return from this digression to the *Guraizi Song :*

9. PRAISE OF THE CONQUEROR SHEIR SHAH ALI SHAH.

Guraizi.		*English.*
Sheir Shah Ali Shah	=	Sheir Shah Ali Shah.
Nōmega djong	=	I wind myself round his name.*
Ká kōlo shing phuté	=	He conquering the crooked Low-lands.
Djar súntsho taréga	=	Made them quite straignt.
Kâne Makponé	=	The great Khan, the Makpon.
Kâno nom mega djong	=	I wind myself round the Khan's name.
Kó Tshamūgar bòsh phuté	=	He conquered bridging over [the Gilgit river] below Tshamûgar.
Sar† súntsho taréga	=	And made all quite straight.

I believe there was much more of this historical song, but unfortunately the paper on which the rest was written down by me as it was delivered, has been lost together with other papers.

"Tshamūgar," to which reference is made in the song, is a village on the other side of the Gilgit river on the Nagyr side. It is right opposite to where I stayed for two nights

* The veneration for the name is, of course, also partly due to the fact that it means "the lion of Ali," Muhammad's son-in-law, to whose memory the Shiah Mussulmans are so devotedly attached. The Little Tibetans are almost all Shiahs.

† "Sar" is Astori for (Gilgiti) "Djor.

under a huge stone which projects from the base of the Niludâr range on the Gilgit side.

There were formerly seven forts at Tshamūgar. A convention had been made between the Rajah of Gilgit and the Rajah of Skardo, by which Tshamūgar was divided by the two according to the natural division which a stream that comes down from the Batkôr mountain made in that territory. The people of Tshamūgar, impatient of the Skardo rule, became all of them subjects to the Gilgit Rajah, on which Sher Shah Ali Shah, the ruler of Skardo, collected an army, and crossing the Makpon-i-shagaron* at the foot of the Haramûsh mountain, came upon Tshamūgar and diverted the water which ran through that district into another direction. This was the reason of the once fertile Tshamūgar becoming deserted; the forts were razed to the ground. There are evidently traces of a river having formerly run through Tshamūgar. The people say that the Skardo Rajah stopped the flow of the water by throwing quicksilver into it. This is probably a legend arising from the reputation which Ahmad Shah, the most recent Skardo ruler whom the Guraizis can remember, had of dabbling in medicine and sorcery.†

CHILASI SONGS.

[The Chilasis have a curious way of snapping their fingers, with which practice they accompany their songs, the thumb running up and down the fingers as on a musical instrument.]

10. CHILASI.

Tù hùn Gítshere bódje sòmmo dímm bamem
Mèy shahínni pashalóto dewà salâm dáute
Rás; Aje gòje bómto méy dùddi aje nush
Hargìnn Zúe déy mo bejómos
Samat Khánay sóni mó báshémm tutàk
Mùugà deyto; mó dabtar dèm

* The defile of the Makpon-i-Shang-Rong, where the Indus river makes a sudden turn southward and below which it receives the Gilgit river.

† The Shiah Rajahs of Skardo believed themselves to be under the special protection of Ali.

11\. A. Tshekòn thónn ; tikki wéy nush, oh Berader
Adòn ; thōn ; madéy nush ; ey Berader
B. Hamírey tshûki, púki thàs, palútọs
Ni rátey ló ne bĕy, oh Berader !

The last word in each sentence, as is usual with all Shín songs, is repeated at the beginning of the next line. I may also remark that I have accentuated the words *as pronounced in the songs* and not as put down in my Vocabulary.

Translation.

MESSAGE TO A SWEETHEART BY A FRIEND.

You are going up to Gitshe, oh my dearest friend,
Give my compliment and salute when you see my hawk.
Speak to her. I must now go into my house ; my mother
is no more
And I fear the sting of that dragon,* my step-mother—
Oh noble daughter of Samat Khan ; I will play the flute
And give its price and keep it in my bosom.

The second song describes a quarrel between two brothers who are resting after a march on some hill far away from any water or food wherewith to refresh themselves.

Younger brother.—Am I to eat now, what am I to say, there is, oh my brother, neither bread nor water.

Am I to fetch some [water], what am I to say, there is no masak [a water-skin], oh my brother !

Elder brother.—The lying nonsense of Hamır (the younger brother) wounds me deeply (tears off the skin of my heart).

There will be no day to this long night, oh my brother !

12\. THE TRANSITORINESS OF THIS WORLD.

Kàka, mosè djò râum | *Mèy dássga nè bèy* | *Tàbàm*
Brother ! I what am to say? | My choice it is not | In the
aresà dáro | *Módje làshga nè béy* | *Dajála*
whole of the present time | To me shame is not | The next
éle jilto | *Jáko udàsóne han*
world near has come | People despairing will be

* The "Harginn," a fabulous animal mentioned elsewhere.

2nd Verse.

Watàn dáro zár | *Tu mashahúre billé* | *Ash*
In my country famous | You famous have become | To-day
bajóni dégi bárri musafiri | *Zari mójo*
to get you prepared on a great journey | Openly me
lai langíddi = íje | *Djíll mey hawallí* | *Sín qatída*
much pains | My soul is in your keeping | The river
phúne | *Sudà chogarong*
is flowing, the large flower | Of silver colour.*

A PRAYER OF THE BASHGELI KAFIRS.

[*In the Kalásha dialect.*]

The ideas and many of the words in this prayer were evidently acquired by my two Kafirs on their way through Kashmir:

"Khudá, tandrusti dé, prushkári rozì de, abattì kari, dewalat man. Tu ghóna asas, tshik intara, tshik tu faidá káy asas. Sat asmán tì, Stru suri mastruk mótshe dé."

MANNERS AND CUSTOMS.

A. AMUSEMENTS.

The Chaughan Bazi or Hockey on horseback, so popular everywhere north of Kashmir, and which is called Polo by the Baltis and Ladakis, who both play it to perfection and in a manner which I shall describe elsewhere, is also well known to the Ghilgiti and Astori subdivisions of the Shina people. On great general holidays as well as on any special occasion of rejoicing, the people meet on those grounds which are mostly near the larger villages, and pursue the game with great excitement and at the risk of casualties. The first day I was at Astor, I had the greatest difficulty in restoring to his senses a youth of the name of

* The beautiful songs of "My little darling ornaments will wear." "Corn is being distributed," "I will give pleasure's price," "My metal is hard," "Come out, oh daughter of the hawk," will be found on pages 2, 4, 10, 11, and 37, of this pamphlet respectively and need not therefore be quoted in this place.

Rustem Ali who, like a famous player of the same name at Mardo, was passionately fond of the game, and had been thrown from his horse. The place of meeting near Astor is called the Eedgah. The game is called TOPE in Astor, and the grounds for playing it are called SHAJARAN. At Gilgit the game is called BULLA, and the place SHAWARAN. The latter names are evidently of Tibetan origin.

The people are also very fond of target practice, shooting with bows, which they use dexterously but in which they do not excel the people of Nagyr and Hunza. Game is much stalked during the winter. At Astor any game shot on the three principal hills—*Tshhamô*, a high hill opposite the fort, *Demídeldèn* and *Tshólokot*—belong to the Nawab of Astor—the sportsman receiving only the head, legs and a haunch—or to his representative, then the Tahsildar Munshi Rozi Khan. At Gilgit everybody claims what he may have shot, but it is customary for the Nawab to receive some share of it. Men are especially appointed to watch and track game, and when they discover their whereabouts notice is sent to the villages from which parties issue, accompanied by musicians, and surround the game. Early in the morning, when the "Lóhe" dawns, the musicians begin to play and a great noise is made which frightens the game into the several directions where the sportsmen are placed.

The guns are matchlocks and are called in Gilgiti "*turmàk*" and in Astór "tumák." At Gilgit they manufacture the guns themselves or receive them from Badakhshan. The balls have only a slight coating of lead, the inside generally being a little stone. The people of Hunza and Nagyr invariably place their guns on little wooden pegs which are permanently fixed to the gun and are called "Dugazá." The guns are much lighter than those manufactured elsewhere, much shorter and carry much smaller bullets than the matchlock of the Maharajah's troops. They carry very much farther than any native Indian gun and are fired with almost unerring accuracy. For "small shot" little stones of any shape—the longest and oval ones being preferred—are used. There is one kind of stone especially which is much used for that purpose; it is called "Balosh Batt," which is found in Hanza, Nagyr, Skardo, and near the "Demídeldèn" hill already noticed, at a village called Pareshinghi near Astor. It is a very soft stone and large cooking utensils are cut out from it, whence the name, "Balósh" Kettle, "Batt" stone, "Balósh Batt." The stone is cut out with a chisel and hammer; the former is called "Gútt" in Astori and "Gukk" in Gilgiti;" the hammer "toá" and "Totshúng" and in Gilgiti "samdenn." The gunpowder is manufactured by the people themselves.*

The people also play at backgammon, [called in Astóri "Patshis," and "TAKK" in Gilgiti,] with dice [called in Astóri and also in Gilgiti "dall."]

Fighting with iron wristbands is confined to Chilasi women who bring them over their fists which they are said to use with effect.

The people are also fond of wrestling, of butting each other whilst hopping, etc.*

To play the Jew's harp is considered meritorious as King David played it. All other music good Mussulmans are bid to avoid.

The "Sitara" [the Eastern Guitar] used to be much played in Yassen, the people of which country as well as the people of Hunza and Nagyr excel in dancing, singing and playing. After them come the Gilgitis, then the Astoris, Chilasis, Baltis, etc. The people of Nagyr are a comparatively mild race. They carry on goldwashing which is constantly interrupted by kidnapping parties from

* "Powder" is called "Jebati" in Astóri and in Gilgiti "Bilen," and is, in both dialects, also the word used for medicinal powder. It is made of Sulphur, Saltpetre and coal. Sulphur = dantzil. Saltpetre = Shór in Astori, and Shorá in Ghilgiti. Coal = Kári. The general proportion of the composition is, as my informant put it, after dividing the whole into six and a half parts to give 5 of Saltpetre, 1 of coal, and ½ of Sulphur. Some put less coal in, but it is generally believed that more than the above proportion of Sulphur would make the powder too explosive.

the opposite Hunza. The language of Nagyr and Hunza is the Non-Aryan Khajuná and no affinity between that language and any other has yet been traced. The Nagyris are mostly Shiahs. They are short and stout and fairer than the people of Hunza [the Kunjûtis] who are described* as "tall skeletons" and who are desperate robbers. The Nagyris understand Tibetan, Persian and Hindustani. Badakhshan merchants were the only ones who could travel with perfect safety through Yassen, Chitral and Hunza.

DANCES†

Fall into two main divisions: "slow" or "Búti Harip" =Slow Instrument" and Quick "Danni Harip,"=Quick Instrument. The Yassen, Nagyr and Hunza people dance quickest; then come the Gilgitis; then the Astóris; then the Baltis, and slowest of all are the Ladakis.

When all join in the dance, cheer or sing with gesticulations, the dance or recitative is called "thapnatt" in Gilgiti, and "Burró" in Astóri.

When there is a solo dance it is called "nàtt" in Gilgiti, and "nott" in Astóri.

"Cheering" is called "Halamush" in Ghilgiti, and "Halamùsh" in Astóri. Clapping of hands is called "tza." Cries of "*Yú*, Yú dea; tza theá, Hiú Hiú dea; Halamush thea; shabâsh" accompany the performances.

There are several kinds of Dances. The PRASULKI NATE, is danced by ten or twelve people ranging themselves behind the bride as soon as she reaches the bridegroom's house. This custom is observed at Astor. In this dance men swing above sticks or whatever they may happen to hold in their hands.

The BURO'NATT is a dance performed on the Nao holiday, in which both men and women engage—the women forming a ring round the central group of dancers, which is composed of men. This dance is called THAPPNATT at

* By the people of Gilgit.

† A few remarks made under this head and that of music have been taken from Part II, pages 32 and 21, of my "Dardistan," in order to render the accounts more intelligible.

Gilgit. In Dareyl there is a dance in which the dancers wield swords and engage in a mimic fight. This dance Gilgitis and Astòris call the *Darelâ nat,* but what it is called by the Dareylis themselves I do not know.

The mantle dance is called "GOJA NAT." In this popular dance the dancer throws his cloth over his extended arm.

When I sent a man round with a drum inviting all the Dards that were to be found at Gilgit to a festival, a large number of men appeared, much to the surprise of the invading Dogras, who thought that they had all run to the hills. A few sheep were roasted for their benefit; bread and fruit were also given them, and when I thought they were getting into a good humour, I proposed that they should sing. Musicians had been procured with great difficulty, and after some demur, the Gilgitis sang and danced. At first, only one at a time danced, taking his sleeves well over his arm so as to let it fall over, and then moving it up and down according to the cadence of the music. The movements were, at first, slow, one hand hanging down, the other being extended with a commanding. gesture. The left foot appeared to be principally engaged in moving or rather jerking the body forward. All sorts of "pas seuls" were danced; sometimes a rude imitation of the Indian Nátsh; the by-standers clapping their hands and crying out "Shabāsh"; one man, a sort of Master of Ceremonies, used to run in and out amongst them, brandishing a stick, with which, in spite of his very violent gestures, he only lightly touched the bystanders, and exciting them to cheering by repeated calls, which the rest then took up, of "Hiù, Hiù." The most extraordinary dance, however, was when about twelve men arose to dance, of whom six went on one side and six on the other. both sides then, moving forward, jerked out their arms so as to look as if they had all crossed swords, then receded and let their arms drop. This was a war dance, and I was told that properly it ought to have been danced with swords, which, however, out of suspicion of the Dogras, did not seem to be forthcoming. They then formed a circle, again separated, the movements becoming more and more violent till almost all the bystanders joined in the dance, shouting like fiends and literally *kicking* up a frightful amount of dust, which, after I had nearly become choked with it, compelled me to retire.* I may also notice that before a song is sung the rhythm and melody of it are given in "solo" by some one, for instance

Dānă dāng dānŭ dăngdā
nădañg dānŭ, etc., etc., etc.

B. BEVERAGES.

BEER.

Fine corn (about five or six *seers* in weight) is put into a kettle with water and boiled till it gets soft, but not pulpy. It is then strained through a cloth, and the grain retained and put into a vessel. Then it is mixed with a drug that comes from Ladak which is called "Papps," and has a salty taste, but in my opinion is nothing more than hardened dough with which some kind of drug is mixed. It is necessary that "the marks of four fingers" be impressed upon the "Papps." The mark of "four fingers" make one stick, 2 fingers' mark ½ a stick, and so forth. This is scraped and mixed with the corn. The whole is then put into an earthen jar with a narrow neck, after it has received an infusion of an amount of water equal to the proportion of corn. The jar is put out into the sun—if summer—for twelve days, or under the fireplace—if in winter—[where a separate vault is made for it]—for the same period. The orifice is almost hermetically closed with a skin. After twelve days the jar is opened and contains a drink possessing intoxicating qualities. The first infusion is much prized, but the corn receives a second and sometimes even a third supply of water, to be put out again in a similar manner and to provide a kind of Beer for the consumer. This Beer is called "Mō," and is much

* The drawing and description of this scene were given in the *Illustrated London News* of the 12th February, 1870, under the heading of 'A Dance at Gilgit."

drunk by the Astóris and Chilasis [the latter are rather stricter Mussulmans than the other Shiná people]. After every strength has been taken out of the corn it is given away as food to sheep, etc., which they find exceedingly nourishing.

WINE.*

The Gilgitis are great wine-drinkers, though not so much as the people of Hunza. In Nagyr little wine is made. The mode of the preparation of the wine is a simple one. The grapes are stamped out by a man who, fortunately before entering into the wine press, washes his feet and hands. The juice flows into another reservoir, which is first well laid round with stones, over which a cement is put of chalk mixed with sheep-fat which is previously heated. The juice is kept in this reservoir; the top is closed, cement being put round the sides and only in the middle an opening is made over which a loose stone is placed. After two or three months the reservoir is opened, and the wine is used at meals and festivals. In Dareyl (and not in Gilgit, as was told to Vigne,) the custom is to sit round the grave of the deceased and eat grapes, nuts and Tshilgōzas (edible pine). In Astor (and in Chilâs ?) the custom is to put a number of Ghi (clarified butter) cakes before the Mulla, [after the earth has been put on the deceased] who, after reading prayers over them, distributes them to the company who are standing round with their caps on. In Gilgit, three days after the burial, bread is generally distributed to the friends and acquaintances of the deceased. To return to the wine presses, it is to be noticed that no one ever interferes with the store of another. I passed several of them on my road from Tshakerkōt onward, but they appeared to have been destroyed. This brings me to another custom which all the Dards seem to have of burying provisions of every kind in cellars that are scooped out in the mountains or near

* Wine is called in Gilgit by the same name as is "beer" by the Astoris, *viz.*: "Mō." The wine press is called "Mōe Kùrr." The reservoir into which it flows is called "Mōe Sán."

their houses, and of which they alone have any knowledge. The Maharajah's troops when invading Gilgit often suffered severely from want of food when, unknown to them, large stores of grain of every kind, butter, ghi, etc., were buried close to them. The Gilgitis and other so-called rebels, generally, were well off, knowing where to go for food. Even in subject Astor it is the custom to lay up provisions in this manner. On the day of birth of anyone in that country it is the custom to bury a stock of provisions which are opened on the day of betrothal of the young man and distributed. The ghi, which by that time turns frightfully sour, and [to our taste] unpalatable and the colour of which is red, is esteemed a great delicacy and is said to bring much luck.

The chalk used for cementing the stones is called "San Bàtt." Grapes are called "Djatsh," and are said, together with wine, to have been the principal food of Ghazanfar, the Rajah of Hunza, of whom it is reported that when he heard of the arrival of the first European in Astor (porbably Vigne) he fled to a fort called Gojal and shut himself up in it with his flocks, family and retainers. He had been told that the European was a great sorcerer, who carried an army with him in his trunks and who had serpents at his command that stretched themselves over any river in his way to afford him a passage. I found this reputation of European sorcery of great use, and the wild mountaineers looked with respect and awe on a little box which I carried with me, and which contained some pictures of clowns and soldiers belonging to a small magic lantern. The Gilgitis consider the use of wine as unlawful; probably it is not very long since they have become so religious and drink it with remorse. My Gilgitis told me that the Mughullí—a sect living in Hunza, Gojal, Yassen and Punyal*—considered the use of wine with prayers to be rather meritorious than otherwise. A Drunkard is called "Máto."

* These are the strange sect of the Muláis about whom more in my "Handbook of Hunza, Nagyr and a part of Yasín."

C. BIRTH CEREMONIES.

As soon as the child is born the father or the Mulla repeats the "Bâng" in his ear "Allah Akbar" (which an Astóri, of the name of Mirza Khan, said was never again repeated in one's life !). Three days after the reading of the "Bâng" or "Namáz" in Gilgit and seven days after that ceremony in Astor, a large company assembles in which the father or grandfather of the newborn gives him a name or the Mulla fixes on a name by putting his hand on some word in the Koran, which may serve the purpose or by getting somebody else to fix his hand at random on a passage or word in the Koran. Men and women assemble at that meeting. There appears to be no pardah whatsoever in Dardu land, and the women are remarkably chaste.* The little imitation of pardah amongst the Ranis of Gilgit was a mere fashion imported from elsewhere. Till the child receives a name the woman is declared impure for the seven days previous to the ceremony. In Gilgit 27 days are allowed to elapse till the woman is declared pure. Then the bed and clothes are washed and the woman is restored to the company of her husband and the visits of her friends. Men and women eat together everywhere in Dardu land. In Astór, raw milk alone cannot be drunk together with a woman unless thereby it is intended that she should be a sister by faith and come within the prohibited degrees of relationship. When men drink of the same raw milk they thereby swear each other eternal friendship. In Gilgit this custom does not exist, but it will at once be perceived that much of what has been noted above belongs to Mussulman custom generally. When a son is born great rejoicings take place, and in Gilgit a musket is fired off by the father whilst the "Bâng" is being read.

* This is said to be no longer the case, except in those Dard republics, where foreigners have not yet interfered. In monarchical Yasin, and, above all, in Hunza, sexual laxity has ever been great. Where Sunni rulers have substituted dancing-boys for the dancing of men (formerly both men and women danced together), a worse evil has been introduced. A most sacred relationship is the one created by the foster-mother. The linguistic portion of "The Hunza-Nagyr Handbook," as also of Parts I. and II. of "Dardistan" solves the questions of whether and where polygamy, endogamy, etc., existed among the Dards, who, in appearance and sentiment as regards women, as also in legendary lore, are very "European," but whom invasion will convert into strict Muhammadans and haters of the "Firenghi."

D. MARRIAGE.

In Gilgit it appears to be a more simple ceremony than in Chilâs and Astór. The father of the boy goes to the father of the girl and presents him with a knife about 1½ feet long, 4 yards of cloth and a pumpkin filled with wine. If the father accepts the present the betrothal is arranged. It is generally the fashion that after the betrothal, which is named: "*Shéir qatar wíye, ballí píye,* = 4 yards of cloth and a knife he has given, the pumpkin he has drunk," the marriage takes place. A betrothal is inviolable, and is only dissolved by death so far as the woman is concerned. The young man is at liberty to dissolve the contract. When the marriage day arrives the men and women who are acquainted with the parties range themselves in rows at the house of the bride, the bridegroom with her at his left sitting together at the end of the row. The Mulla then reads the prayers, the ceremony is completed and the playing, dancing and drinking begin. It is considered the proper thing for the bridegroom's father, if he belongs to the true Shín race, to pay 12 tolas of gold of the value [at Gilgit] of 15 Rupees Nanakshahi (10 annas each) to the bride's father, who, however, generally, returns it with the bride, in kind—dresses, ornaments, &c., &c. The 12 tolas are not always, or even generally, taken in gold, but oftener in kind—clothes, provisions and ornaments. At Astór the ceremony seems to be a little more complicated. There the arrangements are managed by third parties; an agent being appointed on either side. The father of the young man sends a present of a needle and three real (red) "múngs" called "lújum" in Chilâsi, which, if accepted, establishes the betrothal of the parties. Then the father of the bride demands *pro formâ* 12 tolas [which in Astór and Chilâs are worth 24 Rupees of the value of ten annas each.]

All real "Shín" people must pay this dowry for their wives in money, provisions or in the clothes which the bride's father may require. The marriage takes place when the girl reaches puberty, or perhaps rather the age when she is considered fit to be married. It may be mentioned here in general terms that those features in the ceremony which remind one of Indian customs are undoubtedly of Indian origin introduced into the country since the occupation of Astór by the Maharaja's troops. Gilgit which is further off is less subject to such influences, and whatever it may have of civilization is indigenous or more so than is the case at Astór the roughness of whose manners is truly Chilâsi, whilst its apparent refinement in some things is a foreign importation.

When the marriage ceremony commences the young man, accompanied by twelve of his friends and by musicians, sits in front of the girl's house. The mother of the girl brings out bread and Ghi-cakes on plates, which she places before the bridegroom, round whom she goes three times, caressing him and finally kissing his hand. The bridegroom then sends her back with a present of a few rupees or tolas in the emptied plates. Then, after some time, as the evening draws on, the agent of the father of the boy sends to say that it is time that the ceremony should commence. The mother of the bride then stands in the doorway of her house with a few other platefuls of cakes and bread, and the young man accompanied by his bridesman [" Shunèrr " in Astóri and " Shamaderr " in Gilgiti,] enters the house. At his approach, the girl, who also has her particular friend, the " Shaneróy " in Astóri, and " Shamaderoy " in Gilgiti, rises. The boy is seated at her right, but both in Astór and in Gilgit it is considered indecent for the boy to turn round and look at her. Then a particular friend, the " Dharm-bhai "* of the girl's

* The "brother in the faith" with whom raw milk has been drunk, *Vide* page 41.

Betrothal,	= balli = pumpkin in Gilgiti, Soél—Astóri		
Bridegroom,	= hileléo,	Gil.	hiláleo. Astóri.
Bride,	= hilal		
Bridegroom's MEN,	= garóni,	Gil.	hilalée, Astóri.
Marriage شادي	= garr,	Gil.	Kàsh. Astóri
Dowry,	= "dab,"	Gil. and Astóri	

brother asks her if she consents to the marriage. In receiving, or imagining, an affirmative, he turns round to the Mulla, who after asking three times whether he, she and the bridegroom as well as all present are satisfied, reads the prayers and completes the ceremonial. Then some rice, boiled in milk, is brought in, of which the boy and the girl take a spoonful. They do not retire the first night, but grace the company with their presence. The people assembled then amuse themselves by hearing the musicians, eating, &c.

It appears to be the custom that a person leaves an entertainment whenever he likes, which is generally the case after he has eaten enough.

It must, however, not be imagined that the sexes are secluded from each other in Dardistan. Young people have continual opportunities of meeting each other in the fields at their work or at festive gatherings. Love declarations often take place on these occasions, but if any evil intention is perceived the seducer of a girl is punished by this savage, but virtuous, race with death. The Dards know and speak of the existence of "pure love," "pâk âshiqi." Their love songs show sufficiently that they are capable of a deeper, than mere sexual, feeling. No objection to lawful love terminating in matrimony is ever made unless the girl or the boy is of a lower caste. In Gilgit, however, the girl may be of a lower caste than the bridegroom. In Astór it appears that a young man, whose parents—to whom he must mention his desire for marrying any particular person—refuse to intercede, often attains his point by threatening to live in the family of the bride and become an adopted son. A "Shîn" of true race at Astor may live in concubinage with a girl of lower caste, but the

---

(the grain, ghee and sheep that may accompany the betrothal-present is called by the Astóris "sakáro.")

Husband,	= baráo,	Gil.	baréyo,	Astóri.
Wife,	= Greyn,	Gil.	gréyn,	Astóri.

Wedding dinner "garéy tíki" in Gilgiti. "Kajjéyn bai kyas," in Astori (?) ["tikki" is bread, "bai" is a chippati, kyas = food].

relatives of the girl if they discover the intrigue revenge the insult by murdering the paramour, who, however, does not lose caste by the alliance.

The bridegroom dances as well as his twelve companions. The girl ought not to be older than 15 years; but at 12 girls are generally engaged.*

The Balti custom of having merely a *claim to dowry* on the part of the woman—the prosecution of which claim so often depends on her satisfaction with her husband or the rapacity of her relatives—is in spite of the intercourse of the Baltis with the Shîn people never observed by the latter; not even by the Shîn colonists of little Tibet who are called "Brokhpá."

When the bridegroom has to go for his bride to a distant village he is furnished with a bow. On arriving at his native place he crosses the breast of his bride with an arrow and then shoots it off. He generally shoots three arrows off in the direction of his home.

At Astór the custom is sometimes to fire guns as a sign of rejoicing. This is not done at Gilgit.

When the bridegroom fetches his bride on the second day to his own home, the girl is crying with the women of her household and the young man catches hold of her dress in front (at Gilgit by the hand) and leads her to the door. If the girl cannot get over embracing her people and crying with them quickly, the twelve men who have come along with the bridegroom (who in Astóri are called "hilalée" = bridegrooms and "garóni" in Gilgiti) sing the following song :—

INVITATION TO THE BRIDE.

Nikàstalì *quáray kusúni* ("*astali*" *is added to*
Come out hawk's daughter. *the fem. Imp*).
Nikastali *ke* *karanîliè* ("*balanîle*," in Gilgiti).
Come out why delayest thou!
Nikastali *máleyn* *gutîjo.*
Come out (from) thy father's tent.

* The Turks say "a girl of 15 years of age should be either married or buried.

Nikastali ke karanílič.
Come out why delayest thou.
Né ro tsharéyn baráye.
Do not weep waterfall's fairy.
Né ro teyn róng boje.
Do not weep thy colour will go.
Né ro jaro shidati.
Do not weep brethren's beloved.
Né ro téy róng boje.
Do not weep thy colour will go.
Né ro maleyn shidati.
Do not weep father's beloved.
Né ro téy róng boje.
Do not weep thy colour will go.

Translation.

Come out, O daughter of the hawk!
Come out, why dost thou delay?
Come forth from thy father's tent,
Come out and do not delay.
Weep not! O fairy of the waterfall!
Weep not! thy colour will fade;
Weep not! thou art the beloved of us all who are thy brethren,
Weep not! thy colour will fade.
O Weep not! thou beloved of fathers, [or "thy father's darling."]
For if thou weepest, thy face will grow pale.

Then the young man catches hold of her dress, or in Gilgit of her arm, puts her on horseback, and rides off with her, heedless of her tears and of those of her companions.

E. FUNERALS.

Funerals are conducted in a very simple manner. The custom of eating grapes at funerals I have already touched upon in my allusion to Dureyl in the chapter on "Wine." Bread is commonly distributed together with Ghî, etc., three days after the funeral, to people in general, a custom which is called "Nashí" by the Astóris, and "Khatm" by the

Gilgitis. When a person is dead, the Mulla, assisted generally by a near friend of the deceased, washes the body which is then placed in a shroud. Women assemble, weep and relate the virtues of the deceased. The body is conveyed to the grave the very day of the decease. In Astor there is something in the shape of a bier for conveying the dead. At Gilgit two poles, across which little bits of wood are placed sideways and then fastened, serve for the same purpose. The persons who carry the body think it a meritorious act. The women accompany the body for some fifty yards and then return to the house to weep. The body is then placed in the earth which has been dug up to admit of its interment. Sometimes the grave is well-cemented and a kind of small vault is made over it with pieces of wood closely jammed together. A Pîr or saint receives a hewn stone standing as a sign-post from the tomb. I have seen no inscriptions anywhere. The tomb of one of their famous saints at Gilgit has none. I have heard people there say that he was killed at that place in order to provide the country with a shrine. My Gilgiti who, like all his countrymen, was very patriotic, denied it, but. I heard it at Gilgit from several persons, among whom was one of the descendants of the saint. As the Saint was a Kashmiri, the veracity of his descendant may be doubted. To return to the funeral. The body is conveyed to the cemetery, which is generally at some distance from the village, accompanied by friends. When they reach the spot the Mulla reads the prayers standing as in the "Djenazá"—any genuflexion, "ruku" ركوع and prostration are, of course, inadmissible. After the body has been interred the Mulla recites the Fatiha, [opening prayer of the Koran] all people standing up and holding out their hands as if they were reading a book. The Mulla prays that the deceased may be preserved from the fire of hell as he was a good man, etc. Then after a short benediction the people separate. For three days at Gilgit and seven days at Astor the near relatives of the deceased do not eat meat. After that period the grave is again visited by the deceased's friends, who, on reaching the grave, eat some ghí and bread, offer up prayers, and, on returning, slaughter a sheep, whose kidney is roasted and divided in small bits amongst those present. Bread is distributed amongst those present and a little feast is indulged in, in memory of the deceased. I doubt, however, whether the Gilgitis are very exact in their religious exercises. The mention of death was always received with shouts of laughter by them, and one of them told me that a dead person deserved only to be kicked. He possibly only joked and there can be little doubt that the Gilgit people are not very communicative about their better feelings. It would be ridiculous, however, to deny them the possession of natural feelings, although I certainly believe that they are not over-burdened with sentiment. In Astór the influence of Kashmir has made the people attend a little more to the ceremonies of the Mussulman religion.

In Chilâs rigour is observed in the maintenance of religious practices, but elsewhere there exists the greatest laxity. In fact, so rude are the people that they have no written character of their own, and till very recently the art of writing (Persian) was confined to, perhaps, the Rajas of these countries or rather to their Munshis, whenever they had any. Some of them may be able to read the Koran. Even this I doubt, as of hundreds of people I saw only one who could read at Gilgit, and he was a Kashmiri who had travelled far and wide and had at last settled in that country.

F. HOLIDAYS.

The great holiday of the Shîn people happened in 1867, during the month succeeding the Ramazan, but seems to be generally on the sixth of February. It is called the "Shinó náo," "the new day of the Shîn people." The Gilgitis call the day "Shinó bazóno," "the spring of the Shîn people." [The year, it will be remembered, is divided into bazono = spring; walo = summer; shero = autumn;

yono = winter.] The snow is now becoming a little softer and out-of-door life is more possible. The festivities are kept up for twelve days. Visits take place and man and wife are invited out to dinner during that period. Formerly, when the Shîns had a Raja or Nawab of their own, it used to be the custom for women to dance during those twelve days. Now the advent of the Sepoys and the ridiculous pseudo-morality of the Kashmir rule have introduced a kind of Pardah and the chaste Shîn women do not like to expose themselves to the strangers. Then there is the Naurôz, which is celebrated for three, and sometimes for six, days.

There are now five great holidays in the year:

The I'd of Ramazân.
The Shinó-Náo.
The Naurôz.
Kurbanī I'd.
The Kùy Náo,* { Astóri.
Dúmniká, { Gilgiti.

On the last-named holiday the game of Polo is played, good clothes are put on, and men and women amuse themselves at public meetings.

The Shîn people are very patriotic. Since the Maharaja's rule many of their old customs have died out, and the separation of the sexes is becoming greater. Their great national festival I have already described under the head of "Historical Legend of Gilgit" (pages 14 to 16).

G. THE RELIGIOUS IDEAS OF THE DARDS.

If the Dards—the races living between the Hindu-Kush and Kaghán—have preserved many Aryan customs and traditions, it is partly because they have lived in almost perfect seclusion from other Muhammadans. In Chilâs, where the Sunni form of that faith prevails, there is little to relieve the austerity of that creed. The rest of the Muhammadan Dards are Shiahs, and that belief is more elastic and seems to be more suited to a quick-witted race, than the orthodox form of Islam. Sunniism, however, is

* Is celebrated in Autumn when the fruit and corn have become ripe. For a detailed account of this and other festivals see "Hunza-Nagyr Handbook," and Parts II. and III. of the "Languages and Races of Dardistan."

advancing in Dardistan and will, no doubt, sweep away many of the existing traditions. The progress, too, of the present invasion by Kashmir, which, although governed by Hindus, is chiefly Sunni, will familiarize the Dards with the notions of orthodox Muhammadans and will tend to substitute a monotonous worship for a multiform superstition. I have already noticed that, in spite of the exclusiveness of Hinduism, attempts are made by the Maharaja of Kashmir to gather into the fold those races and creeds which, merely because they are not Muhammadan, are induced by him to consider themselves Hindu. For instance, the Siah Posh Kafirs, whom I venture also to consider Dards, have an ancient form of nature-worship which is being encroached upon by Hindu myths, not because they are altogether congenial but because they constitute the religion of the enemies of Muhammadans, their own bitter foes who kidnap the pretty Kafir girls and to kill whom establishes a claim among Kafirs to consideration. In the same way there is a revival of Hinduism in the Buddhist countries of Ladak and Zanskar, which belong to Kashmir, and ideas of caste are welcomed where a few years ago they were unknown. As no one can become a Hindu, but any one can become a Muhammadan, Hinduism is at a natural disadvantage in its contact with an advancing creed and, therefore, there is the more reason why zealous Hindus should seek to strengthen themselves by amalgamation with other idolatrous creeds. To return to the Mussulman Dards, it will be easy to perceive by a reference to my ethnographical vocabulary what notions are Muhammadan and what traces there remain of a more ancient belief. The "world of Gods" is not the mere اخرة which their professed religion teaches, nor is the "serpent world" a Muhammadan term for our present existence. Of course, their Maulvis may read "religious lessons" and talk to them of Paradise and Hell, but it is from a more ancient source that they derive a kindly sympathy with the evil spirits "Yatsh;" credit them with good actions, describe their worship of the sun and moon, and fill the interior of mountains with their palaces and songs. Again, it is not Islam that tells them of the regeneration of their country by fairies—that places these lovely beings on the top of the Himalayas and makes them visit, and ally themselves to, mankind. The fairies too are not all good, as the Yatsh are not all bad. They destroy the man who seeks to surprise their secrets, although, perhaps, they condone the offence by making him live for ever after in fairy-land. Indeed, the more we look into the national life of the Dards the less do we find it tinctured by Muhammadan distaste of compromise. Outwardly their customs may conform to that ceremonial, but when they make death an opportunity for jokes and amusement we cannot refuse attention to the circumstance by merely explaining it away on the ground that they are savages. I have noticed the prevalence of caste among them, how proud they are of their Shîn descent, how little (with the exception of the more devout Chilâsis) they draw upon Scripture for their personal names, how they honour women and how they like the dog, an animal deemed unclean by other Muhammadans. The Dards had no hesitation in eating with me, but I should not be surprised to hear that they did not do so when Mr. Hayward visited them, for the Hinduized Mussulman servants that one takes on tours might have availed themselves of their supposed superior knowledge of the faith to inform the natives that they were making an improper concession to an infidel. A good many Dards, however, have the impression that the English are Mussulmans—a belief that would not deter them from killing or robbing a European traveller in some districts, if he had anything "worth taking." Gouhar-Amán [called "Gôrmán" by the people] of Yasin used to say that as the Koran, the word of God, was sold, there could be no objection to sell an expounder of the word of God, a Mulla, who unfortunately fell into his hands. I did not meet any real Shîn who was a Mulla,* but I have no doubt that, especially in

* I have already related that a foreign Mulla had found his way to Gilgit, and that the people, desirous that so holy a man should not leave

Hunza, they are using the services of Mullas in order to give a religious sanction to their predatory excursions. I have said that the Dards were generally Shiahs—perhaps I ought not to include the Shiah Hunzas among Dards as they speak a non-Aryan language unlike any other that I know*—and as a rule the Shiahs are preyed upon by Sunnis. Shiah children are kidnapped by Sunnis as an act both religious and profitable. Shiahs have to go through the markets of Bokhara denying their religion, for which deception, by the way, they have the sanction of their own priests.† Can we, therefore, wonder that the Muláï Hunzas make the best of both worlds by preferring to kidnap Sunnis to their own co-religionists? A very curious fact is the attachment of Shiahs to their distant priesthood. We know how the Indian Shiahs look to Persia; how all expect the advent of their Messiah, the Imám Mahdi; how the appointment of Kazis (civil functionaries) is made through the Mujtehid [a kind of high priest] and is ratified by the ruling power, rather than emanate direct from the secular authorities, as is the case with Sunnis. The well-known Sayad residing at Bombay, Agha Khan, has adherents even in Dardistan, and any command that may reach them from him [generally a demand for money] is obeyed implicitly. Indeed, throughout India and Central Asia there are men, some of whom lead an apparently obscure life, whose importance for good or evil should not be underrated by the authorities. [See my "Hunza and Nagyr Handbook, 1893."]

What we know about the religion of the Siah-Posh

---

them and solicitous about the reputation that their country had no shrine, killed him in order to have some place for pilgrimage. Similar stories are, however, also told about shrines in Afghanistan. My Sazîni speaks of shrines in Nagyr, Chilâs and Yasin, and says that in Sunni Chilâs there are many Mullahs belonging to all the castes—two of the most eminent being Kramins of Shatiál, about 8 miles from Sazîn. About Castes, *vide* page 62.

* I refer to the Khajuná, or Burishki, a language also spoken in Nagyr and a part of Yasin, whose inhabitants are Dards.

† I refer to the practice of "Taqqîah." In the interior of Kabul Hazara, on the contrary, I have been told that Pathan Sunni merchants have to pretend to be Shiahs, in order to escape being murdered.

Kafirs [whom I include in the term "Dards"] is very little. My informants were two Kafir lads, who lived for some weeks in my compound and whose religious notions had, no doubt, been affected on their way down through Kashmir. That they go once a year to the top of a mountain as a religious exercise and put a stone on to a cairn; that the number of Muhammadan heads hung up in front of their doors indicates their position in the tribe; that they are said to sit on benches rather than squat on the ground like other Asiatics; that they are reported to like all those who wear a curl in front; that they are fair and have blue eyes; that they drink a portion of the blood of a killed enemy—this and the few words which have been collected of their language is very nearly all we have hitherto known about them. What I have been able to ascertain regarding them, will be mentioned elsewhere.*

H. FORMS OF GOVERNMENT AMONG THE DARDS.

Chilâs, which sends a tribute every year to Kashmir for the sake of larger return-presents rather than as a sign of subjection, is said to be governed by a council of elders, in which even women are admitted.† When I visited Gilgit, in 1866, it was practically without a ruler, the invading troops of Kashmir barely holding their own within a few yards of the Gilgit Fort—a remarkable construction which, according to the report of newspapers, was blown up by accident in 1876, and of which the only record is the drawing published in the *Illustrated London News* of the 12th February 1870.‡ There is now (1877) a Thanadar of Gilgit, whose rule is probably not very different from that of his rapacious colleagues in Kashmir. The Gilgitis are kept quiet by the presence of the Kashmir army, and

* Since writing the above in 1867, a third Kafir from Katár has entered my service, and I have derived some detailed information from him and others regarding the languages and customs of this mysterious race, which will be embodied in my next volume. [This note was written in 1872.]

† I have heard this denied by a man from Sazîn, but state it on the authority of two Chilâsis who were formerly in my service.

‡ My Sazîni says that only a portion of the Fort was blown up.

by the fact that their chiefs are prisoners at Srinagar, where other representatives of once reigning houses are also under surveillance. Mansur Ali Khan, the supposed rightful Raja of Gilgit is there; he is the son of Asghar Ali Khan, son of Raja Khan, son of Gurtam Khan—but legitimate descent has little weight in countries that are constantly disturbed by violence, except in Hunza, where the supreme right to rob is hereditary.* The Gilgitis, who are a little more settled than their neighbours to the West, North and South, and who possess the most refined Dardu dialect and traditions, were constantly exposed to marauding parties, and the late ruler of Yasin, Gouhar-Amán, who had conquered Gilgit, made it a practice to sell them into slavery on the pretext that they were Shiahs and infidels. Yasin was lately ruled by Mir Wali, the supposed murderer of Mr. Hayward, and is a dependency of Chitrál, a country which is ruled by Amán-ul-mulk. The Hunza people are under Ghazan Khan, the son of Ghazanfar,† and seem to delight in plundering their Kirghiz neighbours, although all travellers through that inhospitable region, with the exception of Badakhshan merchants, are impartially attacked by these robbers, whose depredations have caused the nearest pass from Central Asia to India to be almost entirely deserted (1866). At Gilgit I saw the young Raja of Nagyr, with a servant, also a Nagyri. He was a most amiable and intelligent lad, whose articulation was very much more refined than that of his companion, who prefixed a guttural to every Khajuná word beginning with a vowel. The boy was kept a prisoner in the Gilgit Fort as a hostage to Kashmir for his father's good behaviour,

* *Vide* "History of Dardistan" for details of the contending dynasties of that region, pages 67 to 110.

† Major Montgomery remarks "the coins have the word Gujanfar on them, the name, I suppose, of some emblematic animal. I was however unable to find out its meaning." The word is غضنفر, Ghazanfar [which means in *Arabic:* lion, hero] and is the name of the former ruler of Hunza whose name is on the coins. In Hunza itself, coined money is unknown. [For changes since 1866, see "Hunza and Nagyr Handbook, 1893."]

and it was with some difficulty that he was allowed to see me and answer certain linguistic questions which I put to him. If he has not been sent back to his country, it would be a good opportunity for our Government to get him to the Panjab in the cold weather with the view of our obtaining more detailed information than we now possess regarding the Khajuná, that extraordinary language to which I have several times alluded. [This was done on my second official mission to Kashmîr in 1886.]

The name of *Rá*, *Rásh*, *Raja*, applied to Muhammadans, may sound singular to those accustomed to connect them with Hindu rulers, but it is the ancient name for "King" at Gilgit (for which "Nawab" seems a modern substitute in that country)—whilst Shah Kathor* in Chitrál, Tham in Hunza and Nagyr, Mitérr (Mihtar) and Bakhté in Yasin and Trakhné in Gilgit offer food for speculation. The Hunza people say that the King's race is Mogholote (or Mogul ?); they call the King *Sawwash* and affirm that he is Aishea (this probably means that he is descended from Ayesha, the wife of Muhammad).† Under the king or chief, for the time being, the most daring or intriguing hold office and a new element of disturbance has now been introduced into Dardistan by the Kashmir faction at every court [or rather robber's nest] which seeks to advance the interests or

* This was the *name* of the grandfather of Amán-ul-Mulk, the present ruler of Chitrál (1877). Cunningham says that the *title* of "Kathor" has been held for 2000 years. I may incidentally mention that natives of India who had visited Chitrál did not know it by any other name than "Kashkar" the name of the principal town, whilst Chitrál was called "a Kafir village surrounded by mountains" by Neyk Muhammad, a Lughmáni Nîmtsha (or half) Mussulman in 1866.

† This is the plausible Gilgit story, which will, perhaps, be adopted in Hunza when it becomes truly Muhammadan. In the meanwhile, my endeavour in 1866 to find traces of Alexander the Great's invasion in Dardistan, has led to the adoption of the myth of descent from that Conqueror by the Chinese Governor or the ancient hereditary "Thàm" of Hunza, who really is "*ayeshö*," or "heaven-born," owing to the miraculous conception of a female ancestor. "Mogholot" is the direct ancestor of the kindred Nagyr line, "Girkis," his twin-brother and deadly foe, being the ancestor of the Hunza dynasty. (See Genealogy on pages 69 and 111.)

ulterior plans of conquest or the Maharaja, our feudatory. Whilst the name of Wazir is now common for a "minister," we find the names of the subordinate offices of Trangpá, Yarfá, Zeytú, Gopá, etc., etc., which point to the reminiscences of Tibetan Government and a reference to the "Official Designations" in Part II. of my "Dardistan" will direct speculation on other matters connected with the subject.

I need scarcely add that under a Government, like that of Chitrál, which used to derive a large portion of its revenue from kidnapping, the position of the official slave-dealer (Diwánbigi)* was a high one. Shortly before I visited Gilgit, a man used to sell for a good hunting dog (of which animal the Dards are very fond), two men for a pony and three men for a large piece of pattú (a kind of woollen stuff). Women and weak men received the preference, it being difficult for them to escape once they have reached their destination. Practically, all the hillmen are republicans. The name for servant is identical with that of "companion;" it is only the prisoner of another tribe who is a "slave." The progress of Kashmir will certainly have the effect of stopping, at any rate nominally, the trade in *male* slaves, but it will reduce all subjects to the same dead level of slavery and extinguish that spirit of freedom, and with it many of the traditions, that have preserved the Dard races from the degeneracy which has been the fate of the Aryans who reached Kashmir and India. The indigenous Government is one whose occasional tyranny is often relieved by rebellion. I think the Dard Legends and Songs show that the Dards are a superior people to the Dogras, who wish to take their country in defiance of treaty obligations,† and I, for one, would almost prefer the continuance of present anarchy which may end in a national solution or in a *direct alliance* with the British, to the *épicier* policy of Kashmir which, without shedding blood,‡ has drained the

* This designation is really that of the Minister of Finances.

† This was written in 1866.

‡ I refer only to the present rule of Kashmir itself and not to the massacres by Kashmir troops in Dardistan, of which details are given elsewhere.

resources of that Paradise on earth and killed the intellectual and moral life of its people. The administration of justice and the collection of the taxes in Dardistan are carried on, the former with some show of respect for religious injunctions, the latter with sole regard to whatever the tax-gatherer can immediately lay his hand upon.

I. HABITATIONS.

Most of the villages, whose names I have given elsewhere, are situate on the main line of roads which, as everywhere in Himalayan countries, generally coincides with the course of rivers. The villages are sometimes scattered, but as a rule, the houses are closely packed together. Stones are heaped up and closely cemented, and the upper story, which often is only a space shielded by a cloth or by grass-bundles on a few poles, is generally reached by a staircase from the outside.* Most villages are protected by one or more wooden forts, which—with the exception of the Gilgit fort — are rude blockhouses, garnished with rows of beams, behind which it is easy to fight as long as the place is not set on fire. Most villages also contain an open space, generally near a fountain, where the villagers meet in the evening and young people make love to each other.† Sometimes the houses contain a subterranean apartment which is used as a cellar or stable—at other times, the stable forms the lower part of the house and the family live on the roof under a kind of grass-tent. In Ládak, a little earth heaped up before the door and impressed with a large wooden seal, was sufficient, some years ago, to protect a house in the absence of its owner. In Dardistan bolts, etc., show the prevailing insecurity. I have seen houses which had a courtyard, round which the rooms were built, but generally all buildings in

* *Vide* my comparison between Dardu buildings, etc., and certain excavations which I made at Takht-i-Bahi in Yusufzai in 1870.

† Seduction and adultery are punished with death in Chilâs and the neighbouring independent Districts. Morality is, perhaps, not quite so stern at Gilgit, whilst in Yasin, Hunza, and even in Nagyr before 1886, great laxity is said to prevail.

Dardistan are of the meanest description—the mosque of Gilgit, in which I slept one night whilst the Sepoys were burying two or three yards away from me, those who were killed by the so-called rebels, being almost as miserable a construction as the rest. The inner part of the house is generally divided from the outer by a beam which goes right across. My vocabulary will show all the implements, material, etc., used in building, etc. Water-mills and windmills are to be found.

Cradles were an unknown commodity till lately. I have already referred to the wine and treasury cellars excavated in the mountains, and which provided the Dards with food during the war in 1866, whilst the invading Kashmir troops around them were starving. Baths (which were unknown till lately) are sheltered constructions under waterfalls; in fact, they are mere sheltered douche-baths. There is no pavement except so far as stones are placed in order to show where there are *no* roads. The rooms have a fire-place, which at Astor (where it is used for the reception of live coals) is in the middle of the room. The conservancy arrangements are on the slope of the hills close to the villages, in front of which are fields of Indian corn, etc.

J. DIVISIONS OF THE DARD RACES.

The name of Dardistan (a hybrid between the "Darada" of Sanscrit writings and a Persian termination) seems now to be generally accepted. I include in it all the countries lying between the Hindu Kush and Kaghan (lat. 37° N. and long. 73° E. to lat. 35° N., long. 74° 30′ E.). In a restricted sense the Dards are the race inhabiting the mountainous country of Shináki, detailed further on, but I include under that designation not only the Chilâsis, Astóris, Gilgitis, Dareylis, etc., but also the people of Hunza, Nagyr, Yasin, Chitrál and Kafiristan.* As is the case with uncivilized races generally, the Dards have no name in common, but call each Dard

* Since writing the above I have discovered that the people of Kandiá —an unsuspected race and country lying between Swat and the Indus— are Dards and speak a Dialect of Shiná, of which specimens are given elsewhere in the " Races of the Hindukush." (See Appendix IV.) The tribe living on the left bank of the Kandiá river is called by its neighbours "Dard."

tribe that inhabits a different valley by a different name. This will be seen in subjoined Extract from my Ethnographical Vocabulary. The name "Dard" itself was not claimed by any of the race that I met. If asked whether they were "Dards" they said "certainly," thinking I mispronounced the word "dáde" of the Hill Panjabi which means "wild" "independent," and is a name given them by foreigners as well as "yaghi," = rebellious [the country is indifferently known as Yaghistan, Kohistan and, since my visit in 1866 as "Dardistan," a name which I see Mr. Hayward has adopted]. I hope the name of Dard will be retained, for, besides being the designation of, at least, *one* tribe, it connects the country with a range known in Hindu mythology and history. However, I must leave this and other disputed points for the present, and confine myself now to quoting a page of Part II. of my "Dardistán" for the service of those whom the philological portion of that work has deterred from looking at the descriptive part.

"SHIN are all the people of Chilâs, Astór, Dareyl or *Darèll*, Gôr, Ghilghit* or *Gilît*. All these tribes do not acknowledge the 'Guraizis,' a people inhabiting the Guraiz valley between Chilâs and Kashmîr, as *Shîn*, although the Guraizis themselves think so. The Guraizi dialect, however, is undoubtedly Shiná, much mixed with Kashmiri.

"The Shîns† call themselves 'Shîn, Shiná lôk, Shinâki,' and are very proud of the appellation, and in addition to the above-named races include in it the people of Tòrr, Hárben, Sazîn, [districts of, or rather near, Chilâs]; Tanyîre [Tangîr] belonging to Darèll; also the people of Kholi-Palus whose origin is Shîn, but who are mixed with Afghans. Some do not consider the people of Kholi-Palus as Shîn.‡

* The word ought to be transliterated "Gilgit" كلكت and pronounced as it would be in German, but this might expose it to being pronounced as "Jiljit" by some English readers, so I have spelt it here as "Ghilghit."

† In a restricted sense "Shîn" is the name of the highest *caste* of the Shîn *race*. "Róno" is the highest official caste next to the ruling families.

‡ My Sazîni says that they are really Shîns, Yashkuns, Dôms and Kramins, but pretend to be Afghans. *Vide* List of Castes, page 62. Kholi-Palus are *two* Districts, Khóli and Palus, whose inhabitants are

They speak both Shiná and Pukhtu [pronounced by the Shîn people 'Postó.'] The Baltis, or Little Tibetans, call the Shîn and also the Nagyr people 'Brokhpá,' or, as a term of respect, 'Brokhpá bábo.'* Offshoots of the 'Shîn' people live in Little Tibet and even the district of Dras, near the Zojilá pass on the Ladâk road towards Kashmîr, was once Shîn and was called by them *Humèss.* I was the first traveller who discovered that there were Shîn colonies in Little Tibet, viz.: the villages of Shingôtsh, Sáspur, Brashbrialdo, Bashó, Danàl djúnele, Tâtshin, Dorôt (inhabited by pure Shîns), Zungót, Tortzé (in the direction of Rongdu) and Durò, one day's march from Skardo."†

The Chilásis call themselves *Boté.*‡

" " " their fellow-countrymen of Takk = "*Kané*" or *Takke-Kané.*

[the *Matshuké* are now an extinct race, at all events in Dardistan proper.]

The Chilâsis call Gilgitis = *Gilîtí.*
" " " Astóris = *Astoríje.*
" " " Gôrş = *Goríje.*
" " " Dureylis = *Darêle.*
" " " Baltis = *Palóye.* Gil. = *Polôle.*
" " " Ladáki = *Botì.* Pl. of Bôt.
" " " Kashmiris = *Kashîre.*
" " " Dogras = *Sikkì* [Sikhs] now "Dôgréy."
" " " Affghans = *Patáni.*
" " " Nagyris = *Khadjunì.*
" " " Hunzas = *Hunzíje.*
" " " Yasînis = *Poré.*
" " " Punyalis = *Punyé.*
" " " Kirghiz = *Kirghìz.*

---

generally fighting with each other. Shepherds from these places often bring their flocks for sale to Gilgit. I met a few.

* This name is also and properly given by the Baltis to their Dard fellow-countrymen. Indeed the Little Tibetans look more like Dards than Ladákis.

† *Place aux dames!* For six years I believed myself "the discoverer" of this fact, but I find that, as regards Kartakchun in Little Tibet, I have been nearly anticipated by Mrs. Harvey, who calls the inhabitants "Dards," "Dâruds" (or "Dardoos.")

‡ My Sazîni calls the people of his own place = Bigé; those of Tórr = *Manuké*, and those of Harbenn = *Jure.*

NOTE.—The Kirghiz are described by the Chilâsis as having flat faces and small noses and are supposed to be very-white and beautiful, to be Nomads and to feed on milk, butter and mutton.

The Chilâsis call the people between Hunza and the Pamêr [our Pamir] on the Yarkand road = Gójâl.

There are also other Gojâls under a Raja of Gojâl on the Badakhshân road.

The Chílâsis call the Siah Pôsh Kâfirs = Bashgalí (Bashgal is the name of the country inhabited by this people who enjoy the very worst reputation for cruelty). They are supposed to kill every traveller that comes within their reach and to cut his nose or ear off as a trophy.*

The Chilâsis were originally four tribes; viz.:

The Bagoté of Buner.
The Kané of Takk.
The Boté of the Chilâs fort.
The Matshuké of the Matshukó fort.

The Boté and the Matshuké fought. The latter were defeated, and are said to have fled into Astor and Little Tibet territory.

A Foreigner is called "ósho."

Fellow-countrymen are called "malêki."

The stature of the Dards is generally slender and wiry and well suited to the life of a mountaineer. They are now gradually adopting Indian clothes, and whilst this will displace their own rather picturesque dress and strong, though rough, indigenous manufacture, it may also render them less manly. They are fairer than the people of the plains (the women of Yasin being particularly beautiful and almost reminding one of European women), but on the frontier they are rather mixed—the Chilâsis with the

* The two Kafirs in my service in 1866, one of whom was a Bashgali, seemed inoffensive young men. They admitted drinking a portion of the blood of a killed enemy or eating a bit of his heart, but I fancy this practice proceeds more from bravado than appetite. In "Davies' Trade Report" I find the following Note to Appendix XXX., page CCCLXII. "The ruler of Chitrál is in the habit of enslaving all persons from the tribes of Kalásh, Dangini and Bashghali, idolaters living in the Chitrál territory."

Kaghanis and Astóris—the Astóris and Gilgitis with the Tibetans, and the Guraizis with the Tibetans on the one hand and the Kashmiris on the other. The consequence is that their sharp and comparatively clear complexion (where it is not under a crust of dirt) approaches, in some Districts, a Tatar or Moghal appearance. Again, the Nagyris are shorter than the people of Hunza to whom I have already referred. Just before I reached the Gilgit fort, I met a Nagyri, whose yellow moustache and general appearance almost made me believe that I had come across a Russian in disguise. I have little hesitation in stating that the pure Shîn looks more like a European than any high-caste Brahmin of India. Measurements were taken by Dr. Neil of the Lahore Medical College, but have, unfortunately, been lost, of the two Shîns who accompanied me to the Panjab, where they stayed in my house for a few months, together with other representatives of the various races whom I had brought down with me.* The prevalence of caste among the Shîns also deserves attention. We have not the Muhammadan Sayad, Sheykh, Moghal, and Pathan (which, no doubt, will be substituted in future for the existing caste designations), nor the Kashmiri Muhammadan equivalents of what are generally mere names for occupations. The following List of Dard Castes may be quoted appropriately from Part II. of my " Dardistan " :—

K. CASTES.

" Raja (highest on account of position).

" Wazîr (of SHÎN race, and also the official caste of ' Róno').

" SHIN the highest caste ; the Shiná people of pure origin, whether they be Astóris, Gilgitis, Chilâsis, etc., etc.*

They say that it is the same race as the ' Moghals ' of India. Probably this name only suggested itself to them when coming in contact with Mussulmans from Kashmir or

* Both my Gilgiti follower, Ghulam Muhammad, and the Astóri retainer, Mirza Khan, claimed to be pure Shîns. The former returned to my service some years afterwards and was measured together with other Dards. (See Appendix V.)

the Panjab. The following castes are named in their order of rank (for exact details, see "Hunza Handbook"):

" *Yáshkunn* [the great land-owning race found in possession by the invading Shîns.]	=a caste formed by the intermixture (?) between the Shîn and a lower [aboriginal ?] race. A Shîn may marry a Yáshkunn woman [called 'Yáshkûni;'] but no Yáshkunn can marry a Shinóy=Shîn woman.
" *Tatshön*	=caste of carpenters.
" *Tshâjjá*	=weavers. The Gilgitis call this caste: '*Byêtshoi.*'
" *Akár*	=ironmonger.
" *Kûlál*	=potter.
" *Dôm**	=musician } (the lowest castes).
" *Kramîn*	=tanner ? }

"*N.B.*—The *Brokhpâ* are a mixed race of Dardu-Tibetans, as indeed are the Astoris [the latter of whom, however, consider themselves very pūre Shîns]; the *Guráïzis* are probably Dardu-Kashmiris; but I presume that the above division of caste is known, if not upheld, by every section of the Shiná people. The castes most prevalent in Guraiz are evidently Kashmiri as:

"Bhat. Lôn. Dâr. Wây. Râter. Thôkr. Bagâ."

* My Sazîni says that the Doms are below the Kramîns and that there are only 4 original castes: Shîn, Yáshkunn, Kramîn [or "Kamînn"] and Dôm, who, to quote his words, occupy the following relative ranks: "The Shîn is the right-hand, the Yáshkunn the left; the Kramîn the right foot, the Dôm the left foot." "The other castes are mere names for occupations." "A Shîn or Yáshkunn can trade, cultivate land or be a shepherd without loss of dignity — Kramîns are weavers, carpenters, etc., but not musicians—as for leather, it is not prepared in the country. Kramîns who cultivate land consider themselves equal to Shîns. Dôms can follow *any* employment, but, if a Dôm becomes a Mulla, he is respected. Members of the several castes who misbehave are called Mîn, Pashgun, Mamîn and Môm respectively. "A man of good caste will espouse sides and fight to the last even against his own brother." Revenge is a duty, as among Afghans, but is not transmitted from generation to generation, if the first murderer is killed. A man who has killed another, by mistake, in a fight or otherwise, seeks a frank forgiveness by bringing a rope, shroud and a buffalo to the relatives of the deceased. The upper castes can, if there are no Kramîns in their villages, do ironmonger's and carpenter's work, without disgrace; but must wait for Kramîns or Dôms for weaver's work. The women spin. The "Dôms" are the "Rôms" of Gipsy lore.

LEGENDS RELATING TO ANIMALS.*

1.—A BEAR PLAYS WITH A CORPSE.

It is said that bears, as the winter is coming on, are in the habit of filling their dens with grass and that they eat a plant, called "ajalí," which has a narcotic effect upon them and keeps them in a state of torpor during the winter. After three months, when the spring arrives, they awake and go about for food. One of these bears once scented a corpse which he disinterred. It happened to be that of a woman who had died a few days before. The bear, who was in good spirits, brought her to his den, where he set her upright against a stone and fashioning a spindle with his teeth and paws gave it to her into one hand and placed some wool into the other. He then went on growling "mû-mû-mû" to encourage the woman to spin. He also brought her some nuts and other provisions to eat. Of course, his efforts were useless, and when she after a few days gave signs of decomposition he ate her up in despair. This is a story based on the playful habits of the bear.

2.—A BEAR MOURNS A GIRL.

Another curious story is related of a bear. Two women, a mother and her little daughter, were one night watching their field of Indian corn "makai," against the inroads of these animals. The mother had to go to her house to prepare the food and ordered her daughter to light a fire outside. Whilst she was doing this a bear came and took her away. He carried her into his den, and daily brought her to eat and to drink. He rolled a big stone in front of the den, whenever he went away on his tours, which the girl was not strong enough to remove. When she became old enough to be able to do this he used daily to lick her feet, by which they became swollen and gradually dwindled down to mere misshapen stumps. The girl eventually died in childbirth, and the poor bear after vain efforts to restore her to life roamed disconsolately about the fields.

3.—ORIGIN OF BEARS.

It is said that bears were originally the offspring of a man who was driven into madness by his inability to pay his debts, and who took to the hills in order to avoid his creditors.†

4.—THE BEAR AND THE ONE-EYED MAN.

The following story was related by a man of the name of Ghalib Shah residing at a village near Astór, called Parishing. He was one night looking out whether any bear had come into his "tromba" field.‡ He

* These legends should be compared with the Chitrál Fables published by Mihtar Nizám-ul-Mulk in the *Asiatic Quarterly Review* of January, 1891, namely: "the vindictive fowl," "the golden mouse," "the mouse and the frog," "the quail and the fox." See Appendix III. as also Legends in "The Hunza-Nagyr Handbook."

† The scrupulousness of the Gipsies in discharging such obligations, when contracted with a member of the same race, used to be notorious. The Dôms or Rôms of the Shins are the "Romany" of Europe and our "Zingari" is a corruption of "Sinkari" or inhabitants on the borders of the River or Sin = the (Upper) Indus.

‡ Tromba, to be made eatable, must be ground into flour, then boiled in water and placed in the "tshamúl" [in Astori] or "popúsh" [Ghilgiti], a receptacle under the hearth, and has to be kept in this place for one night, after which it is fit for use after being roasted or put on a tawa [pan] like a Chupatti [a thin cake of unleavened bread]. "baráo" or tshítti baráo = sour baráo [móro baráo = sweet baráo].

saw that a bear was there and that he with his forepaws alternately took a pawful of "tromba," blew the chaff away and ate hastily. The man was one-eyed [shéo = blind; my Ghilgiti used "Kyor," which he said was a Persian word, but which is evidently Turkish] and ran to his hut to get his gun. He came out and pointed it at the bear. The animal who saw this ran round the blind side of the man's face, snatched the gun out of his hand and threw it away. The bear and the man then wrestled for a time, but afterwards both gave up the struggle and retired. The man, after he had recovered himself went to look for the gun, the stock of which he found broken. The match-string by which the stock had been tied to the barrel had gone on burning all night and had been the cause of the gun being destroyed. The son of that man still lives at the village and tells this story, which the people affect to believe.

5.—WEDDING FESTIVAL AMONG BEARS.

A Mulla, of the name of Lal Mohammad, said that when he was taken a prisoner into Chilás,* he and his escort passed one day through one of the dreariest portions of the mountains of that inhospitable region. There they heard a noise, and quietly approaching to ascertain its cause they saw a company of bears tearing up the grass and making bundles of it which they hugged. Other bears again wrapped their heads in grass, and some stood on their hind-paws, holding a stick in their forepaws and dancing to the sound of the howls of the others. They then ranged themselves in rows, at each end of which was a young bear; on one side a male, on the other a female. These were supposed to celebrate their marriage on the occasion in question. My informant swore to the story and my Ghilgiti corroborated the truth of the first portion of the account, which he said described a practice believed to be common to bears.

6.—THE FLYING PORCUPINE.

There is a curious superstition with regard to an animal called "Harginn," which appears to be more like a porcupine than anything else. It is covered with bristles; its back is of a red-brownish and its belly of a yellowish colour. That animal is supposed to be very dangerous, and to contain poison in its bristles. At the approach of any man or animal it is said to gather itself up for a terrific jump into the air, from which it descends unto the head of the intended victim. It is said to be generally about half a yard long and a span broad. Our friend Lal Mohammad, a saintly Akhunzada, but a regular Münchhausen, affirmed to have once met with a curious incident with regard to that animal. He was out shooting one day when he saw a stag which seemed intently to look in one direction.

* Almost every third man I met had, at some time or other, been kidnapped and dragged off either to Chilás, Chitrál, Badakhshán or Bukhárá. The surveillance, however, which is exercised over prisoners, as they are being moved by goat-paths over mountains, cannot be a very effective one and, therefore, many of them escape. Some of the Kashmir Maharajah's Sepoys, who had invaded Dardistan, had been captured and had escaped. They narrated many stories of the ferocity of these mountaineers; *e.g.*, that they used their captives as fireworks, etc., etc., in order to enliven public gatherings. Even if this be true, there can be no doubt that the Sepoys retaliated in the fiercest manner whenever they had an opportunity, and the only acts of barbarism that came under my observation, during the war with the tribes in 1866, were committed by the Kashmir invaders.

He fired off his gun, which however did not divert the attention of the stag. At last, he found out what it was that the stag was looking at. It turned out to be a huge "Harginn," which had swallowed a large Markhor with the exception of his horns! There was the porcupine out of whose mouth protruded the head and horns of the Markhor!! My Ghilgiti, on the contrary, said that the Harginn was a great snake "like a big fish called Nang." Perhaps, Harginn means a monster or dragon, and is applied to different animals in the two countries of Ghilghit and Astór.

7.—A FIGHT BETWEEN WOLVES AND A BEAR WHO WANTED TO DIG THEIR GRAVE.

A curious animal something like a wolf is also described. The species is called "Kō."* These animals are like dogs; their snouts are of a red colour, and are very long; they hunt in herds of ten or twenty and track game which they bring down, one herd or one Kō, as the case may be, relieving the other at certain stages. A Shikári once reported that he saw a large number of them asleep. They were all ranged in a single long line. A bear approached, and by the aid of a long branch measured the line. He then went to some distance and measuring the ground dug it out to the extent of the line in length. He then went back to measure the breadth of the sleeping troop when his branch touched one of the animals which at once jumped up and roused the others. They all then pursued him and brought him down. Some of them harassed him in front, whilst one of them went behind and sucked his stomach clean out. This seems to be a favourite method of these animals in destroying game. They do not attack men, but bring down horses, sheep and game.

* This is undoubtedly the *canis rutilans*, a species of wild dog, which hunts in packs after the wild goat, so numerously found in the high mountains round Gilgit. The snow-ounce also pursues it. Dardistan, specially Hunza, is the paradise of the ibex, the wild sheep, including the *ovis poli*, and the red bear.

The Flora and Fauna of Dardistan have been so minutely described in Part II. of my "Languages and Races of Dardistan," though mainly from a linguistic standpoint, that I have nothing to say here about the products and animals of that country. Nor need I say anything about the dress of its people, except that its rolled-up woollen cap is, practically, the sign of the brotherhood (sometimes like that of Cain) among all members of the Dard race, and, at once, distinguishes them from Pathans, Affghans, Kashmiris, and others. The beautifully-knit stockings are also a Dard art, and seem to have suggested, rather than followed, Kashmir patterns. Above all, the quasi-Celtic brass brooches of the women, and the family axes of the Hunza-Nagyris denote the antiquity of the Dard race. Curious is also the dress, light as air and softly warm, made of the fluff of the white giant vulture or of that of the wild fowl. I must also refer the reader who wishes to know details about the rivers, mountains, etc., of Dardistan, and the occupations of its peoples, to Part II. of my "Languages and Races of Dardistan," and to the main volume, of which this is a Supplement, namely, the so-called "Hunza and Nagyr Handbook," a volume of 247 folio pages.

DR. LEITNER'S TIBET DOG "CHANG."

GENEALOGIES AND HISTORY OF DARDISTAN.

I do not propose to do more in this place than give the roughest outline of this subject, as sketched in 1866 and 1872, and now rapidly brought up to date. My reason is to prevent those falsifications of History which are inevitable when a conqueror annexes a new country and the vilest in it naturally becomes his first friends, and fabricate their family tree. Therefore, with all its errors, which subsequent enquiries have corrected, there is an element of actuality in the following accounts gathered from Dards in 1866, the value of which will become apparent when I write the history of the events that are drawing Dardistan into the devastating range of European influences and politics:

GENEALOGY OF THE GILGIT, YASIN, CHITRAL. NAGYR, HUNZA, AND OTHER DYNASTIES SINCE 1800.

I.—GILGIT ... ... Gurtam Khan (1800), hereditary ruler of Gilgit, whose dynasty can be traced to the daughter of Shiribadatt, the last, almost mythical, pre-Muhammadan Raja of Gilgit. Killed in 1810 by Suleyman Shah of Yasin.

Raja Khan (?) died 1814.	Muhammad Khan reigns till 1826 and is killed by Suleyman Shah of Yasin.	Abbas Ali, killed in 1815 by Suleiman Shah.

Asghar Ali killed on his flight to Nagyr by Suleyman Shah.

Mansur Ali Khan,
(the rightful Raja of Gilgit, probably still a prisoner in Srinagar).

1827.—Azad Shah, Raja of Gakutsh, appointed ruler of Gilgit by Suleyman Shah whom he kills in 1829.

Tahir Shah of Nagyr conquers Gilgit in 1834 and kills Azad.

Sakandar Khan, killed by Gauhar Aman of Yasin, in 1844.	Kerîm Khan, (Raja of Gôr), (calls in Kashmir troops under Nathe Shah in 1844) was killed in 1848 in Hunza.	Suleyman Khan.

Muhammad Khan died in 1859 when on a visit to Srinagar.	Suleyman Khan.	Sultan Muhammad.	Rustam Khan.
Alidád Khan (son of Muhammad Khan's sister).			Ghulam Hayder.

II.—YASIN DYNASTY. It is said that both the Yasin and the Chitral dynasties are descended from a common ancestor "Kathôr." The Gilgitis call the Yasînis "Poryalé" and the Chitralis "Katoré."

Khushwakt (?) died 1800 (?) from whom the present dynasty derives the name of "Khushwaktia." [A Raja of that name and dignity often met me at Srinagar in 1886.]

He had two sons, *Suleyman Shah and Malik Amán Shah.* The former died about 1829 and left four sons and a daughter whom he married to Ghazanfar, the Rajah of Hunza. The names of the sons are Azmat Shah, the eldest, Ahmad Shah, Rahîm Khan and Zarmast Khan.

Malik Amán Shah was the father of seven or, as some say, of ten sons, the most famous of whom was GAUHAR AMAN, surnamed "Adam farosh" (the man-seller) the third son. The names of the sons are: Khuda Amán, Duda Amán, Gauhar Amán, Khalîl Amán, Akbar Amán (who was killed by his nephew Malik Amán, eldest son of his brother Gauhar-Amán); ISA BAHADUR (son of Malik Amán Shah by a concubine), Gulsher, Mahter Sakhi, Bahadur Khan (who was murdered) and Mir Amán (?) of Mistuch (?).

Gauhar Amán left seven sons: MALIK AMÁN (also called Mîr Kammu? now in Tangîr?) Bahadur Amán, murdered by Lochan Singh, MIR VALI (who killed Hayward), Mir Ghâzi, PAHLWAN (who killed Mir Vali), Khan Daurán and Shajáyat Khan. [The Khushwaktia Dynasty has since been dispossessed by the kindred dynasty of Chitrál in 1884.]

III.—CHITRAL OR "SHAH KATHORIA" DYNASTY.

SHAH KATHOR, the son of Shah Afzal, (who died about 1800) was a soldier of fortune who dispossessed the former ruler, whose grandson, Vigne saw in the service of Ahmad Shah, the independent ruler of Little Tibet in 1835. Cunningham considers that the name of Kathôr is a title that has been borne by the rulers of Chitrál for 2,000 years.

Shah Kathor had a brother, Sarbaland Khan, whose descendants do not concern us, and four sons and a daughter married to Gauhar Amán of Yasin. The names of the sons were: *Shah Afzal* (who died in 1858), Tajammul Shah who was killed in 1865 by his nephew Adam-khor—or man-eater—(so called from his murderous disposition; his real name was Muhtarim Shah), Ghazab Shah (who died a natural death) and Afrasiab (who was killed). The murdered Tajammul Shah left two sons namely Malik Shah (who revenged his father's death by killing Adam Khôr), and Sayad Ali Shah.

Shah Afzal left AMÁN-UL-MULK, his eldest son, the present ruler of Chitrál [1872] Adam-khôr (who usurped the rule for a time); Kohkán Beg, ruler of Drus; a daughter whom he married to Rahmat-ulla-Khan, chief of Dîr; Muhammad Ali Beg; Yadgar Beg; Bahadur Khan; and another daughter whom Gauhar-Amán married as well as Shah Afzal's sister and had Pahlwan by her.

Amán-ul-Mulk married a daughter of the late Ghazan Khan, chief of Dîr, by whom he had Sardar (his eldest son), also called Nizam-ul-Mulk. Amán-ul-Mulk's other sons are Murad and others whose names will be found elsewhere. One of his daughters is married to Jehandar Shah, the former ruler of Badakhshán and the other to the son of the present Chief, Mîr Mahmud Shah. [Full details are given elsewhere of the Yasin-Chitrál house.]

IV.—The names of the principal chiefs of the Chilâsis and of the Yaghistanis (the independent Hill tribes of Darêl, Hôdûr, Tangir, etc.

have already been given in my "history" of their "Wars with Kashmir. Just as in Chilâs and Kandiá, the administration is in the hands of a Board of Elders. The Maharaja of Kashmir only obtains tribute from three villages in Chilaz, *viz.*, the villages of Chilás, Takk and Bundar.

V.—NAGYR,* [is tributary to Ahmad Shah of Little Tibet about the beginning of this century, but soon throws off this allegiance to Ahmad Shah under Alif Khan.] (?) ... ... Alif Khan. 1800 (?)

[See "Historical Legend of the Origin of Gilgit," pages 9 to 16. The Nagyr-Hunza Rajas or Thams similarly claim a divine origin and account for it through the two fairy-brothers who disappeared at Gilgit. See note on page 111.]

["Nagyr," which Col. Biddulph very properly writes "Nager" (like "Pamèr") is now spelt "Nag*a*r," so as to confound it with the Indian "Nagar" for "town," from which it is quite different.]

Alif Khan. 1800 (?)
|
Raja Za'far Khan Záhid (the present Raja of Nagyr).
|
Son (a hostage for his father's adhesion to Kashmîr, whom I saw at Gilgit in 1866). The names of his maternal uncles are Shah Iskandar and Raja Kerîm Khan (?) the elder brother. (The full genealogy of Hunza-Nagyr is given elsewhere.)

VI.—HUNZA ... ... Ghazanfar, died 1865.
|
Ghazan Khan, present ruler.† (1866)

VII.—BADAKHSHAN ... ... *Sultân Shah.*

Sultân Shah.
- Rejeb Shah.
  - Ahmad Shah.
    - Rahmat Shah.
    - Shah Ibrahim Khan.
    - MAHMUD SHAH [1872] (present ruler of Badakhshan under Kabul) stayed a long time with his maternal uncle, the ruler of Kunduz, whence he has often been miscalled "a Sayad from Kunduz."
- Mirza Kalán.
  - NIZAM-UD-DIN (surnamed MIR SHAH).
    - Shajá-ul Mulk.
    - JEHANDAR SHAH, the former ruler, independent of Kabul (now (1872) a fugitive; infests the Kolab road).
    - Suleyman Shah.
    - Shahzada Hasan.
    - Abdulla Khan (by a concubine).
  - Yusuf Ali Khan.
  - Saad-ulla Khan.

Yusuf Ali Khan had seven sons: Mirza Kalán, surnamed Mir Jan; Hazrat Ján; Ismail Khan; Akbar Khan; Umr Khan, Sultan Shah; Abdurrahim Khan (by a concubine).

Saad-ulla Khan had two sons: Baba Khan and Mahmud Khan (by a concubine).

* Only so much has been mentioned of the Genealogies of the rulers of Nagyr, Hunza, and Dîr, as belongs to this portion of my account of Dardistan.

† Full details of the son and successor of Ghazan Khan, Safdar Ali Khan, to the present vassal of the Kashmir (Anglo-Indian) Government, Muhammad Názim Khan, the fugitive Safdar Ali Khan's half-brother, are given elsewhere.

VIII.—DIR ... ... Ghazan Khan (a very powerful ruler. Chitrál is said to have once been tributary to him).

Rahmat-ulla Khan and other eight sons (dispersed or killed in struggles for the Chiefship).

The connection of Little Tibet with the Dard countries had ceased before 1800.

ROUGH CHRONOLOGICAL SKETCH OF THE HISTORY OF DARDISTAN SINCE 1800.

1800.—Gurtam Khan, hereditary ruler of the now dispossessed Gilgit Dynasty, rules 10 years in peace; is killed in an engagement with Suleyman Khan, Khushwaktia, great uncle of the famous Gauhar Amán (or Gormán) of Yasin.

1811.—Muhammad Khan, the son of Gurtam Khan, defeats Suleyman Khan, rules Gilgit for 15 years in peace and perfect independence whilst—

1814.—(Sirdar Muhammad Azim Khan, Barakzai, is ruler of Kashmir).

1819.—Ranjit Singh annexes Kashmir.

1826.—Suleyman Khan of Yasin again attacks Gilgit and kills Muhammad Khan and his brother, Abbas Ali. Muhammad Khan's son, Asghar Ali, is also killed on his flight to Nagyr.

1827.—Suleyman Shah appoints Azad Khan (?), petty Raja of Gakutsh over Gilgit as far as Bunji; Azad Khan ingratiates himself with the people and rebels against Suleyman Shah whom he kills (?) in 1829.

1829.—Suleyman Shah, head of the Khushwaktia family of Yasin, dies.

1833.—Gauhar Amán turns his uncle, Azmat Shah, out of Yasin.

1834.—Azad Khan is attacked by Tahir Shah of Nagyr and killed. Tahir Shah, a Shiah, treats his subjects well. Dies 1839. Vigne visits Astór in 1835, but Tahir Shah will not allow him to cross over to Gilgit. At that time the Sikhs had not conquered any Dard country. Ahmad Shah was independent ruler of Little Tibet (Baltistan) and under him was Jabar Khan, chief of Astór (whose descendants,* like those of Ahmad Shah himself and of the Ladak rulers are now petty pensioners under Kashmir surveillance). (The Little Tibet dynasty had once, under Shah Murad, about 1660, conquered Hunza, Nagyr, Gilgit and Chitrál, where that ruler built a bridge near the fort.) Zorawar Singh conquers Little Tibet in 1840, but no interference in Dard affairs takes place till 1841 when the Sikhs are called in as temporary allies by the Gilgit ruler against Gauhar Amán of Yasin.

1840.—Sakandar Khan, son of Tahir Shah, succeeds to the throne of Gilgit and rules the country—with his brothers, Kerim Khan and Suleyman Khan.

* Abbas Khan (?) now at Srinagur and Bahadur Khan (?).

1841.—Gauhar Amán of Yasin conquers Gilgit. Its ruler, Sikandar Khan, asks Sheikh Ghulam Muhi-ud-din, Governor of Kashmir on behalf of the Sikhs, for help.

1842.—1,000 Kashmir troops sent under Nathe Shah, a Panjabi.

1843.—Sikandar Khan is murdered at Bakrôt at the instigation of Gauhar Amán.

1844.—Gauhar Amán of Yasin re-conquers the whole country, selling many of its inhabitants into slavery.

Nathe Shah, joined by Kerim Khan, younger brother of Sikandar Khan and 4,000 reinforcements, takes Numal Fort, but his subordinate Mathra Das is met at Sher Kila (20 miles from Gilgit) by Gauhar Amán and defeated.

1845.—Karim Khan succeeds his brother as ruler (called "Raja," although a Muhammadan) of Gilgit and pays a small sum for the retention of some Kashmir troops in the Gilgit Fort under Nathe Shah. The Rajas of Hunza, Nagyr and Yasin [Gauhar Amán sending his brother Khalil Amán to Sheikh Iman-ud-din] now seek to be on good terms with Kashmir, especially as its representatives, the tyrannical Nathe Shah and his equally unpopular successor, Atar Singh, are removed by its Muhammadan Governor.

1846.—Karim Khan, Raja of Gor, another son of Tahir Shah, calls in Nathe Shah and defeats Gauhar Amán at Basin, close to Gilgit. A succession of officers of Ghulab Singh then administer the country in connexion with the Raja of Gilgit (Wazir Singh, Ranjit Rai, Bakhshu, Ali Bakhsh and Ahmad Ali Shah, brother or cousin of Nathe Shah). By Treaty (see page 110):

"KASHMIR AND ITS DEPENDENCIES EASTWARD OF THE INDUS" are made over by the British to the Hindu Ghulab Singh. Gilgit, which lies to the *westward* of the Indus, is thus excluded from the dominions of that Maharaja. Gilgit was also, strictly speaking, not a dependency of Kashmir, nor was Chilás.

1847.—The Maharaja restores Nathe Shah, whilst confirming his cousin Nazar Ali Shah as Military Commandant of Gilgit. Raja Kerim Khan sends his brother Suleyman Khan on a friendly mission to Srinagar, where he dies. Vans Agnew arrives at Chalt on the Gilgit frontier towards Nagyr and makes friends with the people, who at first thought that he came accompanied by troops.

1848.—Isa Bahadur, the half-brother of Gauhar Amán by a concubine of Malik Amán Shah, is expelled from Sher Kila, a Fort belonging to Punyal, a dependency of Yasin, and finds refuge with the Maharaja, who refuses to give him up. Gauhar Amán accordingly sends troops under his brother Akbar Amán and captures the Bargu and Shukayôt Forts in Gilgit territory. The Rajas of Hunza and Nagyr combine with Gauhar Amán and assisted by the Gilgit people, with whom Kerim Khan was unpopular because of his friendship for Kashmir, defeat and kill Nathe Shah and Kerim Khan. Gauhar Amán captures the Gilgit and Chaprôt Forts. The Kashmir troops re-invade the country and at the beginning of

1849.—Wrest all the forts in Gilgit territory from Gauhar Amán, and make over the rule of that country to Raja Muhammad Khan, son of Kerim Khan, assisted by the Kashmir representative, Aman Ali Shah as Thanadar, soon removed for oppression.

1850.—The raids of the Chilâsis on Ástór is made the occasion for invading the country of Chilâs, which, *not* being a dependency of Kashmir, is *not* included in the Treaty of 1846. (See page 110.) The Maharaja gives out that he is acting under orders of the British Government. Great consternation among petty chiefs about Muzaffarabad, regarding ulterior plans of the Maharaja. The Sikhs send a large army, which is defeated before the Fort of Chilâs.

1851.—Bakhshi Hari Singh and Dewan Hari Chand are sent with 10,000 men against Chilâs and succeed in destroying the fort and scattering the hostile hill tribes which assisted the Chilâsis.

1852.—The Maharaja's head officers, Santu Singh and Ramdhan, are murdered by the people of Gilgit whom they oppressed. The people again assist Gauhar Amán, who defeats and kills Bhup Singh and Ruknuddin (for details *vide* Appendix), and drives the Kashmir troops across the Indus to Astór.

1853.—The Maharaja now confines himself to the frontier, assigned to him by nature as well as the treaty, at Bunji, on the east of the Indus, but sends agents to sow discord in the family of Gauhar Amán. In addition to Isa Bahadur, he gained over two other brothers, Khalil Amán and Akbar Amán, but failed with Mahtar Sakhi, although an exile. He also attracted to his side Azmat Shah, Gauhar Amán's uncle.

1854.—The Maharaja instigated Shah Afzal of Chitrál to attack Gauhar Amán, and accordingly in

1855.—Adam Khor, son of Shah Afzal of Chitrál, drove Gauhar Amán from the possession of Mistuch and Yasin and restricted him to Punyal and Gilgit.

1856.—The Maharaja sends a force across the Indus under Wazir Zoraweru and Atar Singh assisted by Raja Zahid Jafar of Nagyr,* and Gauhar Amán thus attacked in front and flank, retreats from Gilgit and dispossesses Adam Khor from Yasin and Mistuch.

1857.—Gauhar Amán again conquers Gilgit and drives out Isa Bahadur, officiating Thanadar of that place. Gauhar Amán and the Maharaja intrigue against each other in Chitrál, Nagyr, Hunza, etc.

1858.—Shah Afzal of the Shah Kathor branch, ruler of Chitrál, dies.

Intrigues in Gilgit against Gauhar Amán, by Muhammad Khan, son of Raja Karim Khan, assisted by Kashmir. Muhammad Khan is conciliated by marrying the daughter of Gauhar Amán. The Sai District of Gilgit beyond the Niludar range is still held by the Sikhs.

* I believe that Raja Záhid Za'far's wife was a sister of Rajas Kerîm Khan and Sakandar Khan of Gilgit (also of Nagyr descent). *Vide* page 67 and Heading V. on page 69.
This connexion might account for Za'far helping the Dogras, who had reinstated Kerîm Khan in Gilgit.

1859.—Mir Shah of Badakhshan and Raja Ghazanfar of Hunza assist Gauhar Amán in attacking Nagyr, which is under the friendly Raja Zahid Jafar, and in trying to turn out the Sikhs from Sai and even Bunji. Azmat Shah, uncle of Gauhar Amán, is expelled from Chitrál where he had sought refuge.

Aman-ul-Mulk, King of Chitrál, dispossesses his younger brother, Adam Khor, who had usurped the throne, from the rule of Chitrál and joins Gauhar Amán against Kashmir.

1860.—The Maharaja instigates Adam Khor and Azmat Shah, who were in the country of Dir with Ghazan Khan, a friendly chief to Kashmir, to fight Gauhar Amán—Adam Khor was to have Yasin. Azmat Shah was to take Mistuch and Sher Kila (Payal) was to be given to Isa Bahadur, the Maharaja to have Gilgit. Intrigues of the Maharaja with the Chiefs of Dir, Badakhshan, etc.

Gauhar Amán dies, which is the signal for an attack by the Maharaja co-operating with the sons of Raja Kerim Khan of Gilgit. Gilgit falls easily to Lochan Singh, who murders Bahadur Khan, brother of Gauhar Amán, who was sent with presents from Malik Amán, also called Mulk Amán, son of Gauhar Amán. The Sikhs, under Colonels Devi Singh and Hushiara and Radha Kishen, march to Yasin expelling Mulk Amán from that country (which is made over to Azmat Shah) as also from Mistuch. Isa Bahadur is reinstated as ruler of Payal, but Mulk Amán returns and drives him and Azmat Shah out. The Kashmir troops fail in their counter-attacks on Yasin, but capture some prisoners, including Mulk Amán's wife.

1861.—Malik Amán murders his uncle, Akbar Amán, a partisan of Kashmir.

Badakhshan, Chitrál and Dir ask the Maharaja to assist them against the dreaded invasion of the Kabul Amirs, Afzal Khan and Azim Khan. Amán-ul-Mulk tries to get up a religious war (Jehád) among all the Muhammadan Chiefs. Hunza and Nagyr make friends. Both Adam Khor and Amán-ul-Mulk, who have again become reconciled, send conciliatory messages to the Maharaja, who frustrates their designs, as they are secretly conspiring against him.

Even Mulk Amán makes overtures, but unsuccessfully.

1862.—Kashmir troops take the Fort of Roshan. A combination is made against Mulk Amán, whose uncle Gulsher and brother Mir Ghazi go over to the Maharaja.

1863.—Mulk Amán advancing on Gilgit is defeated in a very bloody battle at the Yasin Fort of Shamîr. Massacre of women and children by the Kashmir troops at Yasin.

1864.—Mir Vali and his Vazir Rahmat become partisans of the Maharaja.

1865.—Ghazanfar, the Raja of Hunza and father-in-law of Mulk-Amán, dies, which causes Mirza Bahadur of the rival Nagyr to combine for an attack on Hunza with Kashmir. Adam Khor murders his uncle, Tajammul Shah, whose son, Malik Shah, murders

1866.—Adam Khor (some say at the instigation of his elder brother, Amán-ul-Mulk). Malik Shah seeks refuge with the Maharaja who will not give him up to Amán-ul-Mulk. Amán-ul-Mulk then sprung the mine he had long prepared, and when the long contemplated campaign against Hunza took place in 1866, all the Mussulman Chiefs who had been adherents of the Maharaja, including Mir Vali, fell away. The Kashmir troops which had advanced on Nummal were betrayed, and defeated by the Hunza people (now ruled by Ghazan Khan, son of Ghazanfar).

All the hill tribes combine against Kashmir and reduce the Dogras to the bare possession of Gilgit, which however held out successfully against more than 20,000 of the allied Dards, headed by Amán-ul-Mulk, Ghazan Khan and Mir Vali. Very large reinforcements were sent by Kashmir,* at whose approach the besiegers retreated, leaving, however, skirmishers all over the country.

Wazir Zoraweru followed up the advantage gained by invading Dareyl. Whilst the place was yet partially invested, Dr. Leitner made his way to the Gilgit Fort and frustrated two attempts made against him by the employés of the Maharaja, who ostensibly were friends.

1867.—Jehandár Shah of Badakhshan is expelled from his country by the Governor of Balkh and seeks refuge in Kabul, where he is restored a year afterwards to his ancestral throne by the influence of Abdurrahman Khan, son of the Amir Afzal Khan and by his popularity. His rival, Mahmud Shah, leaves without a struggle. Mir Vali, joining Mulk Amán, made an unsuccessful attack on Isa Bahadur and Azmat Shah, who beat them off with the help of Kashmir troops from Gilgit. The consequence was general disappointment among the Muhammadan Chiefs and the Hill tribe of Dareyl (which had been subdued in the meantime) and all opened friendly relations with Kashmir, especially.

1868.—Mir Vali rules Yasin with Pahlwan.† Mulk Amán flees to Chitrál.

1869.—Mulk Amán takes service with Kashmir and is appointed on a salary, but under surveillance, at Gilgit.

1870.—Mr. Hayward visits Yasin in March; is well received by the Chief, Mir Vali, but returns, as he finds the passes on to the Pamir closed by snow—visits the country a second time in July, after exposing the conduct and breach of treaty of the Kashmir authorities, and is murdered, apparently without any object, at Darkôt in Yasin, one stage on to Wakhan, by some men in the

* Jewahir Singh went by Shigar with 13,000 Baltis (Little Tibetans), 2,000 light infantry came *viâ* Jagloth under Sirdar Mahmud Khan. The general of all the "Khulle" Regiments was Bakhshi Radha Kishn. Colonel Hoshiára went by the Nomal road to Nagyr, and after destroying 3,000 head of sheep and many villages returned.

Wazir Zoraweru went to Darêl with Colonel Devi Singh and 10,000 men (?). Bija Singh was at Gor (?) and Hussani Ali was in command of the Artillery.

† Mir Vali and Pahlwan are brothers by different mothers. Mulk Amán and Nura Guzá (Mír Ghazi ?) are brothers by the same mother—so one of my men says. Pahlwan is Amán-ul-Mulk's sister's son (*vide* "History of Wars with Kashmir").

service of his former friend, Mir Vali, who, however, soon flies the country in the direction of Badakhshan, then seeks refuge with the Akhund of Swat, and finally returns to Yasin, where he is reported to have been well received by Pahlwan. Whilst in Chitrál, he was seen by Major Montgomerie's Havildar and was on good terms with Amán-ul-Mulk, who is supposed, chiefly on the authority of a doubtful seal, to be the instigator of a murder which was not, apparently, to his interests and which did not enrich him or Mir Vali with any booty, excepting a gun and a few other trifles. Much of the property of Mr. Hayward was recovered by the Kashmir authorities, and a monument was erected by them to his memory at Gilgit, where there is already a shrine, which is referred to on pages 47 and 51.

1871.—Jehandár Shah, son of Mir Shah, who had again been turned out of the rule of Badakhshan in October 1869 by Mir Mahmud Shah with the help of the Afghan troops of Amir Sher Ali, finds an asylum in Chitrál with Amán-ul-Mulk (whose daughter had been married to his son) after having for some time shared the fortunes of his friend, the fugitive Abdurrahman Khan of Kabul. (Chitrál pays an annual tribute to the Chief of Badakhshan in slaves, which it raises either by kidnapping travellers or independent Kafirs or by enslaving some of its own Shiah and Kafir subjects—the ruler being of the Sunni persuasion.)

1872.—Late accounts are confused, but the influence of Amir Sher Ali seems to be pressing through Badakhshán on Chitrál and through Bajaur on Swat on the one hand and on the Kafir races on the other. The Maharaja of Kashmir on the one side and the Amir of Kabul on the other seem to endeavour to approach their frontiers at the expense of the intervening Dard and other tribes. Jehandár Shah infests the Kolab road and would be hailed by the people of Badakhshan as a deliverer from the oppressive rule of Mahmud Shah, as soon as the Kabul troops were to withdraw.

So far my "Dardistan," in which a detailed "History of the Wars with Kashmir" will be found. The events since 1872 need only to be indicated here in rough outline, and, unfortunately, confirm my worst anticipations as to the destruction of the independence of the Dardu tribes, of their legendary lore, and, above all, of the purity of their languages, including the prehistoric Khajuná or "Burishki" spoken in Hunza-Nagyr, and a part of Yasin. What are the admitted encroachments of our Ally, the Maharaja of Kashmir, have been utilized in our supposed interests, and we have stepped in to profit, as we foolishly think, by his sins, whilst he is tricked out of their reward. Falsely alleging that Hunza-Nagyr were rebellious vassals of Kashmir, when Hunza at all events was under Chinese protectorate, we have reduced their patriotic defenders to practical servitude, and, by to-day's *Times* (21st November, 1892), are starting, along with 250 rifles and two guns, some 100 men of a Hunza levy to Chitrál to put down a trouble which our ill-judged interference has created in another independent principality, where we have put aside the rightful heir, Nizám-ul-Mulk, for his younger brother, Afzul-ul-Mulk, on the pretext that the former was intriguing with the Russians. I believe this allegation to be absolutely false, for I know him to be most friendly to British interests. In 1886 he offered to send a thousand men from Warshigum over the passes to the relief of Colonel (now General Sir) W. Lockhart, then a temporary prisoner at Panjah Fort in Affghan hands. As Padishah of Turikoh, Nizám-ul-Mulk was, in his father's life-time, the *acknowledged* heir to the Chitrál throne, and he was made by his father Raja of Yasin in succession to Afzul, who had taken it in 1884 from Mir Amán, the maternal uncle of Pehliwán, who was ruler of Yasin in 1880, when Colonel Biddulph wrote his "Tribes of the Hindukush," and with whom the Khushwaqtia dynasty, as such, came to an end. This Pehliwan killed Mir Wali, the murderer of Hayward, but Pehliwan made the mistake of attacking Biddulph in 1880, and was ousted by Mir Amán. With Nizám-ul-Mulk, therefore, begins the rule over Yasin by the Kathoria Dynasty of Chitrál. He is now a fugitive at Gilgit; had he been intriguing with Russia he would certainly not have sought refuge from his brother in the British lion's mouth at Gilgit. All I can say is that in 1886 he did not even know the name of Russia, and that when he wrote to me in 1887 he referred to the advent of the French explorers Capus, Pepin and Bonvalot, as follows: "they call themselves sometimes French, and at other times Russians." In the "Asiatic Quarterly Review" of January, 1891, there is a paper from Raja Nizám-ul-Mulk on "the Legends of Chitrál." He is thus the first Central Asian prince whose literary effusion has appeared in the pages of a British, or indeed of any other, Review. His first letters, sent in the hollow of a twig, like his latter ones sent through British officers, all breathe a spirit of what might be called the sincerest loyalty to the Queen-Empress, were he not an absolutely independent ruler. There will be an evil day of reckoning when the "meddling and muddling," which has created the Russian Frankenstein, will be followed by the exasperation of princes and people, within and beyond our legitimate frontier. To revert to Hunza and Nagyr, Mr. F. Drew, an Assistant Master of Eton College, who was *in the service of the Maharaja of Kashmir*, wrote in 1877 in his "Northern Barrier of India"—which, alas! our practical annexation of Kashmir, and our interference with the Hindukush tribes are breaking down—as follows: "Hunza and Nagyr are two small INDEPENDENT RAJASHIPS. Nagyr has generally shown a desire to be on friendly terms with the Dogras at Gilgit, while Hunza has been a thorn in their side." There is not a word here of these States being tributaries of Kashmir, whilst Colonel Biddulph, who was our Resident at Gilgit, shows that the last Hunza raid was committed in 1867, and that slavery and kidnapping were unknown in inoffensive, if not "timid," Nagyr. My article in the "Asiatic Quarterly Review" of January, 1892, shows that raiding and slavery had been recently revived in consequence of alike Russian and English advances, and that the fussiness and ambition of our officials have alone *indicated* and *paved* "the nearest way to India."

Woking, 21st November, 1892.

P.S.—In correcting this proof of a paper on the Fairy-land that adjoins "the Roof of the World," which our imprudence has drawn within the range of practical politics. I never anticipated that I should have to refer to my "rough sketch of the History of Dardistan" brought down to 1872 as a refutation of the history written to order by some of our leading journals which, to suit the policy of the moment, would make the Amir of Affghanistan responsible for Badakhshan, and yet blame him for interfering with Chitrál, as is hinted in a telegram in to-day's *Times*. I shall deal with this matter elsewhere. (See also Appendix II.)

Woking, 29th November, 1892.

OUR MANUFACTURED FOES.

A STUDENT FROM TANGÍR.

A NAGYRI PEASANT.

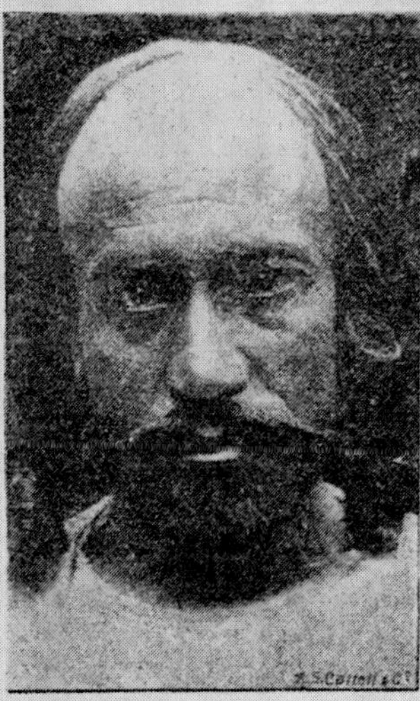

A DAREYLI HERDSMAN.
[*notice fine head and ample forehead.*]

(*Already published.*)
A WELL-KNOWN HUNZA FIGHTER, BROUGHT TO ENGLAND BY DR. LEITNER IN 1887.

KASHMIR SOLDIER (HIGHLANDER),
(Wearing a Great Lama's Hat).

A BALTI COOLIE (LITTLE TIBET).
[The Baltis are used as Coolies by the Kashmir invaders.]

HISTORY OF THE DARD WARS WITH KASHMIR

IN 5 CHAPTERS—(CHAPTER I. CHILÁS)

(*Committed to writing from the statements of a Sazîni Dard who took part in many of the engagements*).

INTRODUCTION. (JULY, 1893.)

Chilás has already been referred to in my "rough Chronological Sketch of the History of Dardistan from 1800 to 1892."* I now propose to re-publish "the History of the Wars of the Dard tribes with Kashmir" beginning with the account given to me by a Sazîni Dard in 1866 of the first war with the Chilásis.† Its importance at the present moment, consists in the fact that these wars with the Dards were almost all provoked by Kashmir, as they, practically, now are by ourselves. The attack on peaceful and pious Nagyr was excused by the usual calumnies that precede and justify annexation, till their exposure comes too late either to prevent aggression or to punish their authors, who, if soldiers, obtain honours, and if writers, an evanescent popularity. Now that the manuscripts of the Hunza Library have been sold by auction, that its fairies have been silenced, that its ancient weapons have been destroyed, that its language and religion have been assimilated to those of its neighbours, a living chapter has disappeared of the most ancient traditions of mankind safe in their mountain recesses for ages, till English and Russian subalterns wanted promotion at the expense of the safety of their respective Asiatic Empires. In 1866, I already pointed out that the Legends and Customs of the Dards were gradually vanishing before the incidental inroads of Orthodox Sunni Muhammadanism and that their preservation was a duty of the civilized world. Now we have simply killed them outright as also a number of interesting Aryan republics, like Chilás and other picturesque and peaceful autonomies. In 1875, Mr. Drew reported that the abhorrence of the Shin race to the cow, which probably marked the almost pre-historical separation of the Dáradas, the lowest of the twice-born, from the Brahmins of Kashmir, was ceasing, and in 1886 I saw a son of the excellent Raja of Nagyr in European garb all except the head-dress. Now that his country is practically annexed, its Chief is called "patriarchal," just as the Chilásis

* *Extract:* "*1850.* The raids of the Chilásis is made the occasion for invading the country of Chilás, which not being a dependency of Kashmir, is not included in the Treaty of 1846. The Maharaja gives out that he is acting under orders of the British Government. Great consternation among petty chiefs about Muzaffarabad regarding ulterior plans of the Maharaja. The Sikhs send a large army, which is defeated before the Fort of Chilás. 1851.—Bakhshi Hari Singh and Dewan Hari Chand are sent with 10,000 men against Chilás, and succeed in destroying the fort and scattering the hostile hill tribes which assisted the Chilásis."

† Extract from Drew's "Northern Barriers of India," 1877: "Until about 1850 they used to make occasional expeditions for plunder, coming round the flanks of the mountain into this Astor Valley. It was these raids that determined Maharaja Gulâb Singh to send a punitive expedition against Chilás. This he did in 1851 or 1852. The Dogrâs at last took the chief stronghold of the Chilásis, a fort two or three miles from the Indus River, and reduced those people to some degree of obedience: and *there has been no raid since.*"

are now patted on the back "as brave and by no means quarrelsome" by journals which a few months ago termed them "raiders," "kidnappers," "robbers" and "slave-dealers," etc., forgetting that there exist the annual reports of our Deputy Commissioners of Abbottabad speaking of them since 1856 as a peaceable people. No doubt *before* that date, the Su'nni Chilásis raided Shiah Astor, just as the Astoris raided what they could.*

The following account, it will be seen, and my own notes, do not, in the least, palliate the shortcomings of the Dards, but I maintain that there were *no* raids since 1856, and that in 1866 *six* Kashmir Seapoys, (not 6,000, as alleged by a recent writer) kept the Astor-Bunji road in a state of perfect safety; there were, no doubt, small detachments of troops at these places themselves, *not* to protect the road against the puritanical peasantry of Chilás, but as Depôts for the *then* War with all the united Dard tribes *except Chilás*. Yet we are told by a recent writer, ignorant of Dard Languages and History, that we took Chilás in order to protect Kashmir from raids (which had ceased for 42 years), that we spend less on the safety of the frontier than Kashmir, that the Nagyr Raja was a slave-dealer, etc., etc. Fortunately, we have official and other reports written before the passions of the moment obscured historical truth, and these Reports will long bear witness against the vandalism and folly by which our Northern Barrier of India was broken down and a military road was constructed for an invader to the heart of the Panjab. This road is the one from Abbottabad to Hunza, of which I obtained the particulars in 1866 (when I was sent on a linguistic Mission by the Panjab Government to Kashmir and Chilás), but which, for obvious reasons, I did not publish. Now that the Indian papers constantly urge and discuss its construction, I have no hesitation in giving the details of this, as I have of other roads and as *now* ought to be done of the various means of communication throughout what was once called, and what should, and could, for ever have remained, the "neutral zone" between the British and the Russian spheres of influence or interference. The first part of the projected road is to Chilás, and extends, roughly speaking, for 125 miles, namely Abbottabad to Mansehra 16 miles; Mansehra to Juba 10 miles; thence to Balakôt 12 miles; Kawaie 12, Jared 12, Kaghan 12, Naran 14, Batakundi 6, Burawaie 6, Sehri 5, Lulusar (where there is a fine lake 11,000 feet over the sea level) 5, Chilás 15. (For details see elsewhere.) Of this 15 miles are on independent territory, so that there was no occasion for the precipitate subjugation of an inoffensive population, whose sense of security is so great that they abandon their houses entirely unprotected during the hottest part of the summer when they leave with their families

* "The Astor people used formerly to do the same thing," and on page 459 of Drew's "Jummoo and Kashmir Territories," the author, who was a high official in the Kashmir service, says: "The Sikhs sent an expedition to Chilás under one Sujah Singh, but it was repulsed. . . . This was about the year 1843 . . . The good effects (of the expedition in 1850 or 1851) . . . have already beep spoken of. Since that time the Chilásis . . . pay yearly to the Maharaja a tribute of 100 goats and about two ounces of gold-dust; *otherwise they are free.*" Since then Major Ommaney in 1868 reports that ever since the advent of British neighbourhood they have never committed any offences: "The people are inoffensive." Mr. Scott calls them "a quiet, peace-loving people," and all the Panjab Administration Reports give them the same reputation.

for the cooler surrounding hills. In another Dard republic, full of Arabic Scholars, Kandiá, there are no forts, and weapons may not be carried. Major Abbott, from whom Abbottabad so deservedly takes its name, reporting to the Lahore Board of Administration in July 1855, when the Maharaja of Kashmir had misinformed him of the successful conclusion of his campaign against Chilás and had asked the British Government, "whether he was to hold it with garrison, or to punish the people by burning their villages and then to retreat," gave as his opinion that the latter course would exasperate the Chilásis into renewing their incursions, and that on the other hand "the possession of Chilás by Jummoo would altogether destroy the hopes of the Syuds of Kaghan. And as the odium of this very unpopular expedition has been carefully attributed to the British Government by the Maharaja's Ministers, so much of advantage may possibly be derived from it." I must now allow my Sazîni and other Dards to give an account of Wars which not only include the struggles for the conquest of Chilás, but detail the expeditions to Hunza-Nagyr, the massacre of women and children at Yasin, the Dareyl and other conflicts, all interspersed with characteristic anecdotes and the names of men and places that have, or may yet, come to the front.

ROUTES TO CHILÁS.

The manners, tribal sub-divisions, and occupations of the Chilásis and the names of the mountains, streams, products, etc., of the country, as also the road from Takk to Kashmir by the Kanagamunn pass, Diúng, Shiril, Koja, Ujatt, etc., are detailed in my "Dardistan," where a Chilási vocabulary, dialogues, songs, etc., will also be found. There are also roads from Abbottabad to Chilás through Agrôr, of Black Mountain fame, practicable for camels. Another road, fit for ponies, goes by Muzafarabad by Sharidi and the lovely Kishenganga and Sargan Rivers in Kashmir, by the Kamakduri Galli, to Niát in Chilás. As already mentioned, the easiest road to our last conquest is by Kaghan through the Takk valley. There is also the long and dangerous road on the banks of the Indus to Bunji, which skirts, as its occupation would irritate, the Kohistani tribes who are Pathans, not Dards, including the rival traders with Gilgit of Koli-Palus. Thence, on that route, comes Jalkot and the road that branches off into learned Kandiá, which I have described at length in the *A.Q.R.* of July 1892. The road, such as it is, constantly crosses and recrosses the Indus (by rafts), and at the Lahtar river is reached the boundary between the true Kohistan and the Dard country, which is there called Shináki, because it is inhabited by the ruling Shiná race. We then come to pretty Sazín, from which my Sazîní informant. Opposite to it runs the Tangir valley and country, whence there is a road to Yasin to which Tangîr owed a sort of loose bond. We then continue by the right bank of the Indus opposite Sazín, passing Shatiál and on to the Dareyl stream, which comes from the Dareyl country that eventually joins on to Gilgit. Crossing the Dareyl stream, we pass Harban on the left bank and a few miles further on, the Tor village, and arrive at the Hôdur village, whence we go on to Chilás, after as bad a road of about 200 miles as it is possible to conceive.

Besides, if we touch the independence of these various republics *en route*, we shall constantly be in a hornets' nest, and provoke the coalition of the Dard with the Pathan or Afghan irreconcilable tribes, whereas, by keeping to the Kashmir route or, at least, confining ourselves to the Kaghan-Chilás road, and prohibiting our men from going to the right or to the left of it, we may yet resume friendly relations with the harmless and religious Chilásis and keep the road open for the eventual advance of Russian troops! In the meanwhile, let us not destroy villages inhabited by hereditary genealogists, who, before our advent, were the living historians of an irrecoverable portion of, perhaps, the earliest Aryan settlements.

I.—STRUGGLES FOR THE CONQUEST OF CHILAS.

"About twenty-three years ago there was a very strong fort at Chilás. Two years before the outbreak of the wars, a man named Lassu came [on the part of Kashmír?] to the frontier of Chilás. This man's ancestors had been in the service of the Dogras and for ninety years had possessed property and the Sirdarship at Goré (?) (probably Guraïz) in the family. It is not known why or whether he was dismissed the Kashmîr service, but he came with his family in 1847 to Chilás and became the cause of all the subsequent disturbances. This man had been renowned for bravery in his youth, but when he came was old and feeble, though full of intrigue. In the valley of Marungá is a place called Neyátt, where he established himself with about twenty families of Kashmiris and others, who had followed him from Guraiz. His two brothers were also with him. Where he fixed his residence there is—at some distance below—a village of the name of Gôsher, inhabited by the people of Takk. The valley is called Karúngá at its exit. In these two years he cultivated his fields and the friendship of the Chilásis. Purchasing also cattle and horses he became a great chief, to whom the Chilásis used to pay visits of ceremony. He also used constantly to visit them, and when he had acquired a decisive influence, he assembled all the Lumberdars of Chilás and said, "What a pity that Astór being so near, whose inhabitants are all Shiahs, you should not attack them according to the Shera' [religious Law]." The ignorant Chilásis then began to go on plundering excursions in the direction of Astor, which were often successful. When the Governor of Astór became unable to resist these attacks, he requested the assistance of the Maharaja of Kashmîr, who refused it to him, but himself advanced direct on Chilás with an army. (In this war I was present for about a month.) One day a battle began in the early morning and lasted till the evening. The Maharaja's army drove us right into the Chilás Fort. We sent off men at once in all directions for help. For two days there was no other engagement. On the 3rd day came allies of the valley of Gîne, from Darêl, Jalkôt, Takk and Torr, Harbànn, Shatiál, Sazîn, Hudúr, Kóli, and 200 Tangîris (we were in all about 20 "thousand" men, women and children, in that great fort*). They poured in all day, and by evening the struggle was renewed in which, as I saw myself, women took part. As the Sikhs were pressing on to the walls, the

* The word "Thousand" may only stand for 400, as explained elsewhere.

TWO CHILÁSIS.

A GILGITI.

women threw bedsteads and planks on their heads; stones and kitchen-utensils were also used. The result was not decisive. A stream was flowing into the fort in which we had four reservoirs kept filled in case of need. Hêmur, a brave man, whose son Sadur is now a Chief, a Yashkunn,* sat there giving a pumpkin full of water (about half a pint) to a man during the day and a pint at night, as it was more quiet then. There was a row of men stationed handing the gourd in and out and taking care that nobody got more than his share. Often we went without food for two days. The Chilási women cooked and cast bullets—the other women chiefly fought. The besiegers diverted the stream from the fort into the valley. We then drank the water of the reservoirs. This lasted for a month. We only lost in killed about three or four a day, as we fought behind cover. The enemy lost from 80 to 120 a day as they were in the open plain. When their provisions failed and supplies did not reach them, they retired with the loss of a third of their army, their treasury and goods. (300 women were appointed for the purpose of working and casting bullets all day.) In the day time we used to exchange shots—at night we would attack their camp, when they were tired or asleep. The walls were loopholed for the guns, and altogether the management of the affair was very good. We looted 100 mule-loads of powder: as much of lead, 40 tents—100 beds (charpoys), 2 boxes filled with money (Chilkis†)—50 sound muskets and 150 injured muskets,—120 brass kettles—50 brass jugs—200 sheets and 400 brass gharras (pitchers)—100 shawls, good and bad—200 Chaplis (sandals)—20 chairs—5 loads of sticks—200 lances—200 bayonets—a heap of 100 swords—20 daggers—20 iron hammers, 130 tent pegs of iron and 800 of wood—2 big guns—3 field guns, and miscellaneous property too numerous and various to detail. Two days after the flight of the Dogras the people assembled and began to divide the spoil. We began by giving 10 Chilkis to each man, but it did not last for all; so, whoever got no money, took a gun, lance, tent, etc. The big guns were put into the fort. I was shot in the leg in that siege. We used to bury our dead in their clothes within two or three days of their death. The Sikhs also used to burn, and the besieging Muslims in their service to bury, the dead for some time. When, however, the casualties increased, the besiegers gave up attending to the dead. It was in the midst of summer; so the stench was very great and disease also spread in the Sikh camp. Seven days after the flight of the enemy, the tribes who had come to help left for their own places. The following is the list of the Sirdars killed in the siege: Deyûri Khan, a Shîn, one-eyed, Sirdar of Chilás; Hashm Shah, a Shîn, of Chilás; Nasr Ali Khan, a Yashkunn, of Chilás; Malik Faulád, a Yashkunn, of Harbenn. The following Sirdars survived: Rahmat Ulla, Shîn, Chilási; Akbari, Shîn, Lamberdar of Takk; Murad Shah, Yashkunn of Tòrr; Adam Shah, Yashkunn of Tòrr; Bahádur (Baghdúr) Shîn of Harbánn; Naik Numa, a Kamìn, Harbann; Faizulla Khan, Shîn, Harbann; Mard Shah, Kamìn of Shatiál; Shah Jehán, Kamìn of Shatiál; Malek

* For divisions of Dard castes see pages 62, 63.

† Of the value of ten annas each, then 1s. 3d.

Nazr-ud-din, Shîn of Sazîn; Hajem Khan. Shîn of Sazîn; Lala Khan, Yashkkunn of Dareyl; Jeldár, Yashkkunn of Dareyl; Izzat, Shîn of Phúgotsh (Dareyl); Rahmi, Shîn of Samagiál in Dareyl; Matshar Khan (a great Sirdár) Shîn, Samagial; Losîn, Shîn of Barzîn; Mirza Khan, Shîn, Barzîn; Shah Merdán, Shîn of Hudúr; Kazilbik, Yashkunn of Búder

After a year had passed, the Chilasis and the Yaghistánis* assembled at Chilás with the intention of plundering Astór, whose Governors then was Jabr Khan and Wazîr Gurbúnd, subjects of Kashmîr and of the Shiah faith, and therefore fit objects for the attack of orthodox Mussulmans (Sunnis). We were in all about 108,000 Yaghistanis (the ideas of number are very vague in those countries—though not so vague as in Lughmáni where there is not a separate name for a number above 400, and the foreign appellation of *hazár* = 1,000 is the equivalent for 400. *Vide* Lughmáni and Kandiá Vocabularies in which numeration is by twenties). The Astóris were only 6,000, but we went in large numbers, as we counted on having to meet the Dogras of Kashmir.

The following is the List of the confederate Yaghistanis: From Koli, 1,000; Palus, 4,000; Jalkót, 3,000; Sazîn, 500; Shatiál, 500; Harbann, 1,000; Takk, 1,000; Chilas, 3,000; Torr, 1,000; Tangir, 4,000; Dareyl, 10,000; Gôrdjan, 5,000 (probably Gôr); Gîne, 100; Bûder, 100; Gormâni, 2,000 (probably auxiliaries from Gauhar-Amán, ruler of Yasin, popularly called Gôrmán); Gilgit, 5,000; Sai, 5,000.

(This only brings the allied Dard forces up to 48,200, perhaps only 19,000, as already explained. Since then the Dards have been more than decimated, and the destruction of Gilgit with all its traditions, etc., is one of the saddest results of the Kashmîr frontier war. There are, however, Gilgit emigrants to be found in Sazîn and other places.) We marched on to the mountains of Astor and Gauhar-Amán with 2,000 men stopped at Jalkôt (j as in French) in the Sái territory, 6 koss far. He told us that when the Dogras came up to assist Astor, he would at once advance with more troops to that place. When we came near Astor, the Governor was informed of our approach. Most of the Astoris fled, many leaving their property behind. The 6,000 fighting men remained; they had, however, sent most of their property away. The people of the Astor village, Dashkin, had not heard of our arrival; so we surprised it about midnight, killed 2 men and wounded 9—100 were captured (men and women). We took 80 cows, 500 goats, clothes to the value of 400 Rupees, 40 hatchets, 100 swords, and 100 muskets. Out of the house of the Wazîr Gorbúnd we got 8 kettles. There are many Yashkunns at Astor, three-fourths being of that race and the remainder being half Shîns and the other half Kamíns.† Our arrival at Astor was announced by a man whom with his companion we surprised seated at the bridge of Sugarkôt. A man of Shatiál killed the companion by throwing a stone at him; the other effected his escape and enabled the Astoris to get away with their property. The reason why we killed so few was because we wanted to make the people our slaves, either

* "Yaghistáni" means inhabitant of the "wild" or "independent" country.

† For Divisions of Dard Castes, see pages 62, 63.

to keep or sell; being Kafirs their lives are forfeited to the Mussulmans, but it is harder on them to be slaves than die and therefore we prefer to enslave them. Besides it is more profitable. In the morning a rumour of the approach of the Maharajah's troops reached us. We were greatly surprised at this and retired on to Hashu Gher (probably the Atsho pîr, a very high mountain which overlooks Bunji, on the Kashmîr side of the Indus) by the Burderikôt road—a very difficult one—on the way to Chilás, which we reached only the 6th day after our retreat. We then divided the spoil. Some sold their slaves in Chilás. Most took them to their homes. We did not lose any one in killed or wounded on this excursion. Jabar Khan of Astor then went to the Maharaja as a suppliant—saying he and his people were children and subjects of Kashmîr and implored help against the marauders, who he urged, should themselves be attacked and punished. The Maharaja advised him to be quiet for a year, as he would then bring a large army. This was satisfactory for Jabar Khan, who was intent on revenge. In fact, 14 months later, when he and his minister with 60 men again presented themselves at Srinagar, in order to urge the fulfilment of the promise, 50,000 men (!!) were sent to Chilás. I was then at Minôr in the Gilgit territory, but my father and brother went into the war and it is from them that I have heard the following particulars. When the Sikh General (whose name I forget) reached the Kashmir river [the Kishnganga (?)] he divided the Army into two parts—one to go by way of Guraiz, the other by the Darau valley which goes straight to Chilas and actually reached Takk. [From Takk there are 2 valleys—the one of Babuserr; the other of Marungâ.] The reason of the division of the forces was that the Kashmîr troops feared to trust their whole body into mountainous country where they might all be cut up. Two days before the enemy came, we were at Sîhil, below Takk, 1,000 strong. The Yaghistanis were collecting at Chilás, but most were still on the roads or starting from their homes. The news of the approach of the Maharajah's troops had also frightened away most of the tribes. Indeed there were only 500 besides the force at Sîhil. The following came: 100 from Sazîn, 200 from Harbàn, 40 from Chitrál, 60 from Dareyl, 40 from Jalkôt, 100 from Tangîr, 200 from Tórr, 40 from Hudúr, 200 from Takk, 100 from Bûder. 800 had collected in Gôr, but never came up, but were at Talpènn on the other side of the Indus, 4 kôs from Chilas. The following Chiefs came: Nazar Khan, Kasîm and Masta Khan of Sazîn. The 2 former were Shîns, the other a Yashkunn. Ravîn, a Yashkunn of Shatial; Der Jihan, Kamin, of Shatial; Alangîr, Kamin, of Harbann; Tapa Khan, Kamin, of Harbann; Jeldar Mama and Sheithing of Dareyl, Shîns; Ametî, Yashkunn, Jalkôt; Keremo, Shin, Khairulla, Yashkunn, Tangîr; Marat Shah Mama, Adam Shah, Great Sirdars of Torr, Shîns; Shahmard Kaka and his brother of Hudûr, Shîns; Akbari and Azád, Kamins, of Takk; Kizilbîk of Búder, Yashkúnn; Sadar Khan, Yashkúnn, Gôr; Wazîr Khan, Yashkúnn, Gôr: Ramanni, Yashkúnn, Gôr; Rahmat ulla Khan, Nasir Ali, and Hasham Shah, Yashkúnns, Chilás.

When the Sikh troops came to the bridge of Sîhil, it was 6 A.M. (before dawn). We were in ambush and rushed upon them sword in hand. There was great fighting till the evening—such as had never been before in Yaghistan. When night broke in, we were beaten and fled. back into the mountains. Then two Sirdars, Ameti Khan and Ser Endáz Khan of Jalkót, rushed in alone on the army of the infidels and after killing some were cut down. Ameti's body fell into the water below the bridge and came up again after one month at Jalkót on the river side, where Jalkót is. A boatman of the name of Mehr Gul, came to the place but did not recognise the body. He told the villagers, who went out with Mira Khan, the uncle of Ametí, who had not gone to the wars as he was very old. Ametí's wife too went to the bank. Nobody recognised the corpse, when the wife knew him from his pijámas. He was buried and a shrine was built over his body, which is known by the name of the "shrine of the martyr." Ametí had said when about to charge the Sikhs that "if he should be killed his body would still get to Jalkôt and be buried there." Many Sirdars testify to this. During the night, the enemy sleeping from fatigue, Mulla Shemshêr, and Mulla Khandád and the Pir Padishah Mîa, a great Sayad, rallied the Yaghistanis and told them of the advantage of assaulting the infidels at night, which wās accounted as a twofold righteousness in this and the next world. When the Yaghis heard this Fatwa (authoritative manifesto) their courage increased and they attacked the enemy's camp in a body. Our men went on slashing at their heads and other limbs. It was winter and the blood clotted our hands and froze them to the sword hilts. Rustam and Afrasiab's wars would be forgotten as trifles, if I could describe the terrors of that night. The slaughter lasted all night. As the day approached and showed the smallness of our numbers we were again defeated and fled from Sihil to Chilás which is at the distance of 6 kôs (or about 9 miles). We were followed by the enemy. Whenever they came up to a suitable place, the fight was renewed and hundreds were killed. At Dasur, Matshuko-Jal and in the valley of Chilás, there being an open space, a stand was made, especially at the last place, which we reached at noon and kept our ground fighting till far into the night (10 o'clock). We were again defeated and fled into the fort, which was surrounded by the Maharajah's army. The following days and nights were occupied in constant fighting. The enemy again cut off the stream. Then the Yaghis again appointed Hemur to undertake the distribution of water from the reservoirs and made the women cook and cast bullets for them, as during the first siege. This siege, however, was greatly protracted -the water became scarce and whilst formerly a man would get three gourdsful (two during the night and one in the day) now only one gourdful was distributed during the whole twenty-four hours. This lasted for three months. At night assaults were made and shots were exchanged during the day through the loopholes. When the enemy approached under the walls, stones, etc., etc., were thrown on him. We did all we could, but were still beaten—the reason God alone knows. Oh God! when the water became scarce, the enemy also put poison into the reservoirs; so some died from thirst and many from poison. When the enemy saw this, he had recourse to another *ruse*. They tied stems of trees together with ropes and using them as ladders, tried to mount on the fort, firing all the day. We had not seen this before and in our surprise lost more men than perhaps was necessary in defending ourselves. Neither water nor an escape was destined for us; so the remainder consulted about evacuating the place and getting into the hills. At midnight two-thirds of the men, taking the women and children with them, left the Fort and began to fly. The voices of the children roused the blood-thirsty enemy, who, like a wolf, came after the lambs. Some of the Sikhs entered the Fort and killed those they found; when they became exhausted with murdering, they took about 680 men, women and children as prisoners for the Sikh General and 120 were destined for the revenge of Jabar Khan and taken away with their property. The fort was at once set on fire and burnt down. Such property as they could take they did take. As for the fugitives, it was a running slaughter till sunrise, when we reached Kitshóri. Here we rallied and renewed the fight. Kitshóri is 2 kôs below Chilas and is a village on the Indus. Our men fought, hungry and tired though they were, till noon and were considerably thinned in numbers. It seemed now useless to us to continue the fight, for we said that we should all be at last overpowered and cut down to a man. We must therefore flee. We, therefore, retraced our march in the direction of the mountains and were not followed up, as the enemy did not perhaps, think it worth while, our numbers being so reduced. The pursuers returned to the Chilás fort. When they got there they agreed to return to Kashmìr. As they reached the place where the two roads branch off, [one for Astor, the other for Kashmìr] the Sikh General gave leave to Jabar Khan, who took his prisoners with him. All were in great joy. The following is the list of the Sirdárs who escaped the slaughter: Alengir, Habba Khan, and Mîr Matta, of Harbenn; Rahmi, of Darêl.

Aladdin of Shatial and Ahmeti and Sir Andaz of Jalkôt were killed; also Azur, and Alahmun of Sazîn. Mard Shah Baba of Torr got away. Azad of Takk was killed. Nasr Ali, Hashm Shah, Paulad and Anwarí of Chilas were all killed. They were all Yashkunns. Serrkushu of Tangir was killed. M...... of Somer, a Shîn, my cousin, was killed by a bullet going through his mouth. 500 were killed and 800 taken prisoners—200 escaped. Among the prisoners was Sirdar Rahmat Ulla Khan, who was sent to Jammu. When he was captured, a Sikh went into the fort after his daughter, who threw herself off the walls in order to escape disgrace and was dashed to pieces on a stone. There is no doubt that we were the first to be in fault, as we attacked Astor without provocation and at the instigation of Lassu seven times before the Maharaja went to war with us. I never joined these plundering excursions but my cousin, M......, went every time and also S......, my brother, who is still alive. Once they brought back a man and 6 women to Minôr—the whole razzia having secured 60 prisoners, 800 goats, etc. Thinking it was "halál" or lawfully acquired property, they divided it with great glee and they ate the goats also as "halál," as they had taken them from Shiahs.

There is a suspicion that Lassu was an agent of Kashmìr sent to foment this discord and bring about the subjection of Chilás. In former times we used to assist Astor, being our neighbour. There is also no difference in our language. That of Khapul (Khapolór) is different. It is Tibetan;

they call a man "shishek" and for "go there" say "gaz yut" and "bakhmula gihrit" (there is a mistake here) and for "bury" say "sùmduk" and for "does he go or not" "yidd mitt." "Son" they call "bhúman." [Some of the words are Kashmîri.] I remember these words, having once known the language, as a woman of Khapul, called Miriam, had fallen to the lot of my brother in the division of the booty. A neighbour of mine also had a slave of the same place called Kolitsh, who used to come to see us. I was very young then and could converse with both. A year after, my brother, in consequence of his greed for money, took her to Kami, a village of Tangir and sold her to Batret Shah, Sirdar, the son of Babar Shah, for 8 tolas of gold (each tolah of the value of 9 Rupees 5 annas). This was a good price as she was very good-looking, but she should not have been sold.

When the Kashmir troops attacked Chilas, Lassu joined us secretly and although himself old and feeble told us what to do—but his two brothers and two nephews openly fought on our side in the battle of the valley of Chilás. Indeed at Sihil, Lassu fought himself and used to send the Sirdars forward with his instructions. In short, as far as he was able, he tried to injure the Sikhs. When the Sikhs had cut the water off the fort, he had arranged about putting only one man in charge of it and fixed the rate at which it should be distributed. He was ever ready with advice. He used to allow the Sikhs to beat up supplies in villages and then would cut them up while encumbered with them. This is how we managed to be fed (the plundered supplies reaching us by a mountain road) for three months. A relative of Lassu was in the Sikh Camp and told the General about Lassú's doings. The attention of the besiegers was then directed towards capturing him, but in vain, and in both wars he escaped being taken prisoner or receiving a wound. His younger brother was shot in the palm of the hand. In short, after the conquest of Chilas, Lassu again resided with his brothers at Neyátt and kept up his visits to Chilas. When the Sirdars arranged to offer their submission to the Maharaja at Jammu, they sent for Lassu and asked him to help them to recover their friends and relatives who had been taken prisoners to Kashmir. Lassu refused on the ground that he had left the Maharajah's service and had been his bitter enemy ever since and that therefore his life was not safe if he ventured into his presence. Finally, Lassu was prevailed upon to go. The following Sirdars went to Jammu to ask for forgiveness: Hashm Shah, Sattari, Baland Khan, and Daria Khan, of Chilas, with 36 Botés (poor people); Buyedad, Daru Khan, and Mir, Shíns of Bûder; Azad and Sakhi, Shîns of Takk; Tatari, Kamìn, and Baghdùr, Shin, also of Takk.

When the Maharaja saw the suppliants, and also noticed Lassu, it was as if an arrow had pierced him. He was greatly indignant, having heard everything from his General about Lassu often defeating his troops and being the origin of the wars and of the numerous plans by which his soldiers had been destroyed by thousands—for instance at the ambush at Sihil. Finally after a long talk, the Maharaja made the forgiveness of the Chilasis conditional on the execution of Lassu. The Chilasis said "By all means, if this man and his ancestors have not been your servants. You expelled him and we received him. In gratitude for this he may have given us sometimes advice, but he has never raised his hands against you. Had he not given us even advice *we* should have killed him. It was his duty to do so. Let His Highness therefore pardon him." The Maharaja refused, and ordered his General to strike off his head there and then, put the blood into a plate and give it to him to drink [this was probably meant metaphorically, as a Hindu would not drink blood, especially not that of a Muhammadan. However, the Chilasi Chiefs appear to have understood the threat literally]. The Sirdars all interposed as they could not witness his death. They offered to pay taxes, if he were spared. [This was probably the object of this comedy.] Then the Maharaja fixed an annual tribute of Rs. 2 per house, in lieu of the blood of Lassu. The Chiefs thought it too much for their poor people, so at last one Rupee per house was settled. He then dismissed them, but wanted them again to appear next year with the tribute, viz. Balang Khan, Deryá Khan, Matshar and Lassu. "When this is done, he added, I will send Lassu with a khilat* to Guraiz and re-instate him as Governor and you shall also receive presents." This was accepted and the Chiefs returned with all the people (men, women and children) who had been taken prisoners. He also sent a letter to Jabar Khan of Astor to restore the 120 prisoners whom he had taken to the Chilas Chiefs. This was done and nearly all returned, excepting the few that had died in course of nature. Thus was Chilas again re-peopled and is inhabited to the present day.

The following villages in Chilas became subject to Kashmir: Chilas, then 300 houses, now only 200, 100 having died out in consequence of disease brought on by the bad water of that place, Bûder, 120 houses, Takk, 131 houses. The rest did not submit, nor will they ever do so, as they have heard about the tyranny and oppression practised in Kashmir. We Yaghistanis have thus become even greater enemies than before, but are helpless. To revert to my story. After a year the following Sirdars went with the tribute to Srinagar, viz.: Deryá Khan, Balang Khan, Satari, Rahmat-ulla, Matshar and Lassu. The Maharaja gave each a present of 120 Rupees and made them stay a month at Jammu. Lassu was sent with much honour to Guraiz and reinstated. On the expiration of the month the Sirdars came to Srinagar and requested leave to go as the harvest-time had come near. The Maharaja received them kindly and requested that in future two Chilasis should come with the tribute and remain for a year as servants (really hostages) when they would be allowed to return and two others be appointed in their stead. The hostages were to receive some pay from the Maharaja. The Sirdars then returned each to his own village. This arrangement is still in force. (For a more chronological account of the conquest of Chilás vide Historical Sketch, page 72.)

* Robe of honor.

II.—WAR WITH GOUHAR AMAN FOR THE POSSESSION OF GILGIT.

A year later, the same Sikh General was despatched with 3,000 horse and foot to Astor and fixed a tribute of one-third of the produce on all. He also established a Thanna at Sógar, a village close to Astor. At the Thanna he laid in ammunition, etc. Next year he went down with his troops along the river of Astor to the Indus and established a Thanna at Bûnji, which is on this side of the Indus and opposite to Sai. Duru was at that time Governor of Bunji on behalf of Gouhar Aman, the ruler of Yasin and Gilgit. He also crossed the Indus at Sai and arranged for a Thanna at Jalkôt, but the Sai country was subject to Gouhar Aman who was residing at Gilgit. When he heard of the encroachments of Kashmir he sent off men to Dareyl and Tangír, asking these tribes to come down on the Sikhs by the mountain paths near Bunji, whilst he would take the road along the Indus and attack Sai. He stated that as he and they were Sunnis, a Jihád [religious war] on the Sikhs became their common duty. 5,000 young men from Dareyl and Tangír at once collected and came down to Bunji in 10 days. Gouhar Aman with 3,000 Gilgiti horse and 2,000 coolies, fell on Sái at 2 o'clock in the afternoon of the day on which the mountaineers reached in the morning. The following Yaghistani Chiefs came: From Dareyl—Kalashmir, Lala Khan Izzetti, Bira Khan, Muhammad Khan, Shaithing, Jaldár; from Tangir—Khairulla, Mansûr, Rustami, Nayûn.

The only son of Gouhar Aman who came was Mulk Aman—Gouhar Aman himself being detained at Minôr by illness. The following also came: From Nómal 200 men, from Bhagrôt 2,000 (!!), from Sakwal 100, and from Minôr 200. These men carried loads of provisions and ammunition. They reached the Niludár range on that day, one kos from the Sai District. Thence preparations were made for an attack—the Sikhs having 8,000 men—the battle began at Chakarkôt which is three kôs from the Indus. There is a field there under cultivation where the fight began. It was summer. The Sikhs had got into the Chakarkôt Fort which was surrounded by the Gilgitis. Mulk Aman dashed into it with his horsemen. The Chakarkoti villagers facilitated their entry and opened the gates for him. The fight lasted all day and night within and without the Fort. The Sikhs were defeated; most were killed fighting and some jumped off the walls and were dashed to pieces. 100 only escaped crossing the river [Indus] back to Bunji. Gouhar Aman only lost 60 horsemen and 40 Dareylis and Tangíris, also Sirdar Muhammad Khan, a Shin of Darêl. Mulk Aman did not cross over to Bunji and dismissed the mountaineers, telling them, however, to be in readiness for renewed fighting. He then returned to Gilgit. A curious circumstance occurred with two Sikhs who were taken away as prisoners by the Dareylis. In taking them over the Jámu rocks,* which on account of their difficulty, we call "ákho" (Atsho?),

[* The stones are so loosely embedded in sandy soil, that treading on or catching hold of one, often brings down an avalanche of stones. When the path is narrow and a river flows beneath, it is, generally, impossible to escape. Stones are often placed in such a way as to cause avalanches to come on the invader who steps on them.]

one fell into the Indus and was never again seen, whilst the other slipped down and rose again to the surface—an event never known to occur with any one who falls into the Indus at that place where it is very rapid. He, however, made his way over to Bunji, and just as he was reaching it, a stone fell on his head and he was drowned.

A year had scarcely elapsed after the battle of Chakarkôt, when, in the spring, about 20,000 Kashmir troops with the former General came to Astor. He sent a letter of defiance to Gauhar Aman, challenging him to do his worst, to assemble the mountaineers and to meet him on an open plain. Gauhar Aman at once told the mountaineers that they should quietly get into Jalkot (Sai District) by way of the valley of Kámberi, over the mountain Hudurga, to the village Kirinjot, and get out by the mountains of Puhût. This was done. Gauhar Aman again fell ill at Minôr. His son just got there in time to meet the Sikhs (10,000 in number) near the Niludar, the mountain ridge which is between Gilgit and Sai. It was night, and so both armies encamped; in the morning the fight began. 7,000 Dareylis and Tangîris had come under Jeldar, and Lala Khan of Gaya in Dareyl and Izzetí, Pátsha Khan of Phogutsh of Dareyl—also Matshar Khan of Samagiál—Bitori, Kalashmir of another Samagial, Kusuti of Manekyál, Arzennu of Dareyl—Rústami, Kâmi of Tangîr, Muhammad Mir, Adab Shah of Gali, Khairulla of Jagôt—Karim, Moya Shah, Mawêshi, Matti of the Deyámur village—Merdumi of Lúrak—Akbaro of Sheikho—[2,000 came from Tangîr, 5,000 from Dareyl]. Gouhar Aman's son had 3.000 infantry and 6,000 horsemen. The Sikhs were on the roads below the mountains, whilst the Yaghistanis were firing from the tops. The Sikhs necessarily wasted their shot in such an encounter, whilst the mountaineers had it all their own way. This lasted the whole day. All (10,000 !!) were destroyed—only one sepoy escaped to Bunji to tell the news to the other half of the army. The General was not present in this as in the Chakarkôt battles, but stayed at Bunji. The Yaghis only lost 2 men, one from Phúgutsh and the other from Samagial, viz. : Shahbaz, also called "Osmin," aud Uzet Shah. The mountaineers then accompanied the victorious army back to Minôr and Gilgit, where they consulted regarding the future safety from the Sikhs. Gauhar Aman thought that the Gilgit Fort could not stand a siege and that it should therefore be strengthened and the walls made higher. This view was shared by the mountaineers who looked upon Gilgit as their centre ; so they all set to work to improve the fort and raised it twenty yards in height and gave six yards of depth to the walls. Bullocks were constantly treading down the stones as the walls were being raised. The Zamindars also helped. The Mountaineers assisted and were fed during the month that it took to strengthen the place. Then all left, when Gauhar Aman fell very ill. He sent Mulk Aman, with 5,000 horsemen against Yasin to fight Mahtar and A'smat Shah, sons of Suleyman Shah, descendants of Pátsha (?), Shins. They came there on the fourth day and surrounded the place. Mahtar would not fight, and surrendered on the tenth day, saying that they all came from one stock and were subjects to Gauhar Aman. A'smat Shah fled to Swat. Mahtar paid his respects with 1,000 young men and was apparently received in a friendly manner by Mulk Aman, who said he wanted to talk to him privately. There is a hall for the princes 100 yards from the Fort, and to this he led Mahtar and after a conversation of two hours struck off his head. Then he came out and killed 20 of Mahtar's relatives and friends. The rest he put into the Fort, as they were merely Zamindars. He then asked Gauhar Aman to come to Yasin with his whole family. On the good news reaching him he assembled the Gilgitis and told them that, as his illness was sure to carry him off, he wanted to be buried in his own country where also his ancestors reposed. In reality, he wanted to marry the widow of Mahtar. When he came near Yasin, some one told him that his son had married the widow. This rendered him furious and made him think of killing his son. In this state of mind he reached Yasin, where he said nothing but ascertained that the widow had been married eight days ago. He then threw Mulk Aman into a prison which was at the top of the highest tower of the Yasin fort and ordered that he should not receive sufficient food. The woman was also placed under surveillance. He left Ghulam as Wazir of Gilgit. Gauhar Aman remained ill for a year, being unable to move and one side being shrivelled up. When he felt his death nigh, he released Mulk Aman and made the woman over to him. A few days after he died and Mulk Aman had accomplished the funeral rites, he ascended the throne. When Isa Baghdùr [Isa Bahadur] and the fugitive A'smat Shah heard this in Swat, they rejoiced as they did not think that Mulk Aman was a hero like his father. Isa Bahadur of Sher Kila' had also fled to Swat having heard of the defeat of the Sikhs and being afraid of being dispossessed by Gauhar Aman—an idea which was confirmed by Akbar Aman, the brother on the father's side of Gauhar Aman—(Isa Bahadur and Akbar were cousins, sons of two sisters) (Isa Bahadur and Gauhar Amán were tarburs ترہور, namely brothers' children). There is a road from Swat to Yâsin which is much used and is near. Mulk Aman, wishing to conquer other countries, enquired who had caused Isa Bahadur's flight and offered a reward for the information. Hayátulla, a servant of Gauhar Amán, told him a month after about his uncle being the cause, as they were related on the women's side (the stronger tie; being related on the father's side is not a strong bond wherever polygamy is common). This convinced Mulk Aman, for having taken the throne from his uncle to whom it by right belonged, he always felt suspicious of him. However, he kept his own counsel, when one day he invited Akbar Aman to go out shooting with him. They went about one kôs from the Yasin fort, where a fine plain comes in view. Mulk Aman advised all retainers to get down from their horses as he wanted to rest a little and then start the game which would come in sight in that place. This they did not do, so he jumped from his horse, pretending that he saw game in different directions and ran after it. Then Akbar Aman also got down from his horse. He had scarcely moved about for a few yards, when a ball, fired by Mulk Aman, struck him dead. Mulk Aman then returned to govern in peace of mind. This news Isa Bahadur had also heard in

Swat. What with wishing to revenge Akbar and thinking of the confusion which would be sure to follow the discord of the brothers of Mulk Aman (Mîr Wali, Pahlivan, etc.) he and Asmár got ready and came back—but I don't know whether he came *via* Kandiá [a hitherto unexplored District, referred to elsewhere] or by what road. Anyhow he appeared at Sai with the 20 followers whom he had taken with him from Sher Kila' on his flight. There he found Sultan, the ex-Wazir of Pohordu Shah, a descendant of the Queen Johari (Jowâri—*vide* 1st Song, page 22) who in ancient times was the ruler of Sai and whose descendants had fled from Gauhar Aman into the hills. When Gauhar Aman died, all these fugitives came back and so Sultan turned up at Sai. When Isa and Asmat met him they contracted an alliance by oath and went together to Jammu by way of Astor in order to offer their services to the Maharajah. Indeed, they offered their allegiance, if he would help them with troops. The Maharajah made them swear on the Koran, because he said, "your religious bigotry may induce you to turn on me and induce you to be again friends with Mulk Aman. Besides, you all belong to one family and I alone shall be the loser." Then they all agreed and he made them swear on the Koran, after getting them to wash themselves first; "that they would never ally themselves or be subject to any one but the Maharaja and consult nobody's interests but his." The three swore most solemnly and assured H. H. that he need not be under any anxiety in future regarding his army and their own movements. They then asked leave in order to avail themselves of the dissensions of the brothers and prevent their becoming friends again. Then H. H. sent 6,000 infantry and 4 guns (mule-batteries) with Isa, Sultan and Asmat—Rs. 200 cash were given to Isa and a dress of honour; Rs. 100 and a gun to Sultan and Rs. 120 and a horse to Asmat Shah. The Maharaja recommended them always to keep the garrisons at Astor and Bunji, which were each 5,000 strong, at half their strength and to take the rest in order to prevent surprises and the loss of places which were difficult to acquire and to reduce to taxation. He thus allowed them to take 11,000 troops with them in all—*viz.* 6,000 men whom he sent direct and 5,000 from the garrisons of Astor and Bunji. Thus they started with the General and the Jîtan Sahib (Adjutant ?) for Astor. There they remained a month to see whether the roads ahead were safe. They sent a Kashmîri, called Abdulla, into Yaghistan, *via* Sai, Minôr, Gilgit, Yasin, Dareyl, Tangîr, Hunza, Nagyr, etc., to enquire what the tribes were doing and going to do. He went to Gilgit and instead of fulfilling his mission himself, he sent Norôz, a Zemindar and a subject of Mulk Aman, who, of course, went to Yasin and told Mulk Aman all he had heard from Abdulla and that Isa and his allies were advancing. On his return he told Abdulla that he had seen the tribes, that they had no idea that anything was impending and that Isa might advance with safety at once. Abdulla returned to Astor, whilst Mulk Aman summoned the Darêl and Tangîr tribes, saying that unless they fought now they would lose their country. He also sent a messenger to Ghazanfar, Raja of Hunza and one to Shah Murad, Wazir o' Nagyr (?) telling them to forget their enmity with him in the advance of a common foe to their country and religion (although the people of Hunza and Nagyr are Shiahs, necessity made Mulk Aman, a Sunni, call them Mussulmans) and asking them to meet him with their young men at Gilgit. Ghazanfar promised to come on the ninth day and asked him to go ahead. Mulk Aman, however, waited nine days and when nobody came, he advanced with the friendly hill tribes of Darêl and Tangîr to Gilgit. Isa Bahadur and his allies, altogether 9,500 men, started from Astor, 2,500 soldiers joined them at Bunji and they all advanced to within the distance of one kôs from the Gilgit Fort, which they surrounded. Wazir Zoraveru commanded in this war on the part of the Sikhs—there were also Sirdar Muhammad Khan of Swat, the Sirdar Jitani (Adjutant) and others whose names I forget. On behalf of the tribes there were: (1) from DAREYL: Lalá Khan, Jeldár Bura Khan of Gayá—with 1,000 Zemindars;—Izzeti and Muhammad Khan of Phugotsh with 700 Zemindars—Matshar Khan and Mahman from Karini (lower) Samegial with 1,000 men—Mirza Khan and Kalashmir from Upper Samegial and 1,000 men—Kasûti from Karini Manikyal with 1,000 men—Hamza Khan and Arzennu from Upper Manikyal and 900 men—Bitori of Yatsho and 40 men—Suryó from Jutyal and 60 men—Tubyó and Syad Amir of Dudishal and 30 men—altogether 5,846 from Dareyl. (2) from TANGIR: Mardumi (is still alive), Talipu of Lurak and 40 men—Moza Shah and Maweshi (still alive) of Dîyamar and 400 men—Khairulla and Mansur (still alive) of Julkôt and 140 Zemindars—Adab Shah and Mansur (still alive), of Gali and 60 men,—Néyo and Rustam Khan of Kami (still alive) and 400 men—Multan of Korgah (still alive) and 60 men—Akbaru of Sheikho and 40 men—altogether 1,153 men and Chiefs. With Mulk Aman there came from YASIN: his brother Mir Vali Khan, the Wazirs Rahmat and Nasir—Hayatalla, Habib—Padisha Mia, Balhi, Syad Khan (of Swat) with 100 Pathans—Muhammad Hussain, a great Chief of Yasin and 10,000 men, horse and foot, from Yasin and friendly countries.

At the dictation of Pehliwan, son of the sister of Aman-ul-Mulk, ruler of Chitral or little Kashghár, a messenger of the name Balli—was sent to Chitrál, saying that Hunza and Nagyr had broken their promise and that, now that their father was dead, all his enemies had assembled to destroy them, 11,000 infidels, described as كافر نابكار ذوكره بي اعتبار, or useless unbelievers and perfidious Dogras, had already surrounded Gilgit with the help of faithless Isa, the fugitive Asmat and the traitor Sultan. "When we shall be dead, what is the use of you, a relative, striking your forehead with a stone (as a sign of grief)"? Balli taking forced marches reached Aman-ul-Mulk speedily, who, at once sent Lakhtar Khan, his nephew, son of Adam Khor (whom he had caused to be killed) with 8,000 men of sorts to Gilgit and wrote to promise further help, if Balli were sent again. Indeed it was said that Aman-ul-Mulk might come himself. So there advanced to the rescue of Gilgit the united forces of Mulk Aman and the auxiliaries from Chitrál. Mulk Aman then told the Dareylis and Tangîris to lay in ambush behind Parmas and Basîn in the valley, as the Sikh troops were there. He himself at 6 o'clock in the evening went to attack these places. About 1,000 Sikhs were there, not suspecting any danger, in their tents. The attack was sudden and 120 were at once despatched to the lowest regions [of hell]; 100 Sikhs were captured. Then he called out to the young horsemen that having done so much they should attack the besiegers and that the infantry would follow them. He himself rode ahead, thereby inspiring his troops with courage. The enemy was attacked, but was now ready for them. A fierce struggle began and the Sikhs were forced on to the fortress with the loss of twenty youths and a loss of three Dareylis on our side, who had rashly followed the Sikhs into the fort. Then Mulk Aman halted in front of the fort and attacked it in the early morning and called out. "If you want to fight, well and good—if not, I will let you depart for Astor." Isa Bahadur replied: "We will certainly not do so till we uproot the foundations of your houses." Saying this, he fired his musket and killed Hayatulla (who had been the cause of his uncle's death). Then volleys were exchanged. So the fight lasted for a month, during the day—Mulk Aman retiring to a short distance at night—the Sikhs, however, picking off stragglers at night also. On the 27th day after the siege, the Raja of Hunza reached with 12,000 soldiers, but did not join the fight. 6,000 soldiers, in addition to the 8,000 already sent, also came from Chitrál who, at once, assisted in the siege. There was plenty of wheat which had been cut and heaped up by the Gilgit Zemindars who had fled at the approach of the Sikhs. The soldiers of Aman-ul-Mulk would take the sheaves, crush them with stones and boil them in water. Food was taken at night. Three days later, when the besiegers still held out, the Chitrál forces thought of returning. On the last day, Makhsat, a servant of Asmat Shah, renowned all over Yaghistan as an incomparable hero, came out of the fort with sword and buckler and called out. "Is there any one who will fight [me] the mountain eating lion?" Then Balli, the servant of Mulk Aman, replied: "Come out and fight with me in the open space, for brave men do not boast." So he, snatching a sword and shield, met him. After boasts and insults on both sides, they closed; but Makhsat's sword could only find Balli's shield to strike, whilst Balli, in protecting himself always found an exposed part of Makhsat to hit. At last Balli struck a blow which not only cut through Makhsat's shield, but falling on his right shoulder caused the sword to pass out on his left side, thus dividing the body into two pieces. On seeing this, Mulk Aman considered that a sufficient victory had been gained and passed on to Yasin, accompanied by the Allies. Of the prisoners he had captured at Barmas, in order to wreak his revenge, having been disappointed in taking the Gilgit fort, he selected twenty four of the officers and ordered them to be executed at Kuffarkôt, four kôs from Gilgit near the Indus. This was accordingly done by some men in Lakhtar Khan, the Chitrál General's army. When their souls had reached the angels of Hell, Mulk Aman ordered the rest also to be killed, for, he said, these infidels have made martyrs of many of our friends and countrymen. Lakhtar Khan interposed on the ground that they were helpless, now that their officers were dead, and made a claim to carry them off himself, as a satisfaction for the losses of his army. "I want," he said, "to bring them to my country and sell them for red gold to the Tájiks. Thus I shall obtain compensation for the blood of the martyrs that has been shed and they will be punished by being sold from place to place by the Tájiks." Then Mulk Aman conferred the desired present on Lakhtar Khan, but kept one (the only officer who was spared) who was called "Commandân Bahádur" and presented him to Jaldár Khan of Gayă (Dareyl), as many martyrs [so called because they were Muhammadans, who had been killed in the war with the "infidel" Dogras] had fallen from that District. When the troops had gone back for another kôs (from Kuffárkôt) to a place called Serga—a very deep valley—Jaldár Khan told the "Commandán" to come near him, as he was in his charge. He caught hold of his hand and led him along. He then noticed a talisman round the Sikh's neck and wanted to snatch it away, forgetting that he was exposing himself to an attack by the movement. The "Commandan" saw a sword hanging on Jaldár's shoulder, so he let Jaldár take his talisman and drawing the sword struck off his head. When the Dareylis saw the death of their chief, they rushed upon the murderer and secured him. Separating in groups to consult as to the best means of putting him to death, the people of Gayá (Jaldár's village) advised his arms and legs being tied to four horses and his body being torn to pieces by the horses being set off at a gallop. This proposal was not favourably received by Khoshál Khan, the brother of Jaldár. The people of Samegiál suggested that his tongue should be torn out with red-hot pincers, then to flay him alive, cover his body afterwards with salt and pepper and finally to burn him and make him over to the ruler of Jahannam [Hell]. This suggestion being favoured by Khoshál Khan, it was ordered to be carried out. Thus the "Commandán Bahádur" died. The Dareylis then rushed on his ashes and half-burnt flesh and taking a handful, secured it in their clothes as a reminiscence of the event. I have mentioned this affair at length, because Jaldár was a very celebrated man for his hospitality, eloquence, good manners and administrative capacity. Rich and poor obeyed him, for he was wise and his death was a great advantage to the Sikhs.

Mulk Aman set out for Yasin, as I have said, and dismissed the Yaghistanis. Lakhtar Khan also asked for his leave through Pahliwan, Mulk Aman's brother and offered to let the army remain if he himself was allowed to go. This was permitted and the army remained with Pahliwan, his mother's brother (a sister of Adamkhor of Chitrál was Gauhar-Aman's wife and Gauhar Aman's sister was Adamkhor's wife). The following is the list of the chiefs killed before Gilgit: [The Sikhs lost 221 killed, wounded and prisoners.] Wazirs Nuseir and Hayatulla of Yasin; Jaldár Khan of Gayá (Dareyl); Talîpu of Tangir; Béra Khan of Gaya; Mirza Khan of Hunîni Samagiál; Sirdar of Hunîni Samagiál; and Padshah Mia of Yasin.

Dareyl lost 203 Zemindars; *Tangîr* 101 men; *Gakutsh* [or *Galkûtsh*] 50; *Tshêr*, 40; *Sherôt* 52; *Shukoyôt* 30; *Guluphúr* 44. Mulk Aman lost 160 of his retainers; (altogether 376 of his subjects.) The Chitrális lost 410, altogether 1,090 were killed on our side. [For a more chronological account of the conquest of Gilgit vide "Chronological History of Dardistan," pages 70-75.

III.—WAR ON YASIN AND THE MASSACRE OF ITS INHABITANTS. [1860]

When Lakhtar Khan informed the ruler of Chitrál of all that had occurred, Aman-ul-Mulk sent a messenger to the ruler of Yasin with the advice to fortify Gakutsh, lest that too should be lost by him and he should be blamed for not advising him in time. He also thought that the Sikhs would not advance before they had strengthened their hold on Gilgit. Therefore he asked for his army to be sent back; next year he promised to send a larger force, as then an attack from the Sikhs might be possible. Mulk Aman delayed the messenger for ten days, but sent Sirdar Mustaán, son of General Hayat-ulla of Yasin, with the Chitrál army to Aman-ul-Mulk. They were 5,880 horse; 7,720 foot and 12 mules with ammunition. Mulk Amán then remained at Yasin, feeling quite safe and established a Thanna of five men at Gakutsh, one day's march from Yasin, in order to scour the country and enquire from travellers and Zemindars about the movements of the Sikhs. He advised them to treat informants well and let him know in time, lest Aman-ul-Mulk's warning should come true. The outpost kept a good look-out, entertained travellers and daily sent in news of the state of affairs. Five months afterwards Wazir Zorawern of Kashmir sent Wazir Mukhtár with twenty young men to Gakutsh to surprise the Thanna at night, and establish themselves as an outpost and intercept all travellers from or to Yasin. He also sent after them Sabûr, a Kashmiri, with ten Hindu Sipahis and Attai, Kashmiri, with ten Muhammadan Sipahis, and ordered Attaï to establish himself at 100 yards above Gakutsh and Sabur at the same distance below Gakutsh and intercept the roads. Three days afterwards, Zoraweru, Isa Bahadur, Ghulam Haydar, Mizra Wazir, Baghdur Shah, Zohrab Khan, Asmat Shah and Saif Ali, the Commandant, with 9,000 infantry and 3,000 cavalry, advanced on Gakutsh. We must now leave them on the road and see what the surprise party is doing. They came there shortly after mid-night, surrounded the Thanna and captured the five men. Mukhtar then established himself as Thannadar and Attai and Sabûr took up their appointed posts and captured all travellers of whatever age and sex, sending them in to the Thanna; in all, three women, four children, two foreign youths and one Yasini were captured. When the army came to Gakutsh, Zoraweru left the Thanna as it was, and advanced the same day without stopping, so as to prevent all notice of his march reaching Yasin before he himself arrived, marching all night, and at about 4 o'clock came to Chamûgar, a village, about twenty nine kôs from Yasin. Accidentally, Muhammad Hussain, a Sayad, had gone out hunting that day. His horse rearing without any apparent cause he looked round and saw clouds of dust at Chamûgar. He, at once, suspected what was taking place, galloped back to Yasin and called out before Mulk Aman's house: "Why are you sitting at your ease? the enemy is on you—now do anything if you can." Mulk Aman at once got his horses saddled and fled with his family over the mountains in the direction of Chitrál. When the army came near Yasin, Isa Bahadur, who knew the country, ordered it to be divided into three corps, one of which marched straight on Yasin—the second to go to the right of Yasin by the village of Martal and the third to go to the left of the place, so that the inhabitants should not be able to escape. When the Sikhs entered Yasin with Asmat Khan preceding them (who got all his friends and relatives out of the way) acts of oppression occurred which I have heard related by the people of Kholi and which have never been surpassed by any nation of infidels. In traditions much is told, but all is nothing compared with the following atrocities which surpass the doings of demons, jins and witches. We, say the Kholi informants, with our own sinful eyes saw these ferocities practised by Mussulmans on Mussulmans. That blood thirsty Kafir, Isa Bahadur, ordered the houses to be entered and all the inhabitants, without regard to sex or age, to be killed. We swear that Isa Bahadur descended from his horse and distinctly ordered the soldiers to snatch the babes from their mothers' arms and kill them, so that his heart might be set at ease. He then put one knee on the ground, putting his hands on his knees and waiting for the babes. As they were brought to him, he put one of their small legs under his foot and tore the other off with his hand. Even the Sikh soldiery could not bear looking on this spectacle. However, this accursed infidel, (infidel, although he was a Sunni) kept on tearing them to pieces. The slaughter lasted five days and nights. The blood of the victims flowed in streams through the roads: there is not a word of exaggeration in all this. After these dreadful five days were over, Zoraweru sent for Asmat Shah and enquired after his relatives, whom he had put in safety. They were brought forward and Yasin committed to their charge, but what was left of Yasin!?* Thus 2,000 men, women, and children above ten years of age and a countless number of infants and babes became martyrs at the hands of the bloody Sikhs—3,000 persons (chiefly women) a very few children as also a few old men were kept as prisoners and brought in three days to Gilgit, Zoraweru being elated with excessive joy which he manifested in various ways *en route*. When he came to Gilgit, Isa Bahadur and Asmat Shah, selecting 1,000 of the more beautiful women, took them to Jammu with 3,000 soldiers. They were so delighted that they took double marches in order to be early with their good news. At a public assembly at Jammu, these scoundrels narrated, with much boasting and eloquence, their own achievements and those of the Sikhs and spoke with the loud tone in which victories are reported.

When they had finished, the Maharaja asked them whether their hearts were pleased with all these doings. Isa Bahadur said that all his heart's desire had not been accomplished, though he certainly had experienced a slight satisfaction in the fate of the people of Yasin, who had been his enemies in the times of Gauhar Aman. "God be praised," he said, "that I have lived to revenge myself on them." The Maharaja enquired what else there remained to afford him complete satisfaction. "Perhaps," he said, "I may be able to meet your views." Isa Bahadur replied. "Alas,

* Here my informant, himself a Sunni Mussulman and always calling his Shiah co-religionists Kafirs, was raving with indignation against the orthodox Sunnis, Isa and Asmat and the Sunni soldiers of Kashmir, for murdering the Shiahs of Yasin. He ascribed the atrocities of the Sikhs entirely to the orders of the ex-fugitives.

Mulk Aman with all his family has escaped unhurt to Chitrál! I should have liked to have treated him as the Commandán Sahib who killed Jaldar was treated, and to have taken his wife for myself and to have killed his children, as I did the infants of Yasin and, moreover, to burn them. Then alone will my heart be at ease. However, in consequence of Your Highness's good fortune, much has been done. If your shadow only continues to protect me, I may, some day, be able to have my heart's desire on Mulk Aman." The Maharaja then bestowed on him a splendid and complete dress of honor, a horse and Rs. 500. He also gave Rs. 100, a dress and a horse to Asmat Shah. He finally placed the 3,000 soldiers whom he had brought under his command and made him Governor of Sher Kila (where he is still). Isa Bahadur, after the usual deprecatory forms of politeness used at oriental Courts, suggested that, in the midst of Yaghistan, he would not be able to hold his own even with 30,000 soldiers, unless the Maharaja placed Pahlivan, the son of the sister of Aman-ul-Mulk at the head of the Government of Yasin even without troops, as he had all the prestige of Aman-ul-Mulk on his side. At last, the Lord of Srinagar said that he agreed to it, if Isa Bahadur could manage to get Pahlivan appointed to Yasin, a matter which, naturally, was out of his own control. Isa Bahadur then asked for troops, not against Chitrál, whose interests would now be conciliated, but against the Dareylis and the other hill tribes. So the Maharaja gave him the troops, warning him at the same time to be on his guard against Pahlivan tampering with his troops and so causing a general revolt against the Maharaja's authority.

His Highness then ordered Asmat Shah to go to Yasin in order to keep a watch on the movements of Pahlivan and to inform Wazîr Zoraweru of all that was going on. Asmat Shah feared that his life would not be safe at Yasin and wished for some other employment. The Maharaja then said his salary should be Rs. 40 per mensem* and he should go with Isa Bahadur, as Thanadar of Gakûtsh. Isa Bahadur, however, thought that it could not be done and that it would be better to send him to Basîn. This was agreed to and the two got ready to depart. The Maharaja advised him to take the 2,000 prisoners left at Gilgit back with him to Sher Kila, so that the place might be well populated, a plan that would not only give him more income from the produce of fields but provide him with assistance against an enemy. "Leave," he added, "your first wife at Gilgit, (as a hostage, no doubt, for Isa's fidelity to the Maharaja) and take your second wife and her children with you to Shêr." So they returned to Gilgît, Asmat Shah setting up with his family at Basîn, where he is still and receives his pay. Isa Bahadur also settled at Shêr in the manner suggested by the Maharaja. He then sent Daulat Shù, a Zemindar of Gulmutti, eight kôs from Shêr, to Aman-ul-Mulk of Chitrál asking him

* I met Lehna Singh, a relative of the Maharaja, in 1866 in command of the Sai forces, who had only Rs. 20 per mensem, with unlimited liberty, however, to make as much besides out of the people, as he could. Bad as this system is, the drain on the rulers and the ruled is not so great, under Oriental methods, as under a highly-paid European administration, and the mismanagement of Kashmîr was far less expensive and less injurious to the Empire than the present "good" management through British officers.

to appoint Pahlivan as Governor of Yasin, who would be quite safe there. Daulat Shù was sent because he knew the roads and had often gone to Chitrál. He reached the place in seven days. Aman-ul-Mulk replied that he could not send Pahlivan, unless Isa Bahadur also agreed to MIR VALI and Wazir Rahmat. He gave Daulat Shu a parting present of a gun, sword and horse. Daulat Shù told Isa Bahadur of the result of his mission. Isa at once set off for Gilgit to consult with Zoraweru. He represented to him that unless Aman-ul-Mulk was allowed to have his way, he himself could not hold his own at Sher Kila. Zoraweru, upon this, gave him full permission to act as he liked, taking the responsibility on his own shoulders in the event of the Maharaja asking any questions, as the only means of securing some peace. Isa then again despatched Daulat Shù in all haste, who reached Chitrál in five days, with the message that Aman-ul-Mulk should do him the favour of sending the three men he had suggested. Aman-ul-Mulk entertained Daulat Shù for twenty days, during which time he assembled 2,000 young men and sent them to Yasin with Pahlivan, Mi Vali and Rahmat. He made those three take an oath on the Koran that they would never intrigue against each other, "for, if you do, you will fall an easy prey to Isa Bahadur." When they reached Yasin, they sent on Daulat Shù to Isa Bahadur. The first thing they did was to get the fugitive Yasinis back to their country which they ruled as in former days. Isa Bahadur was glad at this and gave eight tolahs of gold to the messenger.*

IV.—WAR WITH NAGYR AND HUNZA. [1864]

It is now nine years since these wars have taken place or two years after the conclusion of the war with Yasin. The Maharaja wrote to Zoraweru that after all what he wanted to conquer were the countries of Nagyr and Hunza, as there was no profit to be gained from Gilgit and Yaghistan, whence hitherto, he said, "we have only reaped stony districts and loss of men," [in reality, Gilgit aud Yasin are fertile, whilst Hunza is "stony"]. Zoraweru at once set out for Nômal, which is twelve kôs from Gilgit in the direction of Nagyr and sent Mehdîn Khan of Bunair and Sultan Wazir of the Janheri descendants and Saif Ali, Commandant, with 8,000 infantry. Zoraweru himself remained at Nômal in order to facilitate communications and bring up help, if necessary. The army advanced next day to Chaprôt, Guyétsh and Hini, of which the latter is in Nagyr and the former in Hunza

* The Kholi people from whom the Sazîni heard the account of the massacre were 100 merchants who had come to Gilgit, as is their custom, to sell goats, etc., and had there been arrested and taken along to Yasin by Isa Bahadur, in order to prevent their spreading the news of the impending attack. There were also eight men from Djajiál and five from Patan. The following were the Chiefs with the merchants: Káhar, Kali, Dessa, Amr, Djá—Shîns of Mahrëin in Koli (four miles from Koli). Sabit Shah, Aman, Shudum Khan, Serdàn, Guldán (Kamins); Hajetu, Lola, Shughlu Hákko, Bisat, Puz, Khushir (Yashkunns); Ashmál, Gulu, Subhán Shah, Bilál, Mahsúmu, Yadúla, Najb-ulla of Kóli; Bolós Khan, and Bula Shái, two Patan Sirdars—Wáli, Sirdar of Djajiál, a Shin, with seven Zemindars. I, adds my informant, have also heard it from Mulk Aman who was not present, but who sorrows deeply for the occurrence. (The atrocities related are fully confirmed by Mr. Hayward's account, quoted elsewhere, and by what I saw and heard myself in 1866. Mr. Hayward fixes 1863 as the date of the massacre.)

and encamped between these places on a plain.* (?) Guyétsh and Chaprôt are on the frontier of Hunza. Its inhabitants speak the same language as the people of Hunza. Hini was on the other side of the army and is on the frontier of Nagyr. The Chief of Chaprôt is Shah Murad Wazir, whilst Sirdar Mamal Beg is at Hini and Phagoi, the Lumbardar, at Guyêtsh, whose son is Shukar Beg, a brave young man. The chief command of the invading troops was given to Sultan, who had previously sent a man, Uruz Ali, to the Hunza Raja, to announce his arrival. He told him to lie in ambush at Nilamutsh in order to destroy the troops under the other Kashmir Officers. "I will draw off, he said, half the army in the direction of the Valley." Uruz Ali was by origin a Hunza man who had settled at Gilgit. The Raja of Hunza acted on the advice thus sent. When Wazîr Sultan came to Nilamutsh, he started with some youths towards Chaprôth. Now Nilamutsh is a place so surrounded by inaccessible and high mountains that escape from an enemy who occupies them is impossible and even a great army is helpless. No one prevented or questioned the movements of Sultan, who advanced about one kôs out of Nilamutsh —Mahdin and Saif Ali now entered the place when they were at once assailed with stones and bullets on every side by invisible enemies and lost 400 young men in killed between forenoon and evening. Two Nagyris only were wounded, one being shot through the mouth who is still alive and the other receiving a bullet in his thigh from which he subsequently died at Nagyr. When the surprised Generals consulted at night on the events of the day, they inferred from the absence of Sultan and the fact that he had got safely through Nilamutsh, as well as from the unexpected presence of the enemy, that treachery had been at work. The reason of this conduct was that Sultan, although the bravest to fight on behalf of the Maharaja, had not been rewarded with land as Isa and Azmat had been, but had remained under the direct orders of Zoraweru, who had put him forward in the war in order to get him killed and who had poisoned the Maharaja's mind against him. "However," the Generals added, "at present we must think of getting out of this place; otherwise not a man will remain alive to tell the news at Nômal." They then decided, on the suggestion of Saif Ali, to send two Dareylis, Firôz and Kúweti, into the Hunza lines, as they might have influence with them, being also Yaghistanis, in order to secure the safe return of the Army. The task was reluctantly accepted by the Dareylis whose presence in the Sikh Army naturally compromised them. However, they went and swore on behalf of the Sikhs that if they were allowed to depart no future invasion should ever take place. Naudîn, the Wazir of Nagyr and Ghazanfar of Hunza refused, on which the Dareylis requested that they might be shot and their bodies thrown in the valley, as a proof that they had done their best and failed in their mission. "We are Mussulmans and you should forgive us and as a natural consequence those whom we represent." The men now prepared for death, when Naudîn

* There is a place called Nilamutsh—green mountain ridge—literally a mountain that has fallen off a still higher one. Chaprôt is three kôs above and Guyetsh two kôs below this place. Hîni is on the other side of the river two and a half kos from Nilamutsh. Chaprôt has 150 houses; Guyêtsh 30 and Hini 80 houses.

interposed and got their request sanctioned, on the understanding that the Sikhs would at once return to Gilgit or else he would attack within an hour. The Kashmir Army, which had been re-joined by Sultan in the meanwhile, were only too glad to get away on these terms and returned to Nômal. Sultan gave out that he had gone ahead in order to clear the road in advance. However, Zoraweru was informed of the treachery, and, at once, put Sultan in chains and sent him to Jammu with a detailed letter under strict charge of Sirdars Baghdùr Shah and Ghulam Haidar and ten soldiers.

Zoraweru then took the army back to Gilgit. When the Maharaja read the letter, from which it appeared that no one except Sultan's *confidant*, Urùz Ali, who, the Gilgitis said, was always going backwards and forwards to Hunza, could have gone to inform the Hunza people of an attack, which must have been successful, had they not been forewarned, he condemned Sultan to imprisonment for life. I think that it was a got-up affair, for Zoraweru had often and in vain tried to take Hunza-Nagyr. As a proof of this I may mention that Hilli Shah of Hunza had come to Gilgit a few days before the expedition to buy merchandise. The Wazîr sent for him, gave him money and took him into his confidence. Seven days after he asked Hilli Shah to assist him in an attack on Nilamutsh which he was contemplating a month hence. Hilli said that he and his brother Mirza Khan, an artilleryman famous for his bravery and influence, would guide the Sikh Army through Nilamutsh into Hunza. So they swore to abide by this plan and the Wazir dismissed him with a present of Rs. 40 and a Lungi. He also promised great rewards in the event of the success of the expedition. Hilli Shah told Mirza Khan, who was delighted. Uruz reached Hunza after Hilli Shah and told the Raja of it, who sent for Hilli Shah and enquired from him whether he had heard anything at Gilgit about the movements of the Sikhs or of an attack on Hunza. Hilli Shah said that he had not been to Gilgit and had heard nothing. However, the Raja noticed the Lungi which Hilli wore and which Uruz said had been given by Zoraweru. When he set out to surprise the Sikhs he sent for the brothers: Mirza Khan came at once, but Hilli Shah hid himself at Gakkarkôt, five kôs above Hunza. When Ghazanfar returned from the war, he sent for Hilli Shah. The messenger found him returning from a hunting expedition and brought him to Ghazanfar who asked him, why he had not gone to the war against the infidels; "has the Lungi on your head bribed you?" and added "it is improper that you should live." He was accordingly cut into pieces (literally) before the eyes of Mirza Khan, his brother (who is still alive and braver than Hilli Shah and also a better artilleryman); as for Uruz Ali, he was put in prison for a fortnight by the order of the Maharaja, as soon as he came to Gilgit, although Zoraweru wanted him to share the fate of Sultan. At that time Kalashmir of Dareyl visited Gilgit and was well entertained by Zoraweru for twenty days, when he presented him with a shawl and Rs. 100 and gave cheap shawls to the Sirdars who came with Kalashmir. Zoraweru then asked them, as he had conquered the whole of Yaghistan, to collect tribute for the Maharaja. This was agreed to, but when Kalashmir returned to his country he did nothing. In the war that will ensue I was present all through.

V.—WAR WITH DAREYL [YAGHISTAN] 1866.

When Zoraweru saw that the Hill, or Yaghistan tribes kept quiet he thought it a good opportunity for attacking Dareyl, which, he fancied, would fall easily. He appointed spies to bring to him any Dareylis that might happen to visit Gilgit. Aziz, a Lamberdár of Manikial, came with 100 goats to Gilgit and when he had sold them, visited Zoraweru, who received him kindly and entertained him for two days. When he left, the Kashmir General asked him to remind Kalashmir that he had not sent the tribute of Dareyl and Tangir, which had been promised two years ago and gave him an ultimatum of one month in which to come himself or send the tribute, otherwise Zoraweru would pay Kalashmir a visit with his army. Kalashmir replied that the Kashmiris had better come and take the taxes and that there was no occasion for his fellow-countrymen to take the least notice of the threat. When twenty days of the month had passed, two other messengers, one a Kashmiri, Kurban, residing at Kiner in Chilás; the other, Rahm Nur of Samegial—both traders, happening to be at Gilgit, were sent to announce Zoraweru's immediate attack and to ask the Hill-men to prepare themselves, because, as Zoraweru said, "it is my custom to give my enemy notice three times." Kalashmîr replied he did not care and next day requested the tribes to assemble at Samegiál—*viz:* the people of Tórr, Harbenn, Shatiál, Sazîn, Sômer—and of Tangi, Lurok, Dayamur, Sheikho, Jalkôt, Galli, Kammi, and Korgah. He even sent to the Kandiá people for help, who, however, replied that their harvest was just getting ready and that Dareyl was too far off. He also sent to Jagloth, Chilás, Hudur, Takk, Buder, and Gor. The Chilásis flatly refused on the ground of being subjects of Kashmir and being helpless. Jalkôt also did not send, as the notice had reached them too late and the war was immediately impending. The rest all assembled at Samegiál on the 10th day and were 7,000 in number; there were also 7,000 men from Dareyl itself. The Sikhs also started from Gilgit, on hearing which Kalashmir appointed four scouts at each of the following six posts: in the Kargá valley—at Karóri-Jóji—at Ruro-Dader, fifteen kos off—at Gitshár, at the same distance—at Barîga, sixteen kos distance—and at Naranéiga, fifteen kos.

From Samegial the tribes marched over the Dummu-dummu mountain to the valley of Bariga where they halted. Next morning at about 9 o'clock, after only a few had taken food, the heavens seemed to become dark. Looking round we saw a Dareyli waving his dress at the Karori-Joji post, which was a sign of the approach of the enemy. We all got ready and an hour afterwards the enemy came up, who had taken 11,000 men from Gilgit. A Sirdar of Samegial, Kuwéti, who had fled about four years ago to Gilgit from his village in consequence of the enmity of another fellow-villager, Dodár, now showed the way to the Sikhs. When the forces reached Yatshotsh below Dumnu-dummu on the Gilgit side, he asked Zoraweru to confide the guidance of the troops to him, as he alone knew the paths. Zoraweru assenting, Kuweti divided the forces into three bodies; one under General Har Chand in the direction of the valley of Dutial, the second under Sirdar Shahzada he despatched to the Yatshotsh valley—whilst the third was forwarded with Zoraweru to the Bariga valley —he himself going with the first column. We did not know these tricks and thought we had only to deal with the troops advancing on Barîga and rushed on them at once. The fight lasted till four in the afternoon. Accidentally, a Dareyli looking in the direction of Jadári-Jùt, saw from that "grassy plain" such a cloud of dust arise that the sky was darkened and out of which troops emerged. The Manikialis, whose village is five kos from that plain, fled at once to defend their homes, as they thought the enemy threatened Manikial. This was followed by the flight of the Samegialis by the Dareyl valley—an hour afterwards the people of Phugotsh, then the people of Gayá, also fled in the same direction. Now the fight ceased and night broke in. We remained at Bariga. The fugitives on reaching their villages, fled onwards with their families, some to Sazin, others to Tangîr, others again to Shatial. Yet we only lost five in killed and three in wounded—the losses of the Sikhs it is impossible to estimate. I alone counted twenty from where I stood. The Sikhs during the night surrounded us and cut off our retreat. At day-break, the fight was renewed and lasted till noon, when we discovered a mountain path for flight which we took and came to Samegial. The second day we lost nine men and the Sikhs thirty. The Sikhs remained for ten days at Jadári-Jùt and then advanced on Samegial *via* the District of Manikial, of which they burnt two villages, Shinó Kot and Yashkunó Kot, and killed the old women and children who had not been able to get away; four boys were found ill and also killed. Reaching Samegial, they found that we had fled on to Gayá. In that District the Sikhs also burnt two deserted villages, Dudó Kot and Birió Kot; they found, however, twelve fugitive women and children *en route* and killed them. The Sikhs stayed at Samegial, where 200 of us had remained concealed at about a mile from the place. A fight took place with a loss of four on our side and twelve on the part of the Sikhs. We were not followed up to Gayá. The Sikhs returned to Manikial where they remained ten days and indulged in eating the grapes which had become over-ripe and are very abundant in that District. Many died from disease engendered by this over-indulgence, but the Sikh Sirdars spread a report that the tribes had scattered poison on the grapes. Winter also set in, and snow fell, so the Sikhs returned to Gilgit. *En route* snow-storms set in, which blinded some and froze others. The Sikhs lost in dead about 120 men. The fugitive villagers now returned to their homes and rebuilt the burnt down villages. Six months later, Kalashmîr of Dudokôt (Samegiál) and Duran of Phugôtsh and Surió of Karînokot (Mánikial) and Burshù Sirdar of Biliokôt, (Manikial) and Sirdar of Gayá and Nur Muhammed of Shurôt started for Gilgit and offered allegiance to Zoraweru. He replied; "Oh! Kalashmir, thou hast given me much trouble and inflicted much injury. Now I want a goat per annum from every two houses throughout Dareyl." He then dismissed them with Khilats and now the tribute is regularly paid from those villages that I have named as being represented on that occasion by their Sirdars.

Doulat Shù. It is necessary to say a few words about the treatment of those who had assisted Kashmir. After Doulat Shù had arranged matters with Chitrál, Zoraweru appointed him over the yield of the gold washing of Bakrôt, Sakwár, Jutial, Deyúr, Minôr, Nomal, and Gilgit. The mode of taxation on gold washings is as follows: the men work two months in spring and two months in autumn and have to pay Rs: 3, or 2 gold Rupees = about 5 Chilki Rupees, for each season per head. Taxes are also raised on the produce, viz., a third of the whole. Doulat Shù received 10 Chilkis per mensem for that service. He went one autumn for the first time and brought back the taxes collected, which were sent to the Maharajah through Baghdur Shah. Six weeks later, some gold washers came to Gilgit to pay their respects to Zoraweru, who asked them whether they had had a bad season as the taxes paid had been small. The goldwashers said that it had been as good as usual: so Zoraweru, on referring to the accounts of the preceding year, found a difference of 5 tolas (about 60 Rupees). Doulat Shu was at once thrown into chains and sent to Jammu in charge of Ghulam Haidar and Mirza. The Maharajah sent him to the same place in which Sultan is confined and where both are now. In neither case was there an investigation. When Isa Bahadur heard of the imprisonment of men who had rendered such services as Sultan and Doulat Shu he came to Gilgit, where he found Ghulam Haidar and Mirza and took them to Jammu. They there interceded for the prisoners with the Maharajah and represented that brave and faithful men should not be punished with perpetual imprisonment, one of whom had conquered a country for His Highness, which the other had kept for Kashmir by his admirable arrangement with Chitrál. The Maharajah told them to go about their own business. When they heard this, they left, but, in their correspondence during four years, they constantly urged the release of the prisoners on His Highness. Two years ago they again presented themselves at Jammu and represented that the years that Sultan and Doulat Shu had already passed in prison were a sufficient punishment. They conjured His Highness by his idol, but the Maharajah threatened to send them to keep company with the prisoners if they did not at once desist from their importunities.

When Isa Bahadur heard such words, he left the same night and galloped on without stopping, till he had got to Sher Kila. He still considers that he has been very discourteously treated by Kashmir and his correspondence with the Maharajah has ceased. I have heard him lament over the past. Ghulam Haidar and Mirza kept on for a whole month importuning His Highness, who resolved on imprisoning them, when they fortunately asked and obtained leave to go home to Gilgit. The three Chiefs have not visited Jammu since the affair which I have related.

PRESENT STATE OF MIR VALI.

A year and a half ago Mir Vali (who drugs himself with charas = a preparation of hemp) got offended with Pahlivan, (probably on account of a difference of opinion in *re* Hayward) ;* went to Kandiá (road described elsewhere) and to Manikiál [not the village so often referred to in the account of the Wars] on the borders of Swat. Thence he went to Tall, Ramta, Berahmar and then to Beïkéy, the Akhûn of Swat, who asked him why he had come. Mir Vali said that Pahlivan had annoyed him and as the Akhun was a great Saint he had come to him, having no other friends. The Akhun entertained him for eight months, after which, on a Friday (when service takes place at noon instead of 2 P. M.) he told him to go back to Yasin, "for your heart's desire has been accomplished." Mir Vali at once started off on horseback, taking the bank of the Indus. On the third day he reached Ghorband; thence he went to Damtirey, Bilkái, Ranulia and Jajiál; there he crossed the river to Kúi; thence to Palus, Gagréy Khware (or in Gilgiti, Gabréga), Shogobind (a place for pasture) Jaglôth, Tekkegá, Parbáh (a place for pasture) Latór, Sazin, Dareyl, *viz*: Gayá, Samegial (where he stayed a week in order to consult Mulk Aman, who was there) Manekial, the Matrêt valley (pasture place for Gujers), and finally to Yasin. There he was well received by Pahlivan who could not understand why he had left and now the brothers love each other more than before. The rule is in the hands of Mir Vali who keeps up friendly relations with the Dogras and would strengthen these relations still further were it not for fear of Aman-ul-mulk, who is a great enemy of the Maharajah and who has ordered him to have as little to do with them or Isa Bahadur as possible. [*Vide* note on next page.]

MULK AMAN.

When Mulk Aman remembered his country, Yasin, he fell home-sick in Chitrál and begged Aman-ul-mulk to let him go and, if Aman-ul-mulk would assist him, he would fight the Sikhs or else die as a martyr. Aman-ul-mulk said that Mulk Aman could only do the latter, as he had no army left. "I advise you, he added, to go to Dareyl and ask the Maharajah's forgiveness, who may give you some appointment. Serve him, he said, as Isa Bahadur has done and you may be restored to the throne of your ancestors." Aman-ul-mulk said this in order to get rid of the importunities of Mulk-Aman, who left for Samegial. Baghdur Shah and Kuweti, the Maharajah's agents, happened to be there and actually offered to intercede with the Maharajah on his behalf and to get him an appointment. Mulk Aman was delighted. The agents spoke in his favour to the Maharajah who cheerfully ordered him to present himself. They came to Samegial and brought Mulk Aman to Jammu. His Highness bestowed a dress of honour, a horse and Rs. 200 on him and a monthly salary of Rs. 100 for himself, Rs. 30 for his son and Rs. 50 for the rest of his family and requested him to live at Gilgit outside the fort. "Remain there for 7 years; afterwards I will give you Yasin." This Mulk Aman did and built a house about 100 yards from the fort. He did not, however, for two years

* I sent the Yarkandi, Niaz Muhammad, (whom I had taken to Europe), by the little frequented Shigar route to find out the truth about Hayward's murder. His report is a strange and suggestive one, and will be published in my next volume. (See also pages 74, 75 and 105.)

send for his family from Samegial where he had left them when he started for Jammu. When they came he continued serving Kashmir for four years more. Isa Bahadur, however, happened to tell Zoraweru last year (for Isa was the arch-enemy of Mulk Aman and feared his getting back to Yasin) that Mulk Aman intended to escape with his family to Chitrál, after which, as he had plotted with the Gilgitis, there would be a general revolt which would end in his sharing the Government of Yasin with Pahlivan. When Zoraweru heard this he consulted with Isa Bahadur, who advised him to seize Mulk Aman and send him and his family to Jammu at once, so as not to give him time to rouse the country. This pleased the Governor and a suitable hour was left to Isa's discretion for surrounding the house and bringing Mulk Aman and his family before Zoraweru. Isa Bahadur at once went and selected 400 young men whom he ordered to be in readiness at four in the afternoon. Accidentally a friend of Mulk Aman overheard the conversation between Zoraweru and Isa Bahadur and at once informed him of what was contemplated and of the arrangements made by Isa. The friend advised him to flee at once into the mountains. Mulk Aman, greatly astonished, went to his house and ordered his family to get ready to start. Just as his women were coming out of the house, he saw Isa Bahadur with his soldiers all round it. Mulk Aman drew his sword, ran a-muck among the troops and after killing a few soldiers managed to escape alone into the mountains in the direction of Dareyl.* However swiftly pursued he could not be found; the Sikhs returned from the mountain and took the family prisoners. Mulk Aman, descending on the other side of the mountain, came to Samegial. Isa Bahadur then presented the women and children as hostages to Zoraweru who forwarded them to Jammu, where they still remain. Shortly afterwards the Maharajah heard that Mulk Aman was perfectly innocent of any conspiracy and had been got out of the way by the calumny of Isa Bahadur, the enemy of the house of Gauhar Aman from which he had suffered. The Maharajah was very sorry at what had taken place and ordered Muhammad Khan of Swat to bring the brave and unfortunate man back from Samegial under liberal promises of rewards and appointments. The Swati started and told Mulk Aman that he was responsible that no treachery was intended. All was in vain; he insulted Muhammad Khan and raved about the loss of honour, etc., which he had suffered at the hands of the Maharajah. "If he makes me his greatest Sirdar he can not wipe out the stain of having taken away

* It has also been alleged that in order to get rid of two doubtful friends of the Maharajah, namely, Mir Vali and Mulk-Aman, and to make room for the more trusted Pehliwan, Aman-ul-Mulk, the ruler of Chitrál and supposed instigator of the murder of Hayward through the agency of Mir Vali of Yasin, wrote to the Maharajah to implicate Mulk Aman in the business. Immediately on his flight, his wife and son were temporarily imprisoned in the Fort of Gilgit. Pehliwan and Rahmat interceded for some of the servants, who were set free and sent on to Chitrál. Mir Vali found his way to Chitrál whose ruler had one of Mr. Hayward's guns, though the bulk of his property is said to have been recovered. There he was seen by Major Montgomery's Havildar, who reported that Mir Vali was lame from a kick by a horse. This however, does not seem to have prevented him from resuming the rule of Yasin in conjunction with Pehliwan or, if recent accounts are to be trusted, from turning his nominal suzerain, Aman-ul-Mulk, out of Chitrál. Mulk Aman also figured for a short time on the scene of the war with Aman-ul-Mulk and by the latest report, seems to have fled to Yarkand.

my wife." Muhammad Khan returned to Jammu rrom his fruitless expedition and told the Maharajah, who was very sorry. Twenty eight days after Muhammad Khan's visit, Mulk Aman, considering himself unsafe, went to Harbenn, which is still Yaghistan [independent, wild]. Zoraweru then advised the Maharajah to send for him, as he had got among the Yaghis and might incite them to an attack on Gilgit. "Above all, make him satisfied." When the Maharajah read Zoraweru's letter, he again sent the Swati to Harbenn and told him to swear on the Koran, on his own behalf and that of His Highness, that it was all Isa's fault and that he would give Mulk Amán his revenge for the wrong suffered and allow him double his former salary. This Muhammad Khan did and saw Mulk Aman at Harbenn to whom he brought a shawl as a present from himself. He told him, in private, after "salâming" to him at a public meeting, all that he was charged to say and took an oath in attestation of the sincerity of his promises. Mulk Aman replied that he would not fall a victim to treachery and that if he said another word or came again he would certainly kill him. So Muhammad Khan left and again had to report his failure. "Only an army can bring him, he said, back from Harbenn." The Maharajah is hoping now that he will get tired of wandering about and come back of his own accord. During the last eight months he has sent nobody for him. Mulk Aman is very badly off and is now at Rimon (Dareyl) and I am quite sure that the Yaghistanis will never assist him. His brothers will not help him. His wife (Mahtar's widow) is now at Jammu and reports have spread about her conduct."

In connexion with the Sazîni's account, which in all particulars relating to the tribes is very trustworthy, may be read the following statements of S... S... of Kûner, on the borders of Kafiristan, now a Christian. He relates that he was once a Sepoy in the Maharajah's Army and started on one of the Gilgit expeditions [1860?] with 300 Affghans and 3,000 Dogras, etc., under the command of Samund Khan, Ata Muhammad, Badam Singh, Man Singh and Dula Singh. He believes that Wazir Pannu was with the forces. At any rate, the attack on Gilgit was mere child's play. The Kashmîr troops bombarded it for two or three days, but the Dards had no cannon with which to reply. Wahháb, the Wazir, looked out of one of the fort loopholes and was shot and so was a Bhishti. Wahháb's body was stripped and hung to a tree. S... S.. adds. "We were well entertained by the people who treated us to curds and we found grapes and wallnuts in abundance at Sher Kila'. The women of the country cooked our food, but our soldiers repayed the hospitality which they received by plundering and ill-treating the inhabitants. I remained behind, but when my company came back they told me that the Sikhs wanted to dig out the body of Gauhar Aman, but were prevented from doing so by their own Muhammadan comrades. We found caverns in the mountains which were filled with food for the use of the enemy. It is the custom of this people to heap up food in caverns to which the owners only know the way. After entrusting Sher Kila' (a fort as big as that of Gilgit and constructed of wooden beams and stone) to the administration of native partisans, we went to Gao-Kutsh, where we found plenty of sport. Gauhar

Aman used to sell captured Sepoys for hunting dogs." (This story is repeated from so many trustworthy quarters that it seems to deserve credence. I heard it from many at Gilgit in 1866. The kidnapping propensities of Gauhar Aman were great and one of my own retainers, a petty Chief, had been dragged off for sale, when he escaped by sliding down a mountain side. Yet the people of Gilgit preferred his rule to that of Kashmir and revolted in his favour, when oppressed by Santu Singh in 1852). "We had two Hindustani rebels of 1857 with us and there were also several with the petty Rajahs." [This important statement can be somewhat confirmed by me. What I understood to be the fourth Light Kashmir Cavalry was said to be almost entirely composed of rebels of 1857. I found many of the stations in charge of Swatis and numbers of soldiers of that race at Gilgit. One of the Maharajah's Sepoys, who came to see me, admitted that he was formerly at Hyderabad and then had joined the rebels.]

I can also confirm the statements of the Sazîni with regard to the atrocities committed in the War with Dareyl. In order to be able to report victories, men, said to be innocent of complicity in the war, were hanged and women were dragged into captivity in order to fill the Zananas of the Kashmîr Sepoys. I saw the body of a tall, and powerfully built Dareyli, which had evidently been hacked about a good deal, suspended on a tree by the way-side. It was said to be the body of a man who was quietly returning to Sai, which had long been in the undisturbed occupation of the Maharajah. A little further on near Jaglôth [which is also in long-occupied territory] there is a bridge on one of the poles of which I saw the skeleton head of a Lumberdar of the place, said to be perfectly innocent of all participation in the war with Kashmir. The roofs of the houses in Gilgit had been blown off, and most of the inhabitants had fled into the mountains (*vide* "dance at Gilgit" page 36). On the other hand, dreadful stories were related of the retaliation of the Dard tribes. Sepoys had been sold by hundreds into Badakhshan, etc.; others had been used as fireworks and blown to atoms for the amusement of the Kunjûtis. Personally, I found the Dards pleasant enough and consider them to be superior in many respects to either Dogras or Pathans, but it is by no means improbable that they have been guilty of many of the atrocities which are laid to their charge. At the same time, it must be remembered that the wanton cruelties of the Massacre of Yasin (*vide* page 69) and the fact that their country was invaded by a stranger and an "infidel"—in defiance of treaty obligations—is some palliation for their conduct. The Kashmîr troops, and more particularly the coolies sent with them, were also grossly neglected as regards food, clothing and shelter by their own authorities. It was said that out of 12,000 Kashmiris, impressed for the purpose of carrying loads, only 600 survived in the expedition of 1866. The roads were strewn with the skeletons of horses, etc. I saw men in the most emaciated condition and ready to eat "unlawful" food. Three Mussulmans in a dying condition whom I met below the "Acho" summit,* were

* This peak overlooks Bunji and the whole course of the Indus (with a sight of the Gilgit Valley) from its sudden southward bend at the Makpon-i-Shang-Rong, till it again bends westward beyond Chilás.

ready to take a tin containing pork and could scarcely be restrained till "lawful" food was brought to them by my servants. Men were forced to go with the troops. One Hakím Ali Shah, a teacher at Amritsar, was compelled to serve as a physician, a post to which he had no other claim, except that his name happened to be "Hakím." I rescued him. A virulent fever was destroying the troops at Gilgit, who, even after the siege of the fort had been raised, were liable to be shot down by prowlers from the tribes within a few yards of the fort. I ordered the fort, etc., to be cleaned and, although myself in danger of life from my Kashmír friends, if not from the tribes, I insisted on my orders being obeyed, the assumption of an authoritative tone being often a traveller's only chance of safety among Asiatics. I distributed medicine among the troops and was afterwards told in Durbar by the Maharajah that some medicine which I had sent to Wazir Zoraweru, who was then on his Dureyl expedition, had saved his life.

Since then, the Dards have made the acquaintance of diseases for which there was not even a name in 1866. I refer chiefly to cholera and syphilis, which Kashmíri and Indian troops have introduced. Simultaneously, the indigenous methods of treatment, which are full of lessons for the impartial learner, are dying out. Industrial handicrafts, historical superstitions or reminiscences, national feasts which existed in 1866 exist no longer, and what exists now will soon vanish before the monotony of orthodox Muhammadanism and the vulgarity of so-called European civilization. "*Und der Götter bunt Gewimmel, Hat sogleich das stille Haus geleert.*" The fairies and prophetesses of Dardistan are silent, the Tham of Hunza no longer brings down rain, the family axes are broken, the genealogists have been destroyed, and the sacred drum is heard no longer. The quaint computations of age, of months, seasons, years and half-years, and the strange observations of shadows thrown at various times are dying out or are already dead. Worse than all for enquiry into ancient human history, the languages which contain the words of "*what once was*," are being flooded by foreign dialects, and what may survive will no longer appeal to the national understanding. This result is most lamentable as regards Hunza, where the oldest human speech still showed elementary processes of development. I fear that my attempt to commit, for the first time, to writing, in an adapted *Persian* character, the Khajuná language, has only been followed in a document of honour which the venerable Chief of Nagyr sent me some years ago. Already do some European writers call him and his people "ignorant" when their own ignorance is alone deserving of censure. I deeply regret that the friendship of so many Dard Chiefs for me has made them unsuspicious of Europeans, and may have thus indirectly led to the loss of their independence, but I rejoice that for over twenty-five years I have not attracted the European adventurer to Dardistan by saying anything about Pliny's "*fertilissimi sunt auri Dardæ*," except in Khajuná Ethnographical Dialogues in the "Hunza-Nagyr Handbook," which exploiters were not likely to read. Now others have published the fact, but not the accompanying risks.

As Kandiá is learned, Nagyr pious, Chilás puritanical, and all true Dard tribes essentially peaceful and virtuously republican; so, no doubt, Hunza was the country of free love and of raiding, that had ceased in 1865, which *we* practically revived (see Appendix I.). I doubt, however, whether picturesque vice, which, unfortunately, may form part of indigenous associations, is as reprehensible as the hypocrisy of those hired knights of the pen, who, not practising the virtues which they preach, take away the character of nations and of Chiefs, merely because they are opposed to us, and falsify their history. I do not, for instance, palliate the old Hunza practice of lending one's wife to a guest, or of kidnapping good-looking strangers in order to improve the race, though the latter course may be preferred by a physiologist to a careless marriage, but I do find a reproach on European or Indian morality in the fact that not a single Hunza woman showed herself to the British or Kashmîri invaders, although the men, once conquered, freely joined them in sport and drinking bouts. Europeans have a worse reputation among Orientals than Orientals among Europeans, and, in either case, ignorance, prejudice, want of sympathy and disinclination to learn the truth, are probably among the causes of such regrettable preconceptions. At any rate, it shall not be said that the races which I, so disastrously for them, discovered and named, shall suffer from any misrepresentation so far as I can help it, although the political passions of the moment may deprive my statements of the weight which has hitherto attached to them as authoritative in this speciality. *Væ victis et victoribus*—for history now marches rapidly towards the common disaster. *Finis Dardarum*. "It has been decided that CHILÁS is to be *permanently* held, and consequently the present strength of the garrison in the GILGIT district will be *increased* by one native regiment, while the 23rd Pioneers will complete the road through the Kaghan Valley to Chilás, and will then *remain for duty on the advanced frontier*. This strengthening of the garrison in the sub-Himalayan country will effectually *secure British influence* over CHITRÁL where an Agent is to be *permanently* stationed; it will also insure the *control of the Indus Valley tribes*" (*Times* telegram of the 8th July, 1893—the italics are mine). Alas that British influence should so destroy both itself and the freedom of ancient races!

Quem Deus vult perdere prius dementat. Considering the promises of redress of all grievances made by the Great Northern Emancipator of Oppressed Nationalities,* whose lightest finger is heavier than our entire yoke, it would be a great mistake on our part to still further reduce the independence of Native States, the troops of which are already at our disposal. Even as regards Kashmir, against the mismanagement of which I have protested for so many years, and the Agents of which made several attempts on my life in order to prevent my exposure of their frontier encroachments in 1866, I am bound to say that our procedure has been a great deal too peremptory, if not altogether illegal. The following Treaty between Kashmir and the British Government shows alike that Kashmir had no right to encroach on Chilás and Gilgit (see preceding pages), and still less on Hunza-Nagyr, and that the Government of India has no right to convert Kashmir into a "*semi*-independent State" as called by the *Times* of the 8th July, 1893. Kashmir is an *independent* State, whose independence has been paid for and must be protected by our honour against our ambition, as long as it is loyal to the British Government:

* The last (semi-official) *Moscow Gazette* says: "Russia will not neglect to avail herself of the first convenient opportunity to assist the people of India to throw off the English yoke, with the view of establishing the country under independent native rule."

"TREATY between the British Government on the one part and MAHÂRAJAH GOLAB SING of JUMMOO on the other, concluded on the part of the British Government by FREDERICK CURRIE, ESQUIRE, and Brevet-Major HENRY MONTGOMERY LAWRENCE, acting under the orders of the Right Honourable SIR HENRY HARDINGE, G.C.B., one of Her Britannic Majesty's Most Honourable Privy Council, Governor-General, appointed by the Honourable Company to direct and control all their affairs in the East Indies, and by MAHARAJAH GOLAB SING in person.

ARTICLE I.

The British Government transfers and makes over for ever, in INDEPENDENT POSSESSION, TO MAHARAJAH GOLAB SING AND THE HEIRS MALE OF HIS BODY, all the hilly or mountainous country, with its DEPENDENCIES, situated to the EASTWARD of the River Indus and westward of the River Ravee, including Chumba, and excluding Lahul, being part of the territories ceded to the British Government by the Lahore State, according to the provisions of Article IV. of the Treaty of Lahore, dated 9th March, 1846.

ARTICLE II.

The eastern boundary of the tract transferred by the foregoing Article to Maharajah Golab Sing shall be laid down by Commissioners appointed by the British Government and Maharajah Golab Sing respectively for that purpose, and shall be defined in a separate Engagement after survey.

ARTICLE III.

In consideration of the transfer made to him and his heirs by the provisions of the foregoing Articles, Maharajah Golab Sing will pay to the British Government the sum of seventy-five lakhs of Rupees (Nanukshahee), fifty lakhs to be paid on ratification of this Treaty, and twenty-five lakhs on or before the first October of the current year, A.D. 1846.

ARTICLE IV.

The limits of the territories of Maharajah Golab Sing shall not be at any time changed without the concurrence of the British Government.

ARTICLE V.

Maharajah Golab Sing will refer to the arbitration of the British Government any disputes or questions that may arise between himself and the Government of Lahore or any other neighbouring State, and will abide by the decision of the British Government.

ARTICLE VI.

Maharajah Golab Sing engages for himself and heirs to join, with the whole of his Military Force, the British troops, when employed within the hills, or in the territories adjoining his possessions.

ARTICLE VII.

Maharajah Golab Sing engages never to take, or retain in his service, any British subject, nor the subject of any European or American State, without the consent of the British Government.

ARTICLE VIII.

Maharajah Golab Sing engages to respect in regard to the territory transferred to him, the provisions of Articles V., VI., and VII., of the separate Engagement between the British Government and the Lahore Durbar, dated March 11th, 1846.

ARTICLE IX.

The British Government will give its aid to Maharajah Golab Sing in protecting his territories from external enemies.

ARTICLE X.

Maharajah Golab Sing acknowledges the supremacy of the British Government, and will, in token of such supremacy, present annually to the British Government one horse, twelve perfect shawl goats of approved breed (six male and six female), and three pairs of Cashmere shawls.

This Treaty, consisting of ten Articles, has been this day settled by Frederick Currie, Esquire, and Brevet-Major Henry Montgomery Lawrence, acting under the directions of the Right Honourable Sir Henry Hardinge, G.C.B., Governor-General, on the part of the British Government, and by Maharajah Golab Sing in person; and the said Treaty has been this day ratified by the seal of the Right Honourable Sir Henry Hardinge, G.C.B., Governor-General.

Done at Umritsur, this Sixteenth day of March, in the year of our Lord One Thousand Eight Hundred and Forty-six, corresponding with the Seventeenth day of Rubbee-ool-awal 1262 Hijree.

(Signed) H. HARDINGE [SEAL.]

(Signed) F. CURRIE.
,, H. M. LAWRENCE.

By order of the Right Honorable the Governor-General of India.

(Signed) F. CURRIE,

Secretary to the Government of India, with the Governor-General."

Note on the Genealogy of the divine Rajas of Nagyr (given to me by Raja Habibulla Khan of Nagyr in 1886).—At Doyur, near Gilgit, on the mountain-top, three fairy-brothers shot at a calf, which only the youngest (Azru) hit and was induced to eat, thereby losing his fairy-hood. The two others flew away and settled on another mountain, but the crowing of a cock betrayed them to the people of Gilgit who made one of them, Tura Khan, Raja of Gilgit; the other, Chalis Khan, becoming Raja of Nagyr. [This account is incorrect as *Azru* became Raja of Gilgit, because he had become man by eating meat (*incarnation*), but it is interesting as showing the desire of Nagyris to be connected with the Historical Legend of the origin of the neighbouring and more civilized Gilgit. Some say that Chalis Khan had no son, but that the Rajas of Nagyr are the descendants of the Makpon rulers of Little Tibet (from which the Makpon-i-Shang-rong—see page 107—takes its name). Others say that Alladad was a son of Chalis Khan; at all events, the founders of the Hunza-Nagyr Dynasty, Girkis-Mogholot, two brothers, whether descended from Mogholot or Chalis, are called Mogholoti, Girkis becoming the Tham of Hunza, and Mogholot that of Nagyr. As for Alladad, he was succeeded by Kamal, whom Rahim and Babar (or tiger) followed in turn. Babar's son was Ferdûs, and his son Alif Khan was the father of the present reigning Chief, Zafar Khan, whose progeny is very numerous]. [The above account, although very deficient and confused, supplements, as regards Hunza-Nagyr, the important "historical legend of the origin of Gilgit," which will be found on pages 9 to 16, and which chronicles the change in the Shîn rule in Dardistan. The mystery in the Hunza-Nagyr dynasty fitly entitles it to be called "ayeshó," or "heavenly." I can quite understand that the Chief of Hunza, unable to convince European disbelievers of his divine origin, should have claimed a descent from Alexander the Great, *faute de mieux*, since the more terrestrial chiefs of Badakhshan and other neighbouring countries claim to be descended from that conqueror. (See note on page 55 and page 69.)

Colonel Biddulph gives the following interesting version of the above story:

"The ruling family of Hunza is called Ayeshé (heavenly), from the following circumstance. The two States of Hunza and Nager were formerly one, ruled by a branch of the Shahreis, the ruling family of Gilgit, whose seat of government was Nager. Tradition relates that Mayroo Khan, apparently the first Mahommedan Thum of Nager, some two hundred years after the introduction of the religion of Islamin to Gilgit, married a daughter of Trakhan of Gilgit, who bore him twin sons, named Moghlot and Girkis. From the former the present ruling family of Nager is descended. The twins are said to have shown hostility to one another from their birth. Their father, seeing this, and unable to settle the question of succession, divided his State between them, giving to Girkis the north, and to Moghlot the south, bank of the river.

Age did not diminish their enmity, and Girkis, while out hunting, was one day killed by an adherent of Moghlot, a native of Haramosh, named Mogul Beg, who, under pretence of a quarrel with Moghlot, took service with Girkis, and persuading him to look up at some game on the cliff above him, drove an arrow into his throat. Girkis left only a daughter, who, according to the custom of the country, became Queen or Ganish of Hunza. Her first care was to avenge her father's death. The tradition relates that having sworn to tear the murderer's liver with her teeth, she carried out her vow to the letter. Left without a chaperon, she was not long without getting into a scrape, as young ladies in similar circumstances are apt to do. The young prince Kamal Khan of Nager, a younger son of Moghlot, crossed the river by night, serenaded her and won her heart. Night after night the lovers met, unknown to the rest of the world, till serious consequences ensued; and one fine day it was announced in Hunza that, though Providence had not yet provided the princess with a husband, it had seen fit to bless her with a son. Morals in Hunza are not of the strictest even now, so that few questions were asked, and the good people generally contented themselves with beating their drums, dancing, and the usual festivities proper on the occasion of the birth of the Prince Chiliss Khan. Kamal Khan seems to have 'behaved badly' all through, as the above story is concealed in Hunza under the fiction that a prince of Shighnan became the husband of the princess, but that his name being forgotten he is known only as Ayeshó (Heaven-sent), from which the present ruling family of Hunza takes the name. The present Thum of Hunza is Ghazan Khan" (1880).

APPENDICES.

APPENDIX I.

HUNZA, NAGYR, AND THE PAMIR REGIONS.*

I WISH to record how from small beginnings, owing to carelessness, exclusiveness, and official desire for promotion, Northern India may be lost and British interests in Europe and Asia become subordinate, as they have often been, to Russian guidance; how statesmanship has laboriously invited dangers which physical barriers had almost rendered impossible; and how it may still be practicable to maintain as independent States the numerous mountain strongholds which Nature has interposed between encroachment and intrigue from either the Russian or the English sphere of action in Asia, much to the benefit of these two Powers and of the peace of mankind.

When, after an enormous expenditure of men and money and during campaigns which lasted over thirty-six years, Russia had conquered independent Circassia—a task in which she was largely aided by our preventing provisions and ammunitions from reaching by sea the so-called rebels, although we ourselves were fighting against her in 1856, *quorum pars parva fui*, it was easy to foresee that our conduct, which some called chivalry, others loyalty, and some duplicity or folly, would give her the present command of the Black Sea and lead to the subjugation of Circassia. The same conduct was repeated at Panjdeh, and may be repeated on the Pamir, much to the personal advantage of the discreet officers concerned. We have also recently discovered that the holding of Constantinople by a neutral Power is not essential to British interests, as we had long ago found out that neither Merv nor Herat were keys to India. Indeed,

* I began to write this paper as an introduction to an academical treatment of the history, language, and customs of Hunza-Nagyr, when the apparently, sudden, but, probably, calculated complications on that frontier compelled me to abandon my task for the present and to discuss instead the ephemeral news as they were published from day to day in the press.

as we give up position after position, a crop of honours falls to those who bring about our losses and, like charity, covers a multitude of political sins of ignorance or treason

It seemed, however, that there was one obscure corner which the official sidelight could not irradiate. Valley after valley, plateau after plateau, high mountains and difficult passes separate the populations of India from those of Central Asia. Innumerable languages and warlike races, each unconquerable in their own strongholds if their autonomy and traditions are respected, intervene between invaders from either side who would lead masses of disciplined slaves to slaughter and conquest. It is not necessary to draw an imaginary line on Lord Salisbury's large or small Map of Asia across mountains and rivers, and dividing arbitrarily tribes and kingdoms whose ancestry is the same, call it "the neutral zone." No sign-board need indicate "the way to India," and amid much ado about nothing by ambitious subordinates and puzzled superiors settle to the momentary satisfaction of the British public that Russia can go so far and no farther. Where the cold, the endless marching over inhospitable ground, and starvation do not show the frontier, the sparse population, the unknown tongue, and the bullet of the raider will indicate it sufficiently, without adding to the number of generals or knights for demarcating impossible boundaries.

The reassurances given by Lords Lansdowne and Cross to the native Princes of India indicate the policy that should be adopted with regard to all the Mountain States beyond India proper. It is by everywhere respecting the existing indigenous Oriental Governments that we protect them and ourselves against invasion from without and treachery from within. The loyalty of our feudatories is most chivalrous and touching, but it should be based on enlightened self-interest in order to withstand the utmost strain. The restoration of some powers to the Maharaja of Kashmir came not a minute too soon. Wherever elsewhere reasonable claims are withheld, they should be generously and speedily conceded. The Indian princes know full well that we are arming them, at their own expense, against a common foe who is not wanting in promises, and who is already posing as a saviour to the people of Raushan, Shignan, Wakhan, Hunza, and even Badakhshan, whose native dynasties or traditions we have either already put aside or are believed to threaten.

As for the small States offering a fruitful field for intrigue, their number and internal jealousies (except against a common foreign invader) are in themselves a greater safeguard than the resistance of a big but straggling ally, whose frontier, when broken through at one of its many weak points, finds an unresisting population from which all initiative has disappeared. The intrigue or treachery of a big ally is also a more serious matter than that of a little State. What does it matter if English and Russian agents intrigue or fraternize among the *ovis poli*, and the Kirghiz shepherds of the Pamir, or advocate their respective civilizations in Yasin, Chitrál, Wakhan, Nagyr, Hunza, etc. Ambitious employés of both empires will always trouble waters, in order to fish in them; but their trouble is comparatively innocuous, and resembles that of Sisyphus when it has to be repeated or wasted in a dozen States, before the real defences of either India or of Russia in Asia are reached. Indeed, so far as India is concerned, the physical difficulties on our side of the Himalayas or of the Hindukush, except at a few easily defensible passes, are insuperable to an invader, even after he has crowned the more approachable heights when coming from the North.

The only policy worthy of the name is to leave the Pamir alone. Whatever line is drawn, it is sure to be encroached upon by either side. Races will be found to overlap it, and in the attempt to gather the fold, as with the Sarik and Salor Turkomans, a second Panjdeh is sure to follow. Intrigues will be active on both sides of the line; and, as in Kashmir, the worried people will hail the foreigner as a saviour, so long as he has not taken possession, when they find his little finger heavier than the whole body of the indigenous oppressor. I have suffered so much from my persistent exposure of the misrule and intrigues of Kashmir by those who now hail the *fait accompli* of its practical annexation, that I may claim to be heard in favour of at least one feature of its former native administration. With bodies of troops averaging from 20 to 200, the late Maharaja, who foresaw what has happened after his death, kept the Hunza-Nagyr frontier in order. It certainly was by rule of thumb, and had no dockets, red tape, and reports. Indeed, his frontier guardians were, as I found them, asleep during a state of siege in 1866, or, when war was over, were engaged in storing grain *outside* the forts; but peace was kept as it will never be again, in spite of 2,000 Imperial troops, first-rate roads, and suspension bridges over the "Shaitan Naré," instead of the rotten rope-way that spanned "Satan's Gorge," or of boats dragged up from Srinagar over the mountains to enable a dozen sepoys to cross the Indus at a time, or to convey couriers with a couple of bullets, some dried butter-cakes, and an open letter or two, who ran the siege at Gilgit and brought such effective reinforcements to its defenders!

Nor has our diplomacy been more effectual than our arms, as the encounter at Chalt with Hunza-Nagyr, hereditary foes, but whom our policy has united against us, has shown. To us Nagyr is decidedly friendly; but a worm will turn if trodden on by some of our too quickly advanced subalterns. That, however, the wise and amiable Chief of Nagyr, a patriarch with a large progeny, and preserving the keenness of youth in his old age, is really friendly to us in spite of provocation, may be inferred from the following letter to me, which does credit alike to his head and heart, and which is far from showing him to be our inveterate foe, as alleged by the *Pioneer*. His eldest son began to teach me the remarkable Khajuná language, which I first committed to writing in 1866, during the siege of Gilgit, and another son continued the lessons in 1886.

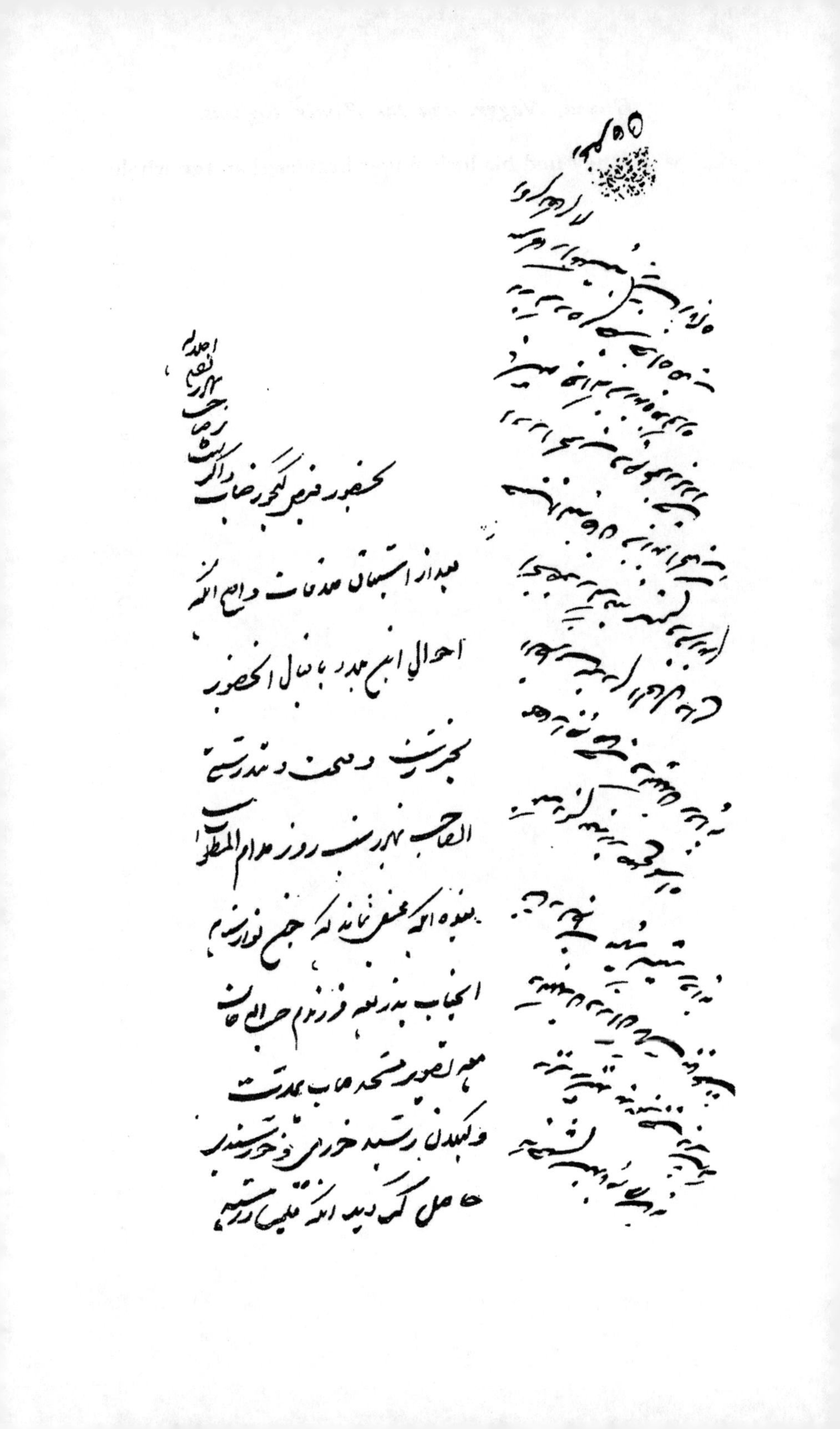

بحضور فیض گنجور صاحب والا دستگاه صاحب مهربان نقش احباب

بعد از اشتیاق ملاقات واضح آنکه

احوال این جانب تا حال الحضور

بخیر است و صحت و تندرستی

آن صاحب مهربان روز مدام المطلوب

بنده آنکه مخفی نماند که چنین نوازش نامه

آنجناب بذریعه فرزندم حاجی

معه التصویر مسجد صاحب بمدت

و کیفیت رسید خرسندی و خورسندی

حاصل گردید الله تعالی

[illegible]

The latter is a hostage in Kashmír, to secure the good behaviour of his tribe, which is really infinitely superior in culture and piety to those around them. The father, who is over 90, writes in Persian to the following effect, after the usual compliments :—"The affairs of this place are by your fortune in a fair way, and I am in good health and constantly ask the same for you from the Throne which grants requests. Your kind favour with a drawing of the Mosque has reached me, and has given me much pleasure and satisfaction. The reason of the delay in its receipt and acknowledgment is due to the circumstance that, owing to disturbances (*fesád*) I have not sent agents to Kashmír this year. After the restoration of peace, I will send [a letter] with them. In the meanwhile, I have caught your hem [seek your protection] for my son Habibullah Khan, a beloved son, about whom I am anxious; the aforesaid son is a well-wisher to the illustrious English Government. —ZA'FAR KHAN." [The letter was apparently written in June last, when *The Times* reported a "rising," because the British Agent was at Chalt with 500 men.]

It seems to me that none but a farseeing man could, in the midst of a misunderstanding, if not a fight, with us, so write to one in the enemy's camp, unless he were a true man alike in war and peace, and a ruler whose good-will was worth acquiring. As for his son, I know him to be indeed well-disposed to our Government. He was very popular among our officers when I saw him in Kashmír, owing to his modesty, amiability, and unsurpassed excellence at Polo. In fact, my friendship with several of the chiefs since 1866 has aided our good relations with them; and it is a pity if they should be destroyed for want of a little "*savoir*," as also "*savoir faire*," on our part.

Between the States of Nagyr and Hunza there exists a perpetual feud. They are literally rivals, being separated by a swift-flowing river on which, at almost regulated distances, one Nagyr fort on one bank frowns at the Hunza fort on the other. The paths along the river sides are very steep, involving at times springing from one ledge of a rock to another, or dropping on to it from a height of six feet, when, if the footing is lost, the wild torrent sweeps one away. Colonel Biddulph does not credit the Nagyris with bravery. History, however, does not bear out his statement; and the defeat inflicted on the Kashmîr troops under Nathu Shah in 1848 is a lesson even for the arrogance of a civilized invader armed with the latest rifle. The Nagyris are certainly not without culture; in music they were proficient before the Muhammadan piety of the Shiah sect somewhat tabooed the art. At all events, they are different in character from the Hunzas with whom they share the same language, and their chiefs the same ancestry. The Hunzas, in whom a remnant of the Huns may be found, were great kidnappers; but under Kashmîr influence they stopped raiding since 1869, till the confusion incidental to our interference revived their gone occupation. Indeed, it is asserted on good authority, that even our ally of Chitrál, who had somewhat abandoned the practice of selling his Shiah or Kalásha Kafir subjects into slavery, and who had so disposed of the miners for not working his ruby mines to profit, has now returned to the trade in men, "with the aid of our present of rifles and our moral support." Nor is Bokhara said to be behind Chitrál in the revival of the slave-trade from Darwáz, in spite of Russian influence; so that we have the remarkable instance of two great Powers both opposed to slavery and the slave-trade, having revived it in their approach to one another. Nor is a third Power, quite blameless in the matter; for when we worried Hunza, that robber-nest remembered its old allegiance to distant Kitái and arranged with the Chinese authorities at Yarkand to be informed of the departure of a caravan. Then, after intercepting it on the Kulanuldi road, the Hunzas would take those they kidnapped from it back for sale to Yarkand!

As a matter of fact, we have now a scramble for the regions surrounding and extending into the Pamirs by three Powers, acting either directly or through States of Straw. The claims of Bokhara to Karategin and Darwáz—if not to Shignán, Raushan, and Wakhan are as little founded as are those of Afghanistan on the latter three districts. Indeed, even the Afghan right to Badakhshan is very weak. The Russian claims through Khokand on the pasturages of the Kirghiz in two-thirds of the Pamirs are also as fanciful as those of Kashmir or China on Hunza. As in the scramble for Africa, the natives themselves are not consulted, and their indigenous dynasties have been either destroyed, or dispossessed, or ignored.

In an Indian paper, received by to-day's mail (29 Nov., 1891), I find the following paragraph : "Col. A. G. Durand, British Agent at Gilgit, has received definite orders to bring the robber tribes of Hunza and Nagar under control. These tribes are the pirates of Central Asia, whose chief occupation is plundering caravans on the Yarkand and Kashgar. Any prisoners they take on these expeditions are sold into slavery. Colonel Durand has established an outpost at Chalt, about thirty miles beyond Gilgit, on the Hunza river, and intends making a road to Aliabad, the capital of the Hunza chief, at once. That he will meet with armed opposition in doing so is not improbable."

For some months past the *mot d'ordre* appears to have been given to the Anglo-Indian Press, to excite public feeling against Hunza and Nagyr, two States which have been independent for fourteen centuries. The cause of offence is not stated, nor, as far as I know, does one exist of sufficient validity to justify invasion. In the *Pioneer* and the *Civil and Military Gazette* I find vague allusions to the disloyalty or recalcitrance of the above-mentioned tribes, and to the necessity of punishing them. As Nagyr is extremely well-disposed towards the British, and is only driven into making common cause with its hereditary foe and rival of Hunza by fear of a common danger,—the loss of their independence,—I venture to point out the impolicy and injustice of interfering with these principalities.

I have already referred to a letter from the venerable chief of Nagyr, in which he strongly commends to my care one of his sons, Raja Habibulla, as a well-wisher of the English Government. Indeed, he has absolutely done nothing to justify any attack on the integrity of his country; and before we invade it other means to secure peace should be tried. I have no doubt that I, for one, could induce him to comply with everything in reason, if reason, and not an excuse for taking his country, is desired. Nagyr has never joined Hunza in kidnapping expeditions, as is alleged in the above-quoted paragraph. Indeed, slavery is an abomination to the pious and peaceful agriculturist of that interesting country. The Nagyris are musical and were fond of dances, polo, ibex *battue*-hunting, archery and shooting from horseback, and other manly exercises; but the growing piety of the race has latterly proscribed music and dancing. The accompanying drawing of a Nagyri dance in the neighbouring Gilgit gives a good idea of similar performances at Nagyr.

The country is full of legendary lore, but less so than Hunza, where Grimm's fairy tales appear to be translated into actual life. No war is undertaken except at the supposed command of an unseen fairy, whose drum is on such occasions sounded in the mountains. Ecstatic women, inhaling the smoke of a cedar-branch, announce the future, tell the past, and describe the state of things in neighbouring valleys. They are thus alike the prophets, the historians, and the journalists of the tribe. They probably now tell their indignant hearers how, under the pretext of shooting or of commerce, Europeans have visited their country, which they now threaten to destroy with strange and murderous weapons; but Hunza is "ayeshó," or "heaven-born," and the fairies, if not the inaccessible nature of the country, will continue to protect it.

The folly of invading Hunza and Nagyr is even greater

than the physical obstacles to which I have already referred. Here, between the Russian and the British spheres of influence in Central Asia, we have not only the series of Pamirs, or plateaux and high valleys, which I first brought to notice on linguistic grounds, in the map accompanying my tour in Dardistan in 1866 (the country between Kashmir and Kabul), and which have been recently confirmed topographically; but we have also a large series of mountainous countries, which, if left alone, or only assured of our help against a foreign invader, would guarantee for ever the peace alike of the Russian, the British, and the Chinese frontiers. Unfortunately, we have allowed Afghanistan to annex Badakhshan, Raushan, Shignan, and Wakhan, at much loss of life to their inhabitants; and Russia has similarly endorsed the shadowy and recent claims of Bokhara on neighbouring provinces, like Darwáz and Karategin.

It is untrue that Hunza and Nagyr were ever tributaries of Kashmír, except in the sense that they occasionally sent a handful of gold dust to its Maharaja, and received substantial presents in return. It is to China or Kitái that Hunza considers itself bound by an ancient, but vague, allegiance. Hunza and Nagyr, that will only unite against a foreign common foe, have more than once punished Kashmír when attempting invasion; but they are not hostile to Kashmír, and Nagyr even sends one of the princes to Srinagar as a guarantee of its peaceful intentions. At the same time, it is not very many months ago that they gave us trouble at Chalt, when we sought to establish an outpost, threatening the road to Hunza and the independence alike of Hunza and Nagyr.

Just as Nagyr is pious, so Hunza is impious. Its religion is a perversion even of the heterodox Mulái faith, which is Shiah Muhammadan only in name, but pantheistic in substance. It prevails in Punyál, Zebak, Darwáz, etc. The Tham, or Raja, of Hunza used to dance in a Mosque and hold revels in it. Wine is largely drunk in Hunza, and like the Druses of the Lebanon, the "initiated" Mulais may consider nothing a crime that is not found out. Indeed, an interesting connection can be established between the doctrines of the so-called "Assassins" of the Crusaders, which have been handed down to the Druses, and those of the Muláis in various parts of the Hindukush. Their spiritual chief gave me a few pages of their hitherto mysterious Bible, the "Kelám-i-Pir," in 1886, which I have translated, and shortly intend to publish. All I can now say is, that, whatever the theory of their faith, the practice depends, as elsewhere, on circumstances and the character of the race.

The language of Hunza and Nagyr solves many philological puzzles. It is a prehistoric remnant, in which a series of simple consonantal or vowel sounds stands for various groups of ideas, relationships, etc. It establishes the great fact, that customs and the historical and other associations of a race are the basis of the so-called rules of grammar. The cradle, therefore, of human thought as expressed in language, whether of the Aryan, the Turanian, or the Shemitic groups, is to be found in the speech of Hunza-Nagyr; and to destroy this by foreign intervention, which has already brought new diseases into the Hindukush, as also a general linguistic deterioration, would be a greater act of barbarism than to permit the continuance of Hunza raiding on the Yarkand road. Besides, that raiding can be stopped again, by closing the slave-markets of Badakhshan, Bokhara, and Yarkand, or by paying a subsidy, say of £1,000 per annum, to the Hunza chief.

Indeed, as has already been pointed out, the recrudescence of kidnapping is largely due to the state of insecurity and confusion caused by our desire to render the Afghan and the Chinese frontiers conterminous with our own, in the vain belief that the outposts of three large and distant kingdoms, acting in concert, will keep Russia more effectively out of India than a number of small independent republics or principalities. Afghanistan may now be big, but every so-called subject in her outlying districts is her inveterate foe. As stated in a letter from Nevsky to the Calcutta *Englishman*, in connection with Colonel Grambcheffsky's recent explorations :

"One and all, these devastated tribes are firm in their conviction that the raids of their Afghan enemies were prompted and supported by the gold of Abdur Rahman's English protectors. They will remember this on the plateau of Pamir, and among the tribes of Kaffiristan."

However colourable this statement may be as regards Shignán, Raushan, and perhaps even Wakhan, I believe that the Kafirs are still our friends. At the same time it should not be forgotten that, owing to the closing of the slave-markets in Central Asia, the sale of Shiah subjects had temporarily stopped in Chitrál. The Kafirs were being less molested by kidnapping Muhammadan neighbours; the Hunzas went back to agriculture, which the Nagyris had never abandoned ; Kashmîr, India, and the Russian side of Central Asia afforded no opening for the sale of human beings. The insensate ambition of officials, British and Russian, the gift of arms to marauding tribes and the destruction of Kashmîr influence, have changed all this, and it is only by a return to "masterly inactivity," which does not mean the continuance of the Cimmerian darkness that now exists as to the languages and histories of the most interesting races of the world, that the peace and pockets of three mighty empires can be saved.

In the meanwhile, it is to the interest of Russia to force us into heavy military expenditure by false alarms; to create distrust between ourselves and China by pretending that Russia and England alone have civilizing missions in Central Asia, with which Chinese tyranny would interfere ; to hold up before us the Will-o'-the-wisp of an impossible demarcation of the Pamirs, and finally, to ally itself with China against India. For let it not be forgotten, that once the Trans-Siberian railway is completed, China will be like wax in her hand ; and that she will be compelled to place her immense material in men and food at the disposal of an overawing, but, as far as the *personnel* is concerned, not unamiable neighbour. The tribes, emasculated by our overwhelming civilization, and driven into three large camps, will no longer have the power of resistance that they now possess separately.

Let us therefore leave intact the two great belts of territories that Nature has raised for the preservation of peace in Asia—the Pamir with its adjacent regions to the east and west, and the zone of the Hindukush with its hives of independent tribes, intervening between Afghanistan on the one side and Kashmír on the other, till India proper is reached. This will never be the case by a foreign invader, unless diplomatists "meddle and muddle," and try to put together what Nature has put asunder. What we require is the cultivation of greater sympathy in our relations with natives; and, comparing big things with small, it is to this feeling that I myself owed my safety, when I put off the disguise in which I crossed the Kashmír frontier in 1866 into countries then wrongly supposed by our Government to be inhabited by cannibals. This charge was also made, with equal error, by one tribe against the other. Then too, as in 1886, the Indian Press spoke of Russian intrigues; but then, as in 1886, I found the very name of Russia to be unknown, except where it had been learnt from a Kashmír Munshi, who had no business to be there at all, as the treaty of 1846, by which we sold Kashmír to Ghulab Singh, assigned the Indus as his boundary on the west. Now, as to the question as to "What and where are the Pamirs?" I have already stated my view in a letter to the Editor of the *Morning Post*, which I trust I may be allowed to quote:

"As some of the statements made at the Royal Geographical Society are likely to cause a sense of false security, as dangerous to peace as a false alarm, I write to say that 'Pamirs' do not mean 'deserts,' or 'broken valleys,' and that they are not uninhabitable or useless for movements of large bodies of men. They may be all this in certain places, at certain periods of the year, and under certain conditions; but had our explorers or statesmen paid attention to the languages of this part of the world, as they should in regard to every other with which they deal, they would have avoided many idle conjectures and the complications that may follow therefrom. I do not wish them to refer to philologists who have never been to the East, and who interpret 'Pamir' as meaning the 'Upa-Meru' Mountain of Indian mythology, but to the people who frequent the Pamirs during the summer months, year after year, for purposes of pasturage, starting from various points, and who in their own languages (Yarkandi, Turki, and Kirghiz) call the high plain, elevated valley, table-land, or plateau which they come across 'Pamir.' There are, therefore, in one sense many 'Pamirs,' and as a *tout-ensemble*, one 'Pamir,' or geographically, *the* 'Pamir.' The legend of the two brothers, 'Alichur and Pamir,' is merely a personification of two plateaux. Indeed, the obvious and popular idea which has always attached to the word 'Pamir,' is the correct one, whether it is the geographical 'roof of the world,' the 'Bám-i-dunya' of the poet, or the 'Pamir-dunya' of the modern journalist. We have, therefore, to deal with a series of plateaux, the topographical limits of which coincide with linguistic, ethnographical, and political limits. To the North, the Pamirs have the Trans-Altaic Mountain range marking the Turki element, under Russian influence; the Panja river, by whatever name, on the West is a Tadjik or Iranian Frontier [Affghan]. The Sarikol on the East is a Tibetan, Mongolian, or Chinese Wall, and the South is our natural frontier, the Hindukush, to go beyond which is physical death to the Hindu, and political ruin to the holder of India, as it also is certain destruction to the invader, except by one pass, which I need not name, and which is accessible from a Pamir. That the Pamirs are not uninhabitable may be inferred from Colonel Grambcheffsky's account [which is published at length elsewhere in this issue of the ASIATIC QUARTERLY REVIEW]. A few passages from it must now suffice:—'The Pamir is far from being a wilderness. It contains a permanent population, residing in it both summer and winter.' 'The population is increasing to a marked extent.' 'Slavery on the Pamir is flourishing: moreover, the principal contingents of slaves are obtained from Chatrar, Jasen, and Kanshoot, chanates under the protectorate of England.' 'On descending into Pamir we found ourselves between the cordons of the Chinese and Affghan armies.' 'The population of Shoognan, numbering 2,000 families, had fled to Pamir, hoping to find a refuge in the Russian Provinces' (from 'the untold atrocities which the Affghans were committing in the conquered provinces of Shoognan,' etc.). 'I term the whole of the tableland "Pamir," in view of the resemblance of the valleys to each other.'

'The climate of the Pamirs is variable, from more than tropical heat in the sun to arctic cold in the shade, and in consequence, is alike provocative and destructive of life. Dr. G. Capus, who crossed them from north to south, exactly as Mr. Littledale has done, but several months in the year before him, says in his 'Observations Météorologiques sur le Pamir,' which he sent to the last Oriental Congress,—'The first general fact is the inconstancy of severe cold. The nights are generally coldest just before sunrise.' 'We found an extreme amplitude of 61 deg. between the absolute minimum and maximum, and of 41 deg. between the minimum and the maximum in the shade during the same day.' 'The thermometer rises and falls rapidly with the height of the sun.' 'Great cold is less frequent and persistent than was believed to be the case at the period of the year dealt with' (March 13 to April 19), 'and is compensated by daily intervals of elevation of temperature, which permit animal life, represented by a fairly large number of species, and including man, to keep up throughout the winter under endurable conditions.' Yet 'the water-streak of snow, which has melted in contact with a dark object, freezes immediately when put into the shadow of the very same object.' . . . The solution of political difficulties in Central Asia is not in a practically impossible, and certainly unmaintainable, demarcation of the Pamirs, but in the strengthening of the autonomy of the most interesting races that inhabit the series of Circassias that already guard the safety alike of British, Chinese, and of Russian dominion or spheres of influence in Central Asia."

WOKING, *Nov.* 29.

It is not impossible that the tribes may again combine in 1892 as they did in 1866 to turn out the Kashmir troops from Gilgit. The want of wisdom shown in forcing on the construction of a road from Chalt to Aliabad, in the centre of Hunza, as announced in to-day's *Times*, must bring on, if not a confederation of the tribes against us, at any rate their awakened distrust. It is doubtful whether it was ever expedient to establish an outpost at Gilgit, and the carrying it still farther to the traditional apple of discord, the holding of Chalt, which commands the Hunza road, is still more impolitic. As in Affghanistan, so here, whatever power does *not* interfere is looked upon as the saviour from present evils. Once we have created big agglomerations under Affghanistan, or China, or Kashmir, we are liable to the dangers following either on collapse, want of cohesion, treachery from within, the ambitions of a few men at the respective courts, or, as with us, to serious fluctuations in foreign politics due to the tactics of English parties. The change, therefore, from natural boundaries to the wirepulling of diplomatists at Kabul, Peking, or Downing Street is not in the interests of peace, of our empire, or of civilization. Besides, it should not be forgotten that we have added an element of disturbance, far more subtle than the Babu, to our frontier difficulties. The timid Kashmîri is unsurpassed as an intriguer and adventurer among tribes beyond his frontier. The time seems to have arrived when, in the words of the well-known Persian proverb,* the sparseness of races round

* "Agàr qahàt rijál uftad az-sî qaum kam gîrî.
Yakùm Affghan, doyum Kambó, soyùm bad-zât Kashmîrî."

If there (ever) should be a scarcity of men, frequent little (beware of) three peoples: one the Affghan, the second the Kambó, and the third the bad-raced Kashmîrî.

the Pamirs should bid us to be on our guard against the Affghan, the "bad-raced" Kashmîrî, and the Kambó (supposed to be the tribe on the banks of the Jhelum beyond Mozaffarabad). Perhaps, however, the Kambó is the Heathen Chinee; and the proverb would then be entirely applicable to the present question. After the construction of the Trans-Siberian Railway, Russia will be able to exert the greatest pressure on China. The Russian strength at Vladivostok is already enormous, and when the time comes she can hurl an overwhelming force on what remains of Chinese Manchuria, before which Chinese resistance will melt like snow. Peking and the north of China are thus quite at the mercy of Russia. She will find there the most populous country of those she rules in Asia, and with ample supplies. China has a splendid raw material, militarily speaking; and Russia could there form the biggest army that has ever been seen in Asia, to hold *in terrorem* over a rival or to hurl at the possessions of a foe.

It is against such possibilities that the maintenance of "masterly inactivity," qualified by the moral and, if need be, pecuniary or other material support of the Anglo-Indian Government is needed. This is the object of this paper, before I enter into the more agreeable task of describing the languages, customs, and country of perhaps the most interesting races that inhabit the globe.

The Times of the 30th November publishes a map of the Pamirs and an account of the questions connected with them that, like many other statements in its articles on "Indian affairs," are incorrect and misleading. Having been on a special mission by the Panjab Government, in 1866, when I discovered the races and languages of "Dardistan," and gave the country that name, and again having been on special duty with the Foreign Department of the Government of India in 1886 in connection with the Boorishki language and race of Hunza, Nagyr, and a part of Yasin, regarding which I have recently completed

Dr. Leitner as a Bukhara Maulvi, when crossing the Frontier in 1866 during the Kashmír War with the Dard Tribes.

Part I. of a large work, I may claim to speak with some authority as regards these districts, even if I had no other claim. The point which I wish to specially contradict at present, is the one relating to the Russians bringing themselves into almost direct contact with "the Hunza and other tribes subject to Kashmîr and, as such, entitled to British protection and under British control."

When I crossed the then Kashmîr frontier in 1866, in the disguise of a Bokhara Maulvi, armed with a testimonial of Muhammadan theological learning, I found that the tribes of Hunza, Nagyr, Dareyl, Yasin, and Chitrâl had united under the leadership of the last-named to expel the Kashmîr invaders from the Gilgit Fort. My mission was a purely linguistic one; but the sight of dying and dead men along the road, that of heads stuck up along the march of the Kashmîr troops, and the attempts made on my life by our feudatory, the late Maharaja of Kashmîr, compelled me to pay attention to other matters besides the languages, legends, songs, and fables of the interesting races with whom I now came in contact under circumstances that might not seem to be favourable to the accomplishment of my task. I had been warned by the then Lieutenant-Governor of the Panjab, Sir Donald McLeod, whose like we have not seen again, not to cross the frontier, as the tribes beyond were supposed to be cannibals; but as I could not get the information of which I was in search within our frontier, I had to cross it. My followers were frightened off by all sorts of wild stories, till our party was reduced from some fifty to three, including myself. The reason for all this was, that the Maharaja was afraid that I should find out and report his breach of the Treaty by which we sold Kashmîr to him in 1846, and in which the Indus is laid down as his boundary on the west. In 1866, therefore, at any rate, even the tenure of Gilgit, which is on the other side of the Indus, was contested and illegal, whilst the still more distant Hunza and Nagyr had more than once inflicted serious punishment on the Kashmîr troops that sought to invade districts that have preserved their autonomy during the last fourteen centuries, as was admitted by *The Times* of the 2nd November, 1891, before its present change with the times, if an unintentional pun may be permitted.

Then, as ever, the Anglo-Indian newspapers spoke of Russian intrigues in those regions. I am perfectly certain that if, instead of the fussiness of our statesmen and the sensationalism of our journals, the languages, history, and relations of these little-known races had been studied by them, we should never have heard of Russia in that part of the East. It is also not by disingenuousness and short cuts on maps or in diplomacy, but by *knowledge*, that physical, ethnographical, and political problems are to be solved; nor will the bold and brilliant robberies of Russia be checked by our handing over the inhabitants of the supposed "cradle of the human race" to Affghan, Kashmīr, or Chinese usurpations. Above all, it is a loss of time to palm off myths as history in order to suit the policy or conceal the ignorance of the moment.

Just as little as Darwaz and Karategin are ancestral dominions of Bokhara, and, therefore, under Russian influence, so little did even Badakhshan, and much less so, Raushan, Shignan, and Wakhan, ever really belong to Affghanistan. As for the Chinese hold on Turkistan, we ourselves denied it when we coquetted with Yakub Khush Begi, though Kitái was ever the acknowledged superior of Eastern Turkistan. If Hunza admits any allegiance, it is to China, and not to Kashmīr; and the designations of offices of rule in that country are of Chinese, and not of Aryan origin, including even "Thàm," the title of its Raja.

As a matter of fact, however, the vast number of tribes that inhabit the many countries between the Indus and the Kuner own no master except their own tribal head or the tribal council. From kidnapping Hunza, where the right to plunder is monarchical, hereditary, and "ayeshó" = "heaven-born," to the peace and learning of republican Kandiá or

Gabriál, all want to be left alone. If a neighbour becomes troublesome, he is raided on till an interchange of presents restores harmony. It is impossible to say that either side is tributary to the other. The wealthier gives the larger present; the bigger is considered the superior in a general sort of way, and so two horses, two dogs, and a handful of gold dust are yearly sent by Hunza to Kashmír or to Yarkand as a cloak for much more substantial exactions in return. Nagyr sends a basket of apricots instead of the horses and dogs. In 1871 Chitrál still paid a tribute to Badakhshan in slaves, but it would be absurd to infer from this fact that Chitrál ever acknowledged the suzerainty of Jehandar Shah, or of the Affghan faction that dispossessed him. Nor were the Khaibaris, or other highway robbers, our rulers, because we paid them blackmail, or they our subjects because they might bring us "sweetmeats."

The points in which most Englishmen are as deficient as Russians are generally proficient, are language and a sympathetic manner with natives. That, however, linguistic knowledge is not useless may be inferred from the fact that it enabled me, to use the words of my Chief, Commissary General H. S. Jones, C. B., during the Russian War in 1855, "to pass unharmed through regions previously unknown and among tribes hitherto unvisited by any European."

Also in topography and geography linguistics are necessary; and the absurd mistakes now made at certain learned societies and in certain scientific journals, regarding the Pamirs, would be avoided by a little study of the Oriental languages concerned. In 1866, the map which accompanies my philological work on "Dardistan" shows, on linguistic grounds, and on the basis of native itineraries, the various Pamirs that have been partially revealed within the last few weeks, or have been laboriously ascertained by expensive Russian and British expeditions between 1867 and 1890. The publication of my material, collected at my own expense and which shall no longer be delayed, would have saved many complications; but when, *e.g.*, I pointed out, in 1866, that the Indus, after leaving Bunji, ran west instead of south, as on the then existing maps, I got into trouble with the Topographical Survey, which "discovered" the fact through its well-known "Mulla" in 1876. The salvation of India that is not made "departmentally" is crucified: and whoever does not belong to the regular military or civil services has no business to know or to suggest. Mr. Curzon, when presiding at a meeting of the late Oriental Congress, assured us that a new era had risen; but only the other night, at the Royal Geographical Society, a complaint was made of the reluctance of official departments in giving the Society information. As a rule, the mysteriousness of offices only conceals their ignorance, of which we have an instance in Capt. Younghusband being sent to shut the passes after the Russians had already stolen a march on, or through, them.

The neutralization of the Pamirs is the only solution of a difficulty created by the conjectural treaties of diplomatists and the ambition of military emissaries. Left as a huge happy hunting-ground for sportsmen, or as pasturage for nomads from whatever quarter, the Pamirs form the most perfect "neutral zone" conceivable. That the wanderings of these nomads should be accompanied by territorial or political claims, whether by Russia, China, Affghanistan, Kashmir, or ourselves, is the height of absurdity. As for Hunza-Nagyr, the sooner they are left to themselves the better for us, who are not bound to help Kashmir in encroaching on them. Kashmir managed them very fairly after 1848; and when it was occasionally defeated, its prestige did not suffer, for the next summer invariably found the tribal envoys again suing for peace and presents. The sooner the Gilgit Agency is withdrawn, the greater will be our reputation for fair dealing. Besides, we can take hostages from the Chiefs' families as guarantees of future tranquillity. Hunza-Nagyr are certainly not favourable to Russia, whilst Nagyr is decidedly friendly to us. The sensational account of

Colonel Grambcheffsky's visit to Hunza, which he places on his map where Nagyr is, seems to be one of the usual traps to involve us in great military expenditure and to alienate the tribes from us. It is also not creditable that, for party or personal purposes, the peaceful and pious Nagyris,—whom our own Gilgit Resident, Colonel Biddulph, has reported on as distinguished for "timidity and incapacity for war," "never having joined the Hunza raids," "slavery being unknown in Nagyr,"—should be described as "kidnappers," "raiders along with Hunza," "slave-dealers," "robbers," and "scoundrels,"—statements made by a correspondent from Gilgit in a morning newspaper of to-day, and to all of which I give an unqualified contradiction.

The establishment of the Gilgit Agency has already drawn attention to the shortest road for the invasion of India; and it is significant that its advocate at Gilgit should admit that all the tribes of the Indus Valley "sympathized with the Hunzas," from whose depredations they are erroneously supposed to have suffered, and that they were likely "to attack the British from behind by a descent on the Gilgit road" to Kashmir. Why should "the only other exit from Gilgit by way of the Indus Valley be through territories held by tribes hostile to the British"? Have the Gilgit doings already alienated the poor, but puritanical Chilásis, tributaries of Kashmir, who adjoin our settled British district of Kaghan? Are we to dread the Republic of Muhammadan learning, Kandiá, that has not a single fort; pastoral Dareyl; the Koli-Palus traders; agricultural Tangir, and other little Republics—one only of eleven houses? As for the places beyond them, our officials at Attock, Peshawur, Rawalpindi, and Abbottabad will deal with the Pathan tribes in their own neighbourhood, which have nothing to do with the adjoining Republics of quiet, brave, and intelligent Dards, on both sides of the Indus, up to Gilgit, to which I have referred, and which deserve our respectful study, sympathy, and unobtrusive support. G. W. LEITNER.

16th December, 1891.

The following account, published by Reuter's Telegram Company, will supplement the preceding article:—

"WOKING, *Dec.* 13.

"A representative of Reuter's Agency interviewed Dr. Leitner at his residence at Woking to-day, with the object of eliciting some information on the subject of the Hunza and Nagyr tribes, with whom the British forces are at present in conflict.

"Dr. Leitner, it is needless to say, is the well-known discoverer of the races and languages of Dardistan (the country between Kabul and Kashmir), which he so named when sent on a linguistic mission by the Punjab Government in 1864, at a time when the various independent tribes, including Hunza and Nagyr, had united in order to turn the troops of the Maharaja of Kashmir out of Gilgit. At that time it was considered that the treaty of 1846, by which Great Britain sold Kashmir to the Maharaja, had confined him to the Indus as his westward boundary, and had therefore rendered his occupation of Gilgit an encroachment and breach of treaty.

"Dr. Leitner, although the country was in a state of war, which is not favourable to scientific research, managed to collect a mass of information, and a fine ethnographical collection, which is at the museum at Woking. He has also made many friends in the country, and is doubtless the highest, if not the only, authority regarding these countries.

"Dr. Leitner, who was quite unprepared for to-day's visit, said that the relations which he had kept up with the natives of Gilgit, Hunza, Nagyr, and Yasin forced him to the conclusion that a conflict had been entered into which might have easily been avoided by a little more sympathy and knowledge, especially of the Nagyr people. Indeed, it was not a light matter that could have induced the venerable chief of Nagyr to make common cause with his hereditary foe of Hunza, unless he feared that the British threatened their respective independence.

"Not many weeks ago Dr. Leitner received a letter from the chief of Nagyr, in which he recommended to his kind attention his son, now in Kashmir, on the ground that he, even more so than any other member of his numerous family, was a well-wisher to the British Government. At that time the chief could not have had any feelings of animosity, although he might have protested, together with his rival of Hunza, against the British occupation of Chalt. In fact, it was not true that Nagyr and Hunza were really subject to Kashmir, except in the vague way in which these States constantly recognised the suzerainty of a neighbouring power in the hope of getting substantial presents for their offerings of a few ounces of gold dust, a couple of dogs, or basket of apricots, etc. Thus Chitrál, the ally of Great Britain, used to pay a tribute of slaves to the Ameers of Badakshan; but it would be absurd on that ground to render Chitrál a part of Afghanistan, because Badakshan now, in a manner, belongs to Abdurrahman. Hunza, again, sends a tribute to China; and, in a general way, China is the only Power that ever had a shadow of claim on these countries, but it is a mere shadow. Dr. Leitner said, the only policy for Great Britain is, in the words of the Secretary of State or Viceroy, 'to maintain and strengthen all the indigenous Governments.' This policy he would extend to the triangle which has Peshawur for its base, and thereby interpose a series of almost impregnable mountainous countries, which would be sufficiently defended by the independence of their inhabitants. If Circassia could oppose Russia for thirty years, even although Russia had the command of the Black Sea, how much more effective would be the resistance of the innumerable Circassias which Providence had placed between ourselves and the Russian frontier in Asia? We ought to have made these tribes look upon us as a distant but powerful friend, ready to help them in an emergency; but now, by attacking two of them, we caused Russia to be looked upon as the coming Saviour; indeed, the people of Wakhan, on the Pamir side of Hunza, were already doing so, whilst Shignan and Roshan, which had been almost depopulated by our friends, the Afghans, had already begun to emigrate into Russian territory. Here Dr. Leitner added that the Russian claims through Bokhara were as illusory as those of Kashmir, and historically even less founded than those of China. Indeed, no one had a right to these countries except the indigenous peoples and chiefs who inhabited them; and in this scramble for the regions round the Pamir, great Britain was simply breaking down her natural defences by stamping out the independence of native tribes and making military roads; for it was the absence of those roads on the British side that rendered it impossible to an invader to do England any real harm or to advance on India proper.

Asked why the trouble had broken out at the present time, Dr. Leitner said, that he had been kept without information of the immediate cause, but he felt certain that it was owing to the attempt to construct a military road to Hunza, whereby England would only facilitate the advent of a possible invader from that direction, besides making Hunza throw in its lot with that invader. It was perfectly untrue, as alleged in some of the Indian papers, that the Nagyris were kidnappers, and that our attack would be an advantage to the cause of anti-slavery. The fact was just the other way. Kidnapping had been stopped in 1869 as far as Hunza was concerned.

The Nagyris never raided at all; Chitrál also gave up selling its Káfir or Shiah subjects into slavery when the markets of Badakshan were closed; but now that confusion had caused the English and Russian advance, Hunza had again taken to raiding, and Chitrál to selling slaves. As for Naygr, the case was quite different; they were an excellent people and very quiet, so much so that Colonel Biddulph, the Resident, described them as "noted for timidity and incapacity for war," whereas in his "Tribes of the Hindu Kush" he also states that the people of Hunza are not warlike in the sense in which the Afghans are said to be so. No doubt the Nagyris dislike war, but would fight bravely if driven to do so. Colonel Biddulph adds: "They are settled agricultural communities, proud of the independence they have always maintained for fourteen centuries, hemmed in by lofty mountains, and living under rulers who boast of long, unbroken descent from princes of native blood." He also bears testimony to the fact that "the Nagyr people were never concerned in these raids, and slavery does not exist among them." At the same time Dr. Leitner fully admitted that the Hunza people were not a model race, since they used to be desperate raiders and kidnappers, and very immoral and impious. The father of the present king used to dance in a state of drunkenness in the mosque; but, on the other hand, we were not bound to be the reformers of Hunza by pulling down one of the bulwarks to our Indian Empire. Hunza was a picturesque country in every sense; it was nominally governed by fairies: ecstatic women were the prophetesses of the tribe, recounted its past glories, and told what was going on in the neighbouring valleys, so they were its historians and journalists as well as its prophetesses. No war was undertaken unless the fairies gave their consent, and the chief fairy, Yudeni, who protects the "Tham" (a Chinese title), has no doubt already struck the sacred drum in order to call the men of the country to defend the "Heaven-born," as their chief is called. The two "Thams" of Hunza and Nagyr, who have a common ancestry, are also credited with the power of causing rain, and there would certainly appear to be some foundation for this remarkable fact.

The two tribes are great polo players; archery on horseback is common amongst them; and they are very fair ibex hunters.

The people of Nagyr are as pious and gentle as those of Hunza are the contrary. Their language went back to simple sounds as indicative of a series of human relations or experiences, and clearly showed that the customs and associations of a race were at the basis of so-called rules of grammar. Nothing more wonderful than their language could be conceived; it went to the root of human thought as expressed in language, but the language had already suffered by foreign influences between 1866, when one son of the Rajah of Nagyr taught him, and 1886, when another son of the Rajah continued his lessons.

As regards religion, the Hunzas are Mulais, a mysterious and heretical sect, akin to the Druses of the Lebanon, practising curious rites, and practically infidels. He had obtained a few pages of their secret Bible, the Kelam-i-pir, which throws much light on the doctrines of the so-called "assassins" during the Crusades. The Nagyris are pious Muhammadans of the Shiah denomination.

Dr. Leitner then showed the map accompanying his linguistic work on Dardistan. After comparing it with the most recent Russian and British maps, that of Dr. Leitner gives the fullest and clearest information, not only as regards Hunza-Nagyr, where all the places where fighting has occurred are marked, but also as regards the various Pamirs, thus anticipating in 1866 on linguistic grounds and native itineraries the different Pamirs that have recently been settled geographically. It shows that the ethnographical frontier of the Pamirs to the north are the Turki-speaking nomads of the trans-Altaic range (now Russian); to the west the Persian, or Tajiks (now Afghan); to the south the Aryan Hindu Kush [British]; and to the east the wall of the Serikol Mountains, dividing or admitting Chinese, Tibetan, or Mongolian influence. The indeterminate river courses through the Pamir, or a line stretched across its plateaux, valleys, and mountains, are obviously an unmaintainable demarcation, which is liable to be transgressed by shepherds under whatever rule; but the whole of the Pamirs together, as a huge and happy hunting-ground, are, no doubt, if neutralized by the three Powers concerned, the best possible frontier, as "no man's land," and a perfect neutral zone. "What matter," continued Dr. Leitner, "if the passes are easy of access on the Russian side, it is on the descent, and on the ascent on our side that almost insuperable difficulties begin. Where we are now fighting in Hunza-Nagyr only the low state of the river which divides Hunza from Nagyr enables us to make a simultaneous advance on both. Otherwise we should have to let ourselves man by man down from one ledge of rock to another, and if we miss our footing be whirled away in the most terrible torrent the imagination can conceive. Why, then, destroy such a great defence in our favour if Hunza is kept friendly, as it so easily can be, especially with the pressure exercised on it by the Nagyris, whose forts frown on those of Hunza all down the river that separates their countries? I cannot conceive anything more wanton or suicidal than the present advance even if we should succeed in removing one of the most important landmarks in the history of the human race by shooting down the handful of Nagyris and Hunzas that oppose us. They preserve the pre-historic remnants of legends and customs that explain much that is still obscure in the life and history of European races. A few hundred pounds a year judiciously spent and the promise of the withdrawal of the Gilgit Agency, which was already once before attacked when under Colonel Biddulph, would be a far better way of securing peace than shooting down with Gatlings and Martini-Henry rifles people who defend their independence within their crags with bows, arrows, battleaxes, and a few muskets; and the promise of the withdrawal of the Gilgit Agency might be made contingent upon the increase of the number of hostages belonging to the chiefs' families that are now annually sent to Kashmir as a guarantee of friendly relations.

The Hunzas and Nagyris are not to be despised as foes; they are very good marksmen. In 1886, when the Kashmir troops thought they had cleared the plain before the Gilgit Fort entirely of enemies, and not a person was to be seen outside it, the tribesmen would glide along the ground unperceived behind a stone pushed in front of them, and resting their old flint muskets on them shoot off the Maharajah's Sepoys whenever they showed themselves outside the fort. Indeed, it was this circumstance that induced Dr. Leitner to abandon the protection of the fort and make friends with the tribesmen outside. All the tribes desired was to be left alone in their mountain fastnesses. They had sometimes internecine feuds, but would unite against the common foe. It was merely emasculating their powers of resistance to subject them, either on the one side to Bokhara, which meant Russia, or to Afghanistan or Kashmir, which meant Great Britain, or to China, which meant dependence on a Power that might be utilized any day against Great Britain after the completion of the trans-Siberian railway. Diplomatists, frontier delimitation commissions, and officers, both British and Russian, anxious for promotion, had, continued Dr. Leitner, created the present confusion; and it was now high time to rely rather on the physical obstacles that guaranteed the safety alike of the British, Russian, and Chinese frontiers than on the chapter of political accidents.

Dr. Leitner, who is going to give a lecture at the Westminster Town-hall to-morrow afternoon on "The Races, Religions, and Politics of the Pamir Regions," then showed our representative Col. Grambcheffsky's map, which put Hunza where Nagyr ought to be, and ignored the latter place altogether, just as did the last map of the Geographical Society in connection with Mr. Littledale's tour. Grambcheffsky's map, however, had since been corrected by evidently an English map, and it was strange that Russians had easier access to English maps than Englishmen themselves. In fact, all this secrecy, Dr. Leitner maintained, was injurious to the acquisition of full knowledge regarding imperfectly known regions. Attention was then directed to a number of maps, that of Mr. Drew, a Kashmir official, showing Hunza-Nagyr to be beyond Kashmir influence. This was practically confirmed by several official maps and the statements of Colonels Biddulph and Hayward, the latter of whom placed the Kashmir frontier towards Hunza at Nomal, whilst the British are now fighting sixteen and a half miles beyond in front of Mayun, where the first Hunza fort is. The Nagyr frontier Dr. Leitner places at Jaglot, which is nineteen miles from Nilt, where we are simultaneously fighting the first Nagyr fort.

Dr. Leitner, in conclusion, expressed his conviction, from his knowledge of the people concerned, that any one with a sympathetic mind could get them to do anything in reason; but that encroachments, whether overt or covert, would be resisted to the utmost. Indeed, England's restlessness had brought on the present trouble.

In 1866, he stated, the very name of Russia was unknown in these parts, and in 1886 was only known to a few. Yet the English Press in both these years spoke of Russian intrigues among the tribes. He did not fear them as long as the Indian Empire relied on its natural defences, its inner strength, and on justice to its chiefs and people, and as long as its policy with the tribes was guided by knowledge and good feeling.

APPENDIX II.

NOTES ON RECENT EVENTS IN CHILÁS AND CHITRÁL.

In 1866 I was sent by the Punjab Government on a linguistic mission to Kashmir and Chilás at the instance of the Bengal Asiatic Society and on the motion of the late Sir George Campbell, who hoped to identify Kailás or the Indian Olympus with Chilás.* Although unable to support that conjecture, I collected material which was published in Part I. of my "Dardistan" and which the Government declared "as throwing very considerable and important light on matters heretofore veiled in great obscurity." That some obscurity still exists, is evident from the *Times* telegram of to-day (5th December, 1892), in which an item of news from the Tak [Takk] valley is described as coming from *Chitrál*, a distant country with which Chilás has nothing to do. The Takk village is fortified, and through the valley is the shortest and easiest road to our British district of Kaghán. It is alleged that some headmen of Takk wished to see Dr. Robertson at Gilgit, who thereupon sent a raft to bring them, but the raft was fired on and Capt. Wallace, who went to its assistance, was wounded. [Chilás is on the Kashmir side of the Indus, and the Gilgit territory is reached by crossing the Indus at Bunji.]

The incident is ascribed either to "*the treachery of the men who professed willingness to* COME IN" or to the mischievousness of "other persons." It is probable from this suggestion of treachery and the unconscious use of the words "to come in," which is the Anglo-Indian equivalent for "surrender," that the headmen of Takk were *not* willing to make over their Fort to the British or to open the road to Gilgit. The Takk incident, therefore, is not a part of the so-called "*Chitrál usurpation*," under which heading it

* I was again on special duty in 1886, and its result was Part I. of the "Hunza-Nagyr Handbook," of which a second and enlarged edition will appear shortly. My material, some of which has been published, has been collected between 1865 and 1889 in my private capacity as a student of languages and customs.

immediately appears, but is a part of *our* usurpation on the tribes inhabiting the banks of the Indus. In 1843, these tribes inflicted a severe loss on the Sikh invaders, and in my "history of the wars with Kashmir" the part taken by the manly defenders of Takk, now reduced from 131 to some 90 houses, is given in detail. It seems to me that as the Gilgit force was unable to support "the Chitrál usurpation" of our protégé, Afzul-ul-Mulk, owing to his being killed by his uncle Sher Afzul, it is to be employed to coerce the Indus tribes to open out a road which ought never to have been withdrawn from their hold. About 50 years ago the Takk men were stirred into so-called rebellion by Kashmir agents in order to justify annexation. It is to be hoped that history will not repeat itself, or that, at any rate, the next 50 years will see the Indus tribes as independent and peaceful as they have been since 1856, especially in Chilás (before 1892), and as mysterious as Hunza ought to have remained till our unnecessary attack on that country caused practically unknown Russia to be looked upon as the Saviour of Nations "rightly struggling to be free" (see Baron Vrevsky's reply to the Hunza deputation). *Quem Deus vult perdere, prius dementat;* and no greater instance of folly can be conceived, than the construction of a military road through countries in which the chamois is often puzzled for its way. Nor was the attention of the Russians drawn to them before we made our own encroachments.

As for the Pamirs, whatever may be the present interpretation of Prince Gortchakoff's Convention, the Russians were unwilling to let political consequences or limits accompany the erratic wanderings of Kirghiz sheep in search of pasturage in that region. Prince Gortchakoff's advocacy of a Neutral Zone and of the autonomy of certain tribes was justified by the facts (which he, however, rather guessed than knew) and was worthy alike of that Diplomatist and of our acceptance in the interests of India and of peace. The incorporation of certain Districts in the domain, or rather the sphere of influence, of Afghanistan, was distasteful to tribes attached to their hereditary rulers or to republican institutions and was not too willingly accepted by the Amir of Afghanistan, who now expects us to defend the white Elephants that we have given him better than we did Panjdeh. Some Muláis that had fled from Russian tyranny to Afghan territory assured me that "the finger of an Afghan was more oppressive than the whole Russian army." Indeed, so far as Central Asia is concerned, Russia, with the exception of certain massacres, has hitherto behaved, on the whole, as a great civilizing power.*

As for Sirdar Nizám-ul-Mulk, this is his *name* and not his *title*. He is the "Mihtar" or "Prince" Nizám-ul-Mulk, and neither an Indian "Sirdár" nor a "Nizám." He is also the "Badshah" of Turikoh, this being the district assigned to him in his father's lifetime as the heir-apparent. He was snubbed by us for offering to relieve that excellent officer, Col. Lockhart, when a prisoner in Wakhan! He has written to me from Turikoh for "English phrases and words with their Persian equivalents as a pleasure and a requirement." This does not look like hostility to the British. He spoke to me in 1886 of his brother Afzul's bravery with affection and pride, though he has ever maintained his own acknowledged right as the successor of his father Amán-ul-Mulk. If he has been alienated from us or has ever been tempted to throw himself into the arms of Russia, it has most assuredly been our fault. Besides, just as we have abandoned the Shiah Hazaras, our true friends during the late Afghan War, to be destroyed by their religious and political foe, the Sunni Amir Abdurrahman, so have the Amir Sher Ali and the Tham of Hunza, Safdar Ali Khan, rued their

* In spite of Russian attempts to conciliate the orthodox Muhammadans of Turkey and thus to take the place of the British as "the Protector of Islám," the news of the revision of the Korán by a Russian Censor and the *bévue* of putting up the Czar's portrait in Central Asian Mosques, have injured Russia's propaganda among Muhammadans, whom also the accounts of the persecution of the Jews have estranged from a Power that began its rule in Central Asia by repairing and constructing Mosques, helping Mosque Schools and even subsidizing an employé to call "the faithful" to fast and *break*-fast during the month of Ramazán.

trust in Russian Agents. I regret, therefore, to find in the *Times* telegram of to-day that "the Nizám" "is acting without the support of the British Agent" "who has not interfered," when he had already interfered in favour of the usurper Afzul-ul-Mulk.

As for the connivance of Amir Abdurrahman, my "rough history of Dardistan from 1800 to 1872" shows that, in one sense, Chitrál is tributary to Badakhshán and as we have assigned Badakhshán to the Amir, he, no doubt, takes an interest in Chitrál affairs. I believe, however, that interest to be somewhat platonic, and he knows that his friend Jehandár Shah (the late wrongfully deposed hereditary ruler of Badakhshán) never paid any tribute to Afghanistan. But Chitrál once also paid tribute to Dír, with whose able Chief, Rahmat-ullah-Khan, "the Nizám" is connected by marriage. Chitrál on the other hand has *received* a subsidy from Kashmir since 1877, but this was as much a tribute from Kashmir to Aman-ul-Mulk, as a sign of his subjection to Kashmir, for shortly after he made offers of allegiance to Kabul. With all alike it is

> "The good old rule, the simple plan,
> That they should take who have the power,
> And they should keep who can."

It is misleading to speak of their relations to neighbouring States as "tributary." Are the Khyberis tributary to us or we to them, because we pay them a tribute to let our merchants travel through their Pass? Have we never ourselves come, first as suppliants, then as merchants, then as guests, then as advisers, then as protectors, and, finally, as conquerors?

The procedure of Afghanistan, of Chitrál, of Kashmir, and of our own is very much alike and so are the several radii of influence of the various factors in "the question." We have our fringe of independent frontier tribes with whom we flirt, or wage war, as suits the convenience of the moment. Afghanistan has a similar fringe of independent Ishmaelites round it and even through it, whose hands are against everybody and everybody's hands against them.

Chitrál is threatened all along its line by the Kafirs, who even make a part of Badakhshán insecure, but are nevertheless our very good friends. Kashmir has its fringe on its extreme border, especially since, in violation of our treaty of 1846, it has attacked countries *beyond the Indus on the west,* including the Kunjûtis of Hunza, who resumed their raiding—which had ceased in 1867—during and after Col. Lockhart's visit in 1886. Yet there can be little doubt about "the loyalty" of those concerned. The Amirs of Afghanistan consider themselves "*shields of India,*" as I have heard two of them say, and so did our Ally of Kashmir, who ought never to have been reduced to a subordinate feudatory position. What wonder then that old Amán-ul-Mulk of Chitrál should also have tried to become a buffer between Afghanistan on the West, Kashmir on the East, India on the South and, latterly, Russia in the North, if indeed the whole story of Russian intrigue in Chitrál be at all truer than a similar mare's nest which we discovered in Hunza? It is the policy of Russia to create false alarms and thereby to involve us in expenditure, whilst standing by and posing as the future saviour of the tribes. Our tendency to compromises and subservient Commissions of delimitation and to "scuttling" occasionally, is also well known and so we are offered in Russian papers "*an Anglo-Russian understanding on the subject of Chitrál,*" as if Chitrál was not altogether out of the sphere of Russia's legitimate influence! It is also amusing to find in the *Novosti* that Russia's sole desire is "to prevent *Afghanistan* from falling into British hands." We are already spending at Gilgit on food etc. for our troops more in one year than were spent in the 40 years of the so-called mismanagement of Kashmir, which I myself steadily exposed, but which kept the frontier far more quiet than it has been since the revival of the Gilgit Agency. There is every prospect now of heavier and continued expenditure, as the policy of the Foreign Department of the Government of India develops. On that policy a *veto* should at once be put by the British Parliament and public, if our present Liberal Administration cannot do so without pressure from without. We should conciliate Nizam-ul-Mulk before it is too late. He is connected with Umra Khan of Jandôl and with the influential Mullah Shahu of Bajaur through his maternal uncle, Kokhan Beg. He has also connections in Badakhshan, Hunza and Dîr, as already stated. Indeed, we ought to have given him our support from the beginning. I doubt whether it would be desirable to subdivide Chitrál as stated in to-day's *Times*, letting Sher Afzul keep Chitrál proper, giving Yasin to "the Nizám" and letting Umra Khan retain what he has already seized of Southern Chitrál. As for Sher Afzul, I believe, that he is also "loyal."

As for Hunza, I am not at all certain that the fugitive, Safdar Ali Khan, really murdered his father. At all events when the deed was committed, I find that it was attributed to Muhammad Khan,* probably not the present

* "By the most recent account, Ghazan Khan, the son of Ghazanfar, has been killed by his own son, Muhammad Khan. Muhammad Khan's mother was the sister of Zafar Khan, the ruler of Nagyr. She was killed by her father-in-law, Ghazanfar, and thrown over a precipice from her house. Ghazan Khan treacherously killed his paternal uncle, Abdullah Khan, ruler of Gojál, who unsuspectingly met him. On ascending the throne, Ghazan Khan is also said to have poisoned his ailing full brother, Bukhtawar Shah, and another (by a different Sayad mother) Nanawal Shah. The fratricidal traditions of Hunza and of the Khush-waqtia family of Yasin have now been somewhat thrown into the shade by the parricide of Muhammad Khan. The father of Ghazan Khan, Ghazanfar, is said to have died from the effects of a suit of clothes, impregnated with small-pox, sent to him by his daughter, the full sister of Ghazan Khan, who was married to Mir Shah of Badakhshan, in order to accelerate her brother's accession to the throne. The father of Ghazanfar, Sullum, also poisoned his own father. This state of things is very different from the gentle rules and traditions of Nagyr, whose aged Chief, Zafar Khan, has nineteen sons, and who sent his rebellious eldest son, Muhammad Khan (whose mother was a full sister of Ghazan Khan of Hunza) to Ramsu in Kashmír territory, where he died. He was married to a daughter of his maternal uncle, and tried to sell some of his Nagyr subjects into slavery, against the traditions of that peaceful country, in consequence of which his father, Zafar Khan, expelled him." (See Part referring to the History and Customs of Hunza and Nagyr.) Yet it is this patriarchal, loyal and God-fearing Záfar Khan, whose letter to me I published last year, whom we accused of kidnapping and aggressiveness, so that we might take his country.

H. H. MIHTAR NIZÁM-UL-MULK AND HIS LATE YASIN COUNCIL.

CHITRÁLI MUSICIANS AND THE BADAKSHI POET, TAIGHÛN SHAH.

Mir Muhammad Nazim who has acknowledged the suzerainty of England (through Kashmir) and of China. The latter power has always had something to say to Hunza, and the very title of its Chief "Tham" is of Chinese origin. The subsidy that China used to pay for keeping open the commercial road from Badakhshan and Wakhan through the Pamirs along Kunjût (Hunza) to Yarkand, was about £380 per annum, and this sum was divided between four States and ensured the immunity of the route from raids.* I doubt whether in future £380 a year on Hunza alone will enable us to keep it quiet, and I am sure that the lofty superciliousness with which Chinese officials discuss the Pamir question, as something that scarcely concerns them, is no evidence of that pertinacious power abandoning claims to a suzerainty in those regions which are historically founded, although their exercise has been more by an appeal to imagination of the glorious and invincible, if distant, "Khitái," than by actual interference.

Indeed, it is China alone that has a grievance—against Russia for the occupation of the Alichur Pamir—against Afghanistan for expelling her troops from Somatash (of subsequent Yanoff fame)—and against England for encroaching on her ancient feudatory of Hunza, whose services in suppressing the Khoja rebellion in 1847 are commemorated in a tablet on one of the gates of Yarkand.

NOTE.—We add a reproduction of the photographs of the Mihtar and Badshah Nizam-ul-Mulk, sitting in Council with his uncle, Bahadur Khan, now at Gilgit, where he represented Afzul-ul-Mulk. On the Nizam's left is his foster-uncle, Maimun Shah, whilst behind him stand our Indian Agent, Wafadár Khan and a Chitráli office-holder, Wazîr Khan, of corresponding rank. We also give the portrait of the Chitrál Court poet and musician, the celebrated Taighûn Shah, one of whose songs, with its notation, was published in our issue of the 1st of January, 1891. He is seated with the two flute-players who always precede the King of Chitrál when on a tour.

---

* Of the £380, Shignán received £170, Sirikul £100, Wakkan £50, and Hunza £60 in Yambus (silver blocks of the value of £17).

Although the period may be past in which a great English Journal could ask, "*what* is Gilgit?" the contradictory telegrams and newspaper accounts which we receive regarding the countries adjoining Gilgit show that the Press has still much to learn. Names of places, as far apart as Edinburgh and London, are put within a day's march on foot. Names of men figure on maps as places and the relationships of the Chiefs of the region in question are invented or confounded as may suit the politics of the moment, if not the capacity of the printer. The injunctions of the Decalogue are applied or misapplied, extended or curtailed, to suit immediate convenience, and a different standard of morality is constantly being found for our friends of to-day or our foes of to-morrow. The youth Afzul-ul-Mulk was credited with all human virtues and with even more than British manliness, as he was supposed to be friendly to us. He had given his country into our hands in order to receive our support against his elder brother, the acknowledged heir of the late Aman-ul-Mulk of Chitrál, but that elder brother, Nizám-ul-Mulk, was no less friendly to English interests, although he has the advantage of being a man of capacity and independence. The sudden death of Aman-ul-Mulk coincided with the presence of our protégé at Chitrál, and the first thing that the virtuous Afzul-ul-Mulk did, was to invite as many brothers as were within reach to a banquet when he murdered them. No doubt, as a single-minded potentate, he did not wish to be diverted from the task of governing his country by the performance of social duties to the large circle of acquaintances in brothers and their families which Providence bestows on a native ruler or claimant in Chitrál and Yasin. A member of the Khushwaqtia dynasty of Yasin, which is a branch of the Chitrál dynasty, told me when I expressed my astonishment at the constant murders in his family: "A real relative in a high family is a person whom God points out to one to kill as an obstacle in one's way, whereas a foster-relative (generally of a lower class) is a true friend who rises and falls with one's own fortune" (it being the custom for a scion of a noble house to be given out to a nurse.)

The dynasty of Chitrál is said to have been established by Baba Ayub, an adventurer of Khorassan. He adopted the already existing name of *Katór*, whence the dynasty is called Katoré. The Emperor Baber refers to the country of Katór in his Memoirs and a still more ancient origin has been found in identifying Katór with "Kitolo, the King of the Great Yuechi, who, in the beginning of the 5th century, conquered Balkh and Gandhara, and whose son established the Kingdom of the Little Yuechi, at Peshawur." (See Biddulph's "Tribes of the Hindoo Koosh," page 148.) General Cunningham asserts that the King of Chitrál takes the title of Shah Kator, which has been held for nearly 2,000 years, and the story of their descent from Alexander may be traced to the fact that they were the successors of the Indo-Grecian Kings in the Kabul valley. If Katór is a corruption of Kaisar, then let it not be said that the remnant of the Katoré exclaimed with the Roman gladiator: "Ave, Kaisar-i-Hind, morituri te salutant."

Amán-ul-Mulk, the late ruler of Chitrál, was, indeed, a terrible man, who to extraordinary courage joined the arts of the diplomatist. He succeeded his elder brother, surnamed Adam-Khôr or "man-eater." His younger brother, Mir Afzul, is said to have been killed by him or to have committed a convenient suicide; another brother, Sher Afzul, who is now in possession of Chitrál, was long a fugitive in Badakhshan whence he has just returned with a few Afghans (such as any pretender can ever collect) and a hundred of the Chitráli slaves that used to be given in tribute to the Mír of Badakhshan, which itself never paid a tribute to Kabul before the late Sher Ali of Afghanistan installed Mahmud Shah, who expelled his predecessor Jehandar Shah, the friend of Abdur-Rahman, the present Amir of Afghanistan. Another brother of Aman-ul-Mulk was Kokhan Beg, whose daughter married the celebrated Mullah Shahu Baba, a man of considerable influence in Bajaur, who is feared by the Badshah of Kunar (a feudatory of Kabul and a friend of the British) and is an enemy of the Kamôji Kafirs, that infest one of the roads to Chitrál. This Kokhan Beg, who was a maternal uncle of Afzul-ul-Mulk, was killed the other day by his brother Sher Afzul coming from Badakhshan. I mention all this, as in the troubles that are preparing, the ramifications of the interests of the various pretenders are a matter of importance. Other brothers of Aman-ul-Mulk are: Muhammad Ali (Moriki), Yádgar Beg, Shádman Beg and Bahádur Khán (all by a mother of lower degree), and another Bahádur Khán, who was on the Council of Nizám-ul-Mulk. Nizám-ul-Mulk has therefore to contend with one or more of his uncles, and by to-day's telegram* is on his way to the Chitrál Fort in order to expel Sher Afzul with the aid of the very troops that Sher Afzul had sent to turn out Afzul-ul-Mulk's Governor from Yasin. I believe that Nizám-ul-Mulk has or had two elder half-brothers, Gholam of Oyôn and Majid Dastagîr of Drôshp; but, in any case, he was the eldest legitimate son and, according to Chitrál custom, was invested with the title of Badshah of Turikoh, the rule of which valley compelled his absence from Chitrál and not "his wicked and intriguing disposition" as alleged by certain Anglo-Indian journals. Of other brothers of Nizám-ul-Mulk was Shah Mulk (of lower birth), who was Governor of Daraung and was killed by Afzul-ul-Mulk. He used to live at Dros (near Pathan in Shashi). Afzul-ul-Mulk of Drasun, whom we have already mentioned as a wholesale fratricide, was killed in his flight to one of the towers of the Chitrál Fort from the invading force of his uncle, Sher Afzul of Badakhshan. A younger half-brother is also Behram-ul-Mulk (by a lower mother), called "Viláyeti," of Moroi in Andarti. Other brothers are: Amin-ul-Mulk, a brother of good birth of Oyôn (Shoghôt), who was reared by a woman of the Zondré or highest class; Wazîr-ul-Mulk (of low

* *Times*, 5th December, 1892.

birth) of Brôz; Abdur-Rahman (low-born) at Owir (Barpèsh), and Badshah-i-Mulk, also of Owir, who was reared by the wife of Fath-Ali Shah. There are no doubt other brothers also whose names I do not know. Murid, who was killed by Sher Afzul, is also an illegitimate brother.

A few words regarding the places mentioned in recent telegrams may be interesting: Shogôth is the name of a village, of a fort, and of a district which is the north-western part of Chitrál, and it also comprises the Ludkho and tributary valleys. Through the district is the road leading to the Dara and Nuqsàn passes, to the right and left respectively, at the bottom of which is a lake on which official toadyism has inflicted the name of Dufferin in supersession of the local name. Darushp (Drôshp) is another big village in this district and in the Ludkho valley, and Andarti is a Fort in it within a mile of the Kafir frontier. The inhabitants of Shogôth are descendants of Munjanis, whose dialect (Yidgah) I refer to elsewhere, and chiefly profess to be Shiahs, in consequence of which they have been largely exported as slaves by their Sunni rulers. Baidam Khan, a natural son of Aman-ul-Mulk, was the ruler of it. The Ludkho valley is traversed by the Arkari river which falls into that of Chitrál. At the head of the Arkari valley are three passes over the Hindukhush, including the evil-omened "Nuqsán," which leads to Zeibak, the home of the heretical Maulais (co-religionists of the Assassins of the Crusades) in Badakhshán. It is shorter, more direct, and freer from Kafir raids than the longer and easier Dora pass. *Owir* is a village of 100 houses on the Arkari river, and is about 36 miles from Zeibak. *Drasan* is both the name of a large village and of a fort which commands the Turikoh valley, a subdivision of the Drasan District, which is the seat of the heir-apparent to the Chitrál throne (Nizám-ul-Mulk). Yet the *Pioneer*, in its issue of the 5th October last, considers that Lord Lansdowne had settled the question of succession in favour of Afzul-ul-Mulk, that Nizám-ul-Mulk would thus be driven to seek Russian aid, but that any such aid would be an infringement of the rights of Abdur-Rahman. Now that Abdur-Rahman is suspected, on the flimsiest possible evidence, to have connived at Sher Afzul's invasion of Chitrál, we seek to pick a quarrel with him for what a few weeks ago was considered an assertion of his rights. Let it be repeated once for always that if ever Abdur-Rahman or Nizám-ul-Mulk, or the Chief of Hunza or Kashmir or Upper India fall into the arms of Russia, it will be *maxima nostra culpa.* I know the Amir Abdur-Rahman, as I knew the Amir Sher Ali, as I know Nizám-ul-Mulk, and of all I can assert that no truer friends to England existed in Asia than these Chiefs. Should Abdur-Rahman be alienated, as Sher Ali was, or Nizám-ul-Mulk might be, it will be entirely in consequence of our meddlesomeness and our provocations. Russia has merely to start a will-o'-the-wisp conversation between Grombcheffsky and the Chief of Hunza, when there is internal evidence that Grombcheffsky was never in Hunza at all, and certainly never went there by the Muztagh Pass, that we, ignoring the right of China and of the treaty with Kashmír in 1846, forgetful of the danger in our rear and the undesirability of paving for an invader the road in front, fasten a quarrel on Hunza-Nagyr, and slaughter its inhabitants. No abuse or misrepresentation was spared in order to inflame the British public even against friendly and inoffensive Nagyr. What wonder that a Deputation was sent from Hunza to seek Russian aid and that it returned contented with presents, and public expressions of sympathy which explained away the Russian official refusal as softened by private assurances of friendship? Whatever may be the disaster to civilization in the ascendancy of Russian rule, the personal behaviour of Russian agents in Central Asia is, generally, pleasant. As in Hunza, so in Afghanistan, some strange suspicion of the disloyalty of its Chief, suggested by Russia, may involve us in a senseless war and inordinate expense, with the eventual result that Afghanistan must be divided between England and Russia, and their frontiers in

Asia become conterminous. Then will it be impossible for England ever to oppose Russia in Europe, because fear of complications in Asia will paralyze her. Then the tenure of India will depend on concessions, for which that country is not yet ripe, or on a reign of terror, either course ending in the withdrawal of British administration from, at any rate, Northern India. Yet it is "*Fas ab hosti doceri,*" and when Prince Gortschakoff urged the establishment of a neutral zone with autonomous states, including Badakhshan, he advocated a policy that would have conduced to centuries of peace and to the preservation of various ancient forms of indigenous Oriental civilization by interposing the mysterious blanks of the Pamirs and the inaccessible countries of the Hindukush between Russian and British aggression

Instead of this consummation so devoutly to be wished, and possible even now, though late, if action be taken under good advice and in the fulness of knowledge, either Power—

> "Thus with his stealthy pace
> With Tarquin's ravishing strides, towards his design
> Moves like a ghost."

If ever the pot called the kettle black, it is the story of Anglo-Russian recriminations. Russian intrigues are ever met by British manœuvres and Muscovite earth-hunger can only be paralleled by English annexations. *Here* a tribe is instigated to revolt, so that its extermination may "rectify a boundary," *there* an illusory scientific frontier is gradually created by encroachments on the territories of feudatories accused of disloyalty, if not of attempts to poison our agents. By setting son against father, brother against brother and, in the general tumult, destroying intervening republics and monarchies, Anglo-Russian dominions are becoming conterminous. Above all

> "There's not a one of them but in his house
> I keep a servant fee'd."

And it is this unremitting suspicion which is alike the secret of present success and the cause of eventual failure in wresting and keeping Asiatic countries and of the undying hatred which injured natives feel towards Europeans.

The attempt to obtain the surrender of the Takk fort, and of the Takk valley, a short and easy road to the British District of Kaghán, has merely indicated to Russia the nearest way to India, just as we forced her attention to Hunza and are now drawing it to Chitrál. David Urquhart used to accuse us of conspiracy with Russia in foreign politics. Lord Dufferin in his Belfast speech sought the safety of India in his friendship with M. de Giers and his Secretary popularized Russia in India by getting his work on "Russia" translated into Urdu. Certainly the coincidence of Russian as well as British officials being benefited by their respective encroachments, Commissions, Delimitations, etc., would show their "mutual interest" to consist in keeping up the farce of "Cox and Box" in Central Asia, which must end in a tragedy.

As an official since 1855, when I served Her Majesty during the Russian War, I wish to warn the British public against the will-o'-the-wisp of our foreign policy, especially in India. I can conceive that a small, moral and happy people should seek the ascendancy of its principles, even if accompanied by confusion in the camps of its enemies. I can understand that the doctrines of Free Trade, of a free Press, a Parliamentary rule, the Anti-Slavery propaganda and philanthropic enterprises generally, with which the British name is connected, should have been as good as an army to us in every country of the world in which they created a Liberal party, but these doctrines have often weakened foreign Executive Governments, whilst "Free Trade" ruined their native manufacture. What I, however, cannot understand is that a swarming, starving and unhappy population should seek consolation for misery at home in Quixotism abroad, especially when that Quixotism is played out. If bread costs as much now as in 1832, although the price of wheat has fallen from 60s. to 27s. a quarter, it is, indeed, high time that we should lavish no more blood and treasure on the stones of foreign politics, but that we should first extract the beam from our own eye before we try to take out the mote from the eye of others.

What these foreign politics are worth may be inferred from the growing distrust on the Continent of British meddlesomeness or from what we should ourselves feel if even so kindred a race as the Prussians sought to monopolize British wealth and positions. It would be worse, if they did so without possessing a thorough knowledge of the English language or of British institutions. Yet we are not filled with misgivings when our Indian Viceroys or Secretaries of State cannot speak Hindustani, the *lingua franca* of India or when an Under-Secretary has a difficulty in finding Calcutta on the Map.

India should be governed in the fulness of knowledge and sympathy, not by short cuts. It should not be the preserve of a Class, but the *one* proud boast of its many and varied peoples. When Her Majesty assumed Her Indian title. it was by a mere accident, in which *pars magna fui*, at the last moment, that the Proclamation was translated to those whom it concerned at the Imperial Assemblage. This superciliousness, wherever we can safely show it, the cynical abandonment of our friends, the breach of pledges, the constant experimentalizing on the natives, the mysteriousness that conceals official ignorance, is the enemy to British rule in India, not Russia. A powerful Empire can afford to discard the arts of the weak, and *should* even "show its hand." India should be ruled by a permanent Viceroy, a member of the Royal family, not by one whom the exigencies of party can appoint and shift. When in 1869 the Chiefs and people of the Panjab deputed me to submit their petition that H.R.H. the Prince of Wales be pleased to visit India, it was because they felt that it was desirable in the interests of loyalty to the Throne. If it be true that H.R.H. the Duke of Connaught is going out as the next Viceroy, I can only say that the longer his admirers miss him in England, the better for India, which requires its best interests to be grouped round a permanent Chief.

Dec. 7th.—As for the wanton aggression on Chilás which never gave us the least trouble, as all our Deputy Commissioners of Abbottabad can testify, it is a sequel of our interference last year with Hunza-Nagyr. The Gilgit Residency has disturbed a peace that has existed since 1856 and now continues in its suicidal policy of indicating and paving the nearest military road to British territory to an invader. In November 1891 I wrote of the possibility of driving even the peaceful, if puritanical, Chilásis into aggression and now the *Times* telegraphs the cock-and-bull story of the raft, enlarged in to-day's *Times* telegram into an attack of the Chilási tribesmen aided by those of Darêl (another newly-created foe) on our convoy proceeding from Bunji—the extreme frontier of Kashmir according to the treaty of 1846—to Dr. Robertson's Camp at (now) Talpenn (spelt "Thalpin" in the telegram) and (then) Gôr, with, of course, the inevitable result of the victory of the heroism of rifles against a few old muskets and iron wrist-bands (which the Chilásis use in fighting).

There are still other realms to conquer for our heroes. There is the small Republic of Talitsha of 11 houses; there is Chilás itself which admits women to the tribal Councils and is thus in advance even of the India Office and of the Supreme Council of the Government of India; there is the Republic of Muhammadan learning, Kandiá, that has not a single fort; there is, of course, pastoral Dareyl; there are the Koli-Palus tribes, agricultural Tangîr and other little Republics. Soon may we hear of acts of "treachery," "disloyalty," etc. from Hôdur and Sazîn, till we shoot down the supposed offenders with Gatlings and destroy the survivors with our civilization. I humbly protest against these tribes being sacrificed to a mistaken Russophobia. I have some claim to be heard. I discovered and named Dardistan and am a friend of its peoples. Although my life was attempted more than once by agents of the Maharaja of Kashmir, I was the means of saving that of his Commander-in-Chief, Zoraweru, when on his Dareyl expedition. This is what the Gilgit Doctor did in 1866 and what the Gilgit Doctor should do in 1892. This is how friendship for the British name was, and should be, cemented, and not by shedding innocent blood or by acts worthy of *agents provocateurs.*

As for the "*toujours perdrix*" of the Afghan advance from Asmár (*Times*, December 8th) it is better than the telegram in the *Standard* of the 2nd December 1892, in which the Amir makes Sher Afzul Ruler of Kafiristan, a country that has yet to be conquered, and which says "Consequently there is now no buffer-state between Afghanistan and the Pamirs"!! "Goods carried from India to Russian Turkestan, through Chitrál and *Kafiristan*, will pay *duty to the Amir.*" Such journalistic forecasts and geography are inevitable when full and faithful official information, such as it is, is, in a free country, not obtainable by Parliament, the Press, and the Public. Reuter's Central Asian Telegrams, though meagre, are more correct than those of certain correspondents of the *Times* and *Standard.*

Dec. 9th.—Dr. Robertson has, at last, entered Chilás, and found it deserted. *Solitudinem faciunt, pacem appellant.* The *Times* Correspondent now admits that Chilás has no connexion with Chitrál, but he still gives us "Tangail" for "Tangir," and omits the name of the member of the ex-royal family of Yasin, who is supposed to have stirred up against us the tribes of Darel and "Tangail," among whom he has resided for years. This is one of the Khushwaqtias, though not the loyal chief to whom I have referred, and who has rendered us good service. So we have now an excuse for entering Tangir also. In the meanwhile, the Russian *Svet* points out that the Russians "would only have to march some 250 miles along a good road to enter Cashmere," "since it is impossible to invade India viâ Afghanistan." Yet are we nibbling at the Amir

Abdurrahman, whose troops merely occupy the *status quo ante* at Asmar, confronted by Umra Khan on the other side of the Kuner river. We are forgetting the lessons of the Afghan campaigns, and especially that, although Abdurrahman allowed himself to be proclaimed by us, in his absence, as Amir, he marched in at one side of Kabul, whilst we marched out at the other. We forget that, with the whole country against us in a revived Jehád, with the discontent among our native troops and with a crushing expenditure, we preferred a political fiasco in order to avoid a still greater military fiasco. The Russians also urge "the construction of a military road on their side from Marghelan across the Pamirs" leaving us to finish it for them on our side of the Hindukush. The pretension to Wakhan, however, is already disposed of in Prince Gortchakoff's Convention with Lord Granville in 1872, and no notice need be taken of the preposterous claim of the *Svet* to place Chitrál under a Russian protectorate! Thus have we sown the wind and reaped the whirlwind. Our real defence of India lies, as Lord Lawrence ever held, in its good government, and to this I would respectfully add, in justice to its Chiefs, wherever they have a legitimate grievance. Mere speeches of Viceroys, unaccompanied by acts, will not convince them of our "good intentions." It is also not by emasculating the Dard tribes and breaking down their powers of resistance to the level of Slaves to the British, that we can interpose an effectual barrier to the invading Myriads of Slavs that threaten the world's freedom. By giving to the loyalty of India the liberty which it deserves, on the indigenous bases that it alone really understands and in accordance with the requirements of the age, we can alone lead our still martial Indian Millions in the defence of the Roman Citizenship which should be the reward of their chivalrous allegiance to the Queen.

G. W. LEITNER.

P.S.—15 Dec. 1892. The just cause of Nizám-ul-Mulk appears to have triumphed. Sher Afzul is said to have fled. So far Chitrál. As for Chilás, the people have come to Dr. Robertson's Camp and express friendliness.

LETTERS FROM MIHTAR NIZAM-UL-MULK TO DR. LEITNER:

My kind and true friend and dear companion, may you know:

That before this, prompted by excess of friendship and belief in me, you had written to me a letter of sincerity full of pleasing precepts and words of faithfulness. These were received and caused joy to my heart. My true friend, whatever words of faith and sincere regard there were, these have been written in my mind. For I am one of your disciples and well-wishers here, and have no other care but that of serving and well-wishing my friends. My heart sorrows at separation from friends, but there is no remedy except resignation. *As I consider your stay there [in London] as my own stay, I hope from your friendship that you have expressed words of my well-being and my sincerity towards the Lord Bahadoor and the Great Queen and thus performed the office of friendship and caused joy there.* Another request is that if you have found a good dog like "Zulu," when you come to Delhi please send it to Jummoo. My men are there, and shall bring it to me. Further, the volume of papers on the customs of Chitrár and the old folk-tales have been written partly in Persian and partly in the Chitrári language. We are frontier and village people, and are deficient in intelligence and eloquence. They have not been very well done, and I don't know if they will please you or not. But we have no better eloquence or practice as we are hillmen.

Tuesday 11th Shavval 1304 despatched from Turikoh to London.

The standard of affection and friendship, the foundation-stone of kindness and obligation, my friend, may his kindness increase!

After expressing the desire of your joy-giving meeting be it known to your kind self, that the condition of *this* your faithful friend is such as to call for thanks to the Almighty. The safety and good health of *that* friend [yourself] is always wished for. As you had sent me several volumes of bound papers to write on them the customs of the Chitrar people and their folk-tales, partly in Persian and partly in Chitrari language, I have in accordance with this request of *that* true friend got them written partly in Persian and partly in Chitrari and sent to you. Inshallah, they will reach you, but I do not know whether they will please you or not; in any case you know, that whatever may be possible to do by a faithful friend or by his employés I will do, with the help of God, if you will forgive any faulty execution of your wishes, and continue to remember me for any services in my power, and keep me informed continually of your good health so as to dispel my anxiety. The condition here is of all news the best, as no new event has happened; but three persons, wayfarers and travellers, have come from Wakhan to Mastuch and two of these persons I have sent on to Chitrar, and one of these wanderers has remained (behind) at Mastuch. They don't know anybody. Sometimes they say we are Russians, and sometimes they say we are Frenchmen. And I with my own eye have not seen them. If I had seen them, they might have told me. Another desire is that you send me something worth reading in English words and write opposite to them their translation into Persian, so that it may be a pleasure and useful to me. I have another request to make which is that you may be pleased to give an early fulfilment to your kind promise of visiting Chitrar with your lady for the purpose of sight-seeing and sport and study. I have been waiting ever since for your arrival. It is really only right that you should come now when the weather is very delightful, game is abundant, and I have made every arrangement for our hunting together. Everything is tranquil and you will be able to return before the winter, greatly pleased. Let this become a fact. The writer Sirdar Nizam-ul-Mulk, Tuesday the 11th of Shevvál, from Turikoh to London. May it be received!

APPENDIX III.

FABLES, LEGENDS, AND SONGS OF CHITRAL *

(called Chitrár by the natives).

Collected by H. H. SIRDAR NIZÁM-UL-MULK, Raja of Yasin, etc., and by Dr. G. W. LEITNER, and translated from Persian or Chitráli.

I. FABLES.

1. THE VINDICTIVE FOWL.

A FOWL sat near a thistle, and opened a rag, in which corals were tied up. Suddenly one fell into the thistle; the fowl said, "O thistle, give me my coral." The thistle said, "This is not my business." The fowl said, "Then I will burn thee.". The thistle agreed. The fowl then begged the fire to burn the thistle. The fire replied, "Why should I burn this weak thorn?" The fowl thereupon threatened to extinguish the fire by appealing to water: "O water, kill this fire for my sake." The water asked, "What is thy enmity with the fire, that I should kill it?" The fowl said, "I will bring a lean cow to drink thee up." The water said, "Well"; but the cow refused, as it was too lean and weak to do so. Then the fowl threatened to bring the wolf to eat the cow. The wolf refused, as he could feed better on fat sheep. The fowl threatened the wolf with the huntsman, as he would not eat the lean cow. The huntsman refused to shoot the wolf, as it was not fit to eat. The fowl then threatened the huntsman with the mouse. The huntsman replied, "Most welcome." But the mouse said that it was feeding on almonds and other nice things, and had no need to gnaw the leather-skin of the huntsman. The fowl then said, "I will tell the cat to eat thee." The mouse said, "The cat is my enemy in any case, and

* *Asiatic Quarterly Review*, January, 1891.

will try to catch and eat me, wherever it comes across me, so what is the use of your telling the cat?" The fowl then begged the cat to eat the mouse. The cat agreed to do so whenever it was hungry: "Now," it added, "I do not care to do so." The fowl then became very angry, and threatened to bring little boys to worry the cat. The cat said, "Yes." The fowl then begged the little boys to snatch the cat one from the other, so that it might know what it was to be vexed. The boys, however, just then wanted to play and fight among themselves, and did not care to interrupt their own game. The fowl then threatened to get an old man to beat the boys. The boys said, "By all means." But the old man refused to beat the boys without any cause, and called the fowl a fool. The fowl then said to the Pîr (old man), "I will tell the wind to carry away thy wool." The old man acquiesced; and the wind, when ordered by the fowl, with its usual perverseness, obeyed the fowl, and carried off the old man's wool. Then the old man beat the boys, and the boys worried the cat, and the cat ran after the mouse, and the mouse bit the huntsman in the waist, and the huntsman went after the wolf, and the wolf bit the cow, and the cow drank the water, and the water came down on the fire, and the fire burnt the thistle, and the thistle gave the coral to the fowl, and the fowl took back its coral.

---

2. The Story of the Golden Mouse who tells the Story of a Mouse and a Frog.

There was a kind of mice that had a golden body. They never went out of their hole. One day one of them thought: "I will go out and see the wonders of God's creation." So it did; and when thirty or forty yards from its hole, a cat, prowling for game, saw it come out from the hole. The cat, that was full of wiles, plotted to get near the hole, awaiting the return of the mouse, who, after its peregrinations, noticed the mouth of the hole closed by the wicked cat. The mouse then wished to go another way, and turned to the left, towards a tree, on which sat concealed a crow, expecting to devour the mouse when it should run away from the cat. The crow then pounced on the mouse, who cried out to God, "O God, why have these misfortunes overtaken such a small being as myself? My only help is in thee, to save me from these calamities." The mouse was confused, and ran hither and thither, in vain seeking a refuge, when it saw another cat stealthily approaching it; and, in its perplexity, the mouse nearly ran into the cat's paws; but that cat had been caught in a hunter's net, and could do nothing. The crow, and the cat which was watching at the hole, saw that the mouse had got near another cat between the two. They thought that the mouse had fallen a victim to the second cat, and that it was no use remaining. It was the fortune of the mouse that they should be so deceived. The trembling mouse saw that the two enemies had gone. It thanked the Creator for having escaped from the cat and the crow, and it said, "It would be most unmanly of me not to deliver the cat in the net, as it has been the instrument of my safety; but then, if I set it free, it will eat me." The mouse was immersed in thought, and came to the conclusion to gnaw the net at a distance from the cat, and that as soon as the hunter should come in sight, the cat then, being afraid of the hunter, would seek its own safety, and not trouble itself about the mouse. "Thus I will free the cat from the hunter and the net, and deliver my own life from the cat," was the thought of the mouse. It then began to gnaw the net at a distance. The cat then said to the mouse, "If you want to save me, for God's sake, then gnaw the net round my throat, and not at a distance; that is no use to me when the hunter will come. You err if you think that I will eat you as soon as I get out. For all the faults, hitherto, have been on the side of cats, which you mice have never injured, so that, if you are magnanimous and release me, there is no such ungrateful monster in the world as would return evil for the unmerited good that I implore you to bestow on me." The golden mouse, which was very wise, did not attend to this false speech, but continued to gnaw the net at a distance, so that, when the hunter came, there only remained the threads round the neck of the cat, which the mouse bit asunder at the last moment and then ran back into its hole. The cat bolted up the tree where the crow had sat, the huntsman saw that the cat had escaped, and that his net was gnawed in several places, so he took the net to get it repaired in the Bazaar.

Then the cat descended from the tree and said to herself, "The time of meals is over, it is no use to go home; I had better make friends with the mouse, entice it out of the hole, and eat it." This she did, and going to the hole, called out: "O faithful companion and sympathizing friend, although there has been enmity between cats and mice for a long time, thou hast, by God's order, been the cause of my release, therefore come out of the hole, and let us lay the foundation of our friendship." The mouse replied: "I once tried to come out, and then I fell from one danger into another. Now it is difficult for me to comply with your request. I have cut the threads encircling your throat, not out of friendship for you, but out of gratitude to God. Nor is our friendship of any use in this world, as you will gather from the story of

3. "The Frog and the Mouse."

The mouse then narrated: "There was once a mouse that went out for a promenade, and going into people's houses, found food here and there, and in the dawn of the next morning it was returning to its home. It came to a place where there was a large tank, round which there were flowers and trees; and a voice was heard from out of the tank. Coming near, it saw that it emanated from a being that had no hair on its body, no tail, and no ear. The mouse said to itself: 'What is this ill-formed being?' and thanked God that it was not the ugliest of creatures. With this thought the mouse, that was standing still, shook its head to and fro. The frog, however, thought that the mouse was smitten with astonishment at his beauty and entranced with pleasure at his voice, and jumping out of the corner of the tank came near: 'I know, beloved, that you are standing charmed with my voice; we ought to lay the firm basis of our friendship, but you are sharper than I am, therefore go to the house of an old woman and steal from it a thread, and bring it here.' The mouse obeyed the order. The frog then said: 'Now tie one end to your tail and I will tie the other end to my leg, because I want to go to your house, where you have a large family and there are many other mice, so that I may know you from the others. If again you visit me, the tank is large, my friends many, and you too ought to distinguish me from the rest. Again, when I want to see you I will follow the thread to your hole, and when you want to see me you will follow it to the tank.' This being settled, they parted. One day the frog wanted to see the mouse. Coming out of the tank he was going to its hole, when he saw the mouse-hawk, who pounced upon the frog as he was limping along, and flew up with him in its claws. This pulled the end to which the mouse was tied. It thought that its lover had come to the place and wanted to see it; so it came out, only to be dragged along in the air under the mouse-hawk. As the unfortunate mouse passed a Bazaar it called out: 'O ye Mussulmans, learn from my fate what happens to whoever befriends beings of a different species.'

"Now," said the golden mouse to the cat, "this is the story which teaches me what to do; and that is, to decline your friendship and to try never again to see your face.

---

4. The Quail and the Fox.

The Quail said: I teach thee art.
Night and day I work at art;
Whoever lies, the shame is on his neck.

A quail and a fox were friends. The fox said: "Why should you not make me laugh some day?" The quail replied, "This is easy." So they went to a Bazaar, where the quail, looking through the hole in the wall of a house, saw a man sitting, and his wife turning up and down the "samanak" sweetmeat with a big wooden ladle (much in the same way as the Turkish *rakat lokum*, or lumps of delight, are made). The quail then settled on the head of the man. The woman said to him, "Don't stir; I will catch it." Then the quail sat on the woman's head, so the man asked the woman to be quiet, as he would catch the quail, which, however, then flew back to the head of the man. This annoyed the wife, who struck at the quail with the wooden ladle, but hit instead the face of her husband, whose eye and beard were covered with the sweetmeat, and who thereupon beat his wife. When the fox saw this, he rejoiced and laughed greatly; and both the fox and quail returned to their home. After a time the fox said to the quail: "It is true that you have made me laugh, but could you feed me?" This the quail undertook to do, and with the fox went to a place where a woman was carrying a plate of loaves of bread to her husband in the fields. Then the quail repeated her tactics, and sat on the head of the woman, who tried to catch it with one hand. The quail escaped and settled on one shoulder, then on another, and so on till the woman became enraged, put the plate of bread on the ground, and ran after the quail, who, by little leaps, attracted her further and further away till she was at a considerable distance from it, when the fox pounced on the bread and appeased his hunger.

Some time after, the fox wanted to put the cleverness of the quail again to the test, and said: "You have made me laugh, you have fed me, now make me weep." The quail replied, "Why, this is the easiest task of all," so she took the fox to the gate of the town and called out: "O ye dogs of the Bazaar, come ye as many as ye are, for a fox has come to the gate!" So all the dogs, hearing this good news, assembled to hunt the fox, which, seeing the multitude of its enemies, fled till he reached a high place. Turning round, he saw the dogs following, so he jumped down and broke his back. The fox therefore helplessly sat down and said to the approaching quail: "O sympathizing companion, see how my mouth has become filled with mud and blood, and how my back has been broken. This is my fate in this world; now, could you kindly clean my mouth from mud and blood, as my end is near?" The intention of the fox was, that he should take the opportunity of this artifice to swallow the quail in revenge of her being the cause of its death. The quail, in her unwise friendship, began to clean the fox's mouth. The accursed fox caught her in his mouth; but the quail, which was intelligent and clever, said, "O beloved friend, your eating me is lawful, because I forgive you my blood, on condition that you pronounce my name, otherwise you will suffer an injury." The base fox, although full of wiles, clouded by approaching death, fell into the trap, and as soon as he said "O quail," his teeth separated, and the quail flew away from him and was safe, whilst the fox died.

II. Stories and Legends.

There is a story which seems to illustrate the fact that private hatred is often the cause of the injury that is ascribed to accident A man slaughtered a goat, and kept it over-night in an outhouse. His enemy put a number of cats through the airhole, and when their noise awoke the master of the house he only found the bones of his goat. But he took their bones, and scattered them over the field of his enemy the same night; and the dogs came, smelling the bones, searched for them, and destroyed the wheat that was ripe for reaping. One blamed the cats, the other blamed the dogs; but both had the reward of their own actions.

Sulei was a man well known on the frontier of Chitrál for his eloquence. One day, as he was travelling, he met a man from Badakhshan, who asked him whether he knew Persian. Sulei said, "No." "Then," replied the Badakhshi, "you are lost" [nobody, worthless]. Sulei at once rejoined, "Do you know Khowár?" (the language of Chitrál). "No," said the Badakhshi. "Then you too are lost," wittily concluded Sulei (to show that personal worth or eloquence does not depend on knowing any particular language).

It is related that beyond Upper Chitrár there is a country called *Shin* or Rashan. It is very beautiful, and its plains are gardens, and its trees bear much fruit, and its chunars (plane trees) and willows make it a shaded land. Its earth is red, and its water is white and tasty. They say that in ancient times the river of that district for a time flowed with milk without the dashing (of the waves) of water.

Besir is a place near Ayin towards Kafiristan. The inhabitants were formerly savage Kafirs, but are now subjects of the Mehter (Prince) of Chitrár. They carry loads of wood, and do not neglect the work of the Mehter. They are numerous and peaceful, and in helplessness like fowls, but they are still Kafirs; though in consequence of their want of energy and courage they are called "Kalàsh." The people of Ayin say that in ancient times five savages fled into the Shidi Mount and concealed themselves there.

Shidi is below Ayin opposite Gherát on the east (whence Shidi is on the west). Between them is a river. It is said that these savages had to get their food by the chase. One day word came to them from God that "today three troops of deer will pass; don't interfere with the first, but do so with the others." When, however, the troops came, the savages forgot the injunctions of God, and struck the first deer. Now there was a cavern in the mountain where they lived, into which they took the two or three deer that they had killed and were preparing to cook, two being sent out to fetch water. By God's order the lips of the cavern were closed, and the three men imprisoned in it. God converted the three into bees, whilst the two who had gone to fetch water fled towards Afghanistan. Thus were created the first honey-bees, who, finding their way out of the cavern, spread themselves and their sweet gift all over the world. This is a story told by the Kalàsh, who credit that the bees are there still; but it is difficult to get there, as the mountains are too steep, but people go near it and, pushing long rods into the hole of the cavern, bring them back covered with honey.

Shah Muhterim is the name of a Mehter (prince), the grandfather of the present Ruler of Chitrár. This Mehter was renowned as a descendant of fairies, who all were under his command. Whatever he ordered the fairies did. Thus some time passed. From among them he married a fairy, with whom he made many excursions. She bore him a daughter. Seven generations have passed since that time. This daughter is still alive, and her sign among the fairies is that her hair is white, which does not happen to ordinary fairies. Whenever a descendant of the Shah Muhterim leaves this transitory world for the region of permanence, all the fairies, who reside in the mountains of Chitrár, together with that white-haired lady, weep and lament, and their voices are clearly heard. This statement is sure and true, and all the men on the frontiers of Chitrár are aware of the above fact.

The People of Aujer (the Bœotia of Chitral).

There is a country "Aujer," on the frontier of Chitrár (or Chitrāl as we call it), the inhabitants of which in ancient times were renowned for their stupidity. One had taken service at Chitrár, and at a certain public dinner noticed that the King (Padishah) ate nothing. So he thought that it was because the others had not given anything to the king. This made him very sorry. He left the assembly, and reached home towards evening; there he prepared a great amount of bread, and brought it next day to the council enclosure, beckoning to the king with his finger to come secretly to him. The king could not make this out, and sent a servant to inquire what was the matter; but the man would not say anything except that the king should come himself. On this the king sent his confidant to find out what all this meant. The man answered the inquiries of the confidant by declaring that he had no news or claim, but "as they all ate yesterday and gave nothing to the king, my heart has become burnt, and I have cooked all this bread for him." The messenger returned and told the king, who told the meeting, causing them all to laugh. The king, too, smiled, and said: "As this poor man has felt for my need, I feel for his;" and ordered the treasurer to open for him the door of the treasury, so that he might take from it what he liked. The treasurer took him to the gate, next to which was the treasurer's own house, where he had put a big water-melon, on which fell the eye of that stupid man from Aujer. He had never seen such a thing, and when he asked, "What is it?" the treasurer, knowing what a fool he had to deal with, said, "This is the egg of a donkey." Then he showed him the gold, silver, jewels, precious cloths, and clean habiliments of the treasury from which to select the king's present. The man was pleased with nothing, and said, "I do not want this; but, if you please, give me the egg of the donkey, then I shall indeed be glad." The treasurer and the king's confidant, consulting together, came to the conclusion that this would amuse the king to hear, and gave him the melon, with the injunction not to return to the king, but to take the egg to his house, and come after some nights (days). The fool was charmed with this request, went towards his home, but climbing a height, the melon fell out of his hand, rolled down towards a tree and broke in two pieces. Now there was a hare under that tree, which fled as the melon touched the tree. The fool went to his house full of grief, said nothing to his wife and children, but sat mournfully in a corner. The wife said, "O man, why art thou sorry? and what has happened?" The man replied: "Why do you ask? there is no necessity." Finally, on the woman much cajoling him, he said: "From the treasury of the prince (mehter) I had brought the egg of the donkey; it fell from me on the road, broke, and the young one fled out from its midst. I tried my utmost, but could not catch it." The woman said: "You silly fellow! had you brought it, we might have put loads on it." The man replied, "You flighty thing! how could it do so, when it was still so young? Why, its back would have been broken." So he got into a great rage, took his axe, and cut down his wife, who died on the spot.

Once, a donkey having four feet, in this country of donkeys having two feet, put his head into a jar of jáo (barley), but could not extricate it again. So the villagers assembled, but could not hit on a plan to effect this result. But there was a wise man in that land, and he was sent for and came. He examined all the circumstances of the case, and finally decided that they should do him Bismillah"; that is to say, that they should cut his throat with the formula, "in the name of God," which makes such an act lawful. When they had done this to the poor donkey, the head remained in the jar, and the wise man ordered them now to break the jar. This they did, and brought out the head of the donkey. The wise man then said: "If I had not been here, in what manner could you have been delivered of this difficulty?" This view was approved by all, even by the owner of the donkey.

Two brothers in that country of idiots, being tired of buying salt every day, decided on sowing it over their fields, so that it may bring forth salt abundantly. The grass grew up, and the grasshoppers came; and the brothers, fearing that their crop of salt would be destroyed, armed themselves with bows and arrows to kill the grasshoppers. But the grasshoppers jumped hither and thither, and were difficult to kill; and one of the brothers hit the other by mistake with an arrow instead of a grasshopper, and he got angry, and shot back and killed his brother.

A penknife once fell into the hands of this people, so they held a council in order to consider what it was. Some thought it was the young one of a sword, the others that it was the baby of an axe, but that its teeth had not yet come out. So the argument waxing hot, they fell to fight one another, and many were wounded and killed.

A number of these people, considering that it was not proper that birds alone should fly, and that they were able to do so, clad themselves in posteens (some of which are made from the light down of the Hindukush eagle), and threw themselves down from a great height, with the result that they reached the ground killed and mangled.

III. Songs.

A Song (of evidently recent date, as the influence on it of Persian poetry is obvious).

The Confession of the Soul.

1. (*He.*) If thy body be as lithe as (the letter) Alif (ا),
   thy eye is as full as (the letter) Nûn (ن).
   If thou art Laila, this child (or lover) is Majnûn (referring to the well-known story of these true lovers).
2. (*She.*) If thou art the Prince of the Sultan of Rûm (Turkey)
   Come and sit by me, free from constraint;
   My eye has fallen on thee, and I now live.
3. My friend had scarcely come near me—why, alas, has he left?
   My flesh has melted from these broken limbs.
4. How could I guard against the enmity of a friend?
   May God now save me from such grief!

5. (*He.*) Were I to see 200 Fairies and 100,000 Houris,
I should be a Káfir (infidel), O my beloved!
If my thoughts then even strayed from thee.
6. Yea, not the Houri nightingale, nor my own soul and eyes as Houris,
Would, on the day of judgment, divert my thought from thee.
7. I envy the moth, for it can fly
Into the fire in which it is burnt (whereas I cannot meet thee).
8. (*She.*) My friend, who once came nigh me, suddenly left me—to weep.
My grief should move the very highest heaven.
A coral bed with its root has been torn out and gone.
9. A ship of pilgrims (Calendárs) has suṇk, and yet the world does not care.
The end of all has been a bad name to me.
10. (*He.*) On this black earth how can I do (sing) thy praise?
Imbedded in the blue heaven (of my heart) thou wilt find it;
And yet, O child (himself), how great a failure (and below thy merits)!
11. Before thy beauty the very moon is nothing,
For sometimes she is full and sometimes half.
May God give thee to me, my perfect universe!
12. (*She.*) If an angel were a mortal like myself,
It would be ashamed to see my fate (unmoved).
13. (*He.*) O angel! strangely without pity,
Thou hast written her good with my evil (linked our fates).
14. (*Both.*) All have friends, but my friend is the Chief (God),
And of my inner grief that friend is cognizant;
His light alone loves our eyes and soul.
15. Break with the world, its vanities, its love;
Leave ignorance, confess, and let thy goal be heaven!

The following is an attempt to render the pretty tune of a more worldly Laila and Majnûn song, which reminds one of the "Yodeln" of the Tyrolese. It was sung to me by Taighûn Shah, the poet-minstrel of the Raja, to the accompaniment of a kind of guitar. The Çhitráli language, it will be perceived, is musical.

APPENDIX IV.

GROUP OF DARDS AND CENTRAL ASIATICS WITH DR. LEITNER.

Standing Nos. 1 2 3 4 5 6 (*see next page.*)

Sitting Nos. 7 8 9 10 11 (*see next page.*)

Standing—1. Khundayár, son of a Shiah Akhun (priest) at Nagyr; 2. Maulvi Najmuddin, a poet from Koláb; 3 and 4. Khudádád and Hatámu, pilgrims from Nagyr; 5. A Chitráli soldier; 6. Matavalli, of Hunza.

Sitting—7. Mir Abdullah, a famous Arabic scholar and jurist from Gabriál; 8. Hakim Habibullah, a Tájik, a physician from Badakhshán; 9. Ghulam Muhammad, Dr. Leitner's Gilgit retainer; 10. Ibrahim Khan, a Shiah, Rôno (highest official caste), of Nagyr; 11. Sultan Ali Yashkun, of Nagyr.

APPENDIX IV.

THE RACES AND LANGUAGES OF THE HINDU-KUSH.

By Dr. G. W. Leitner.

The accompanying illustration was autotyped some years ago from a photograph taken in 1881, and is now published for the first time. Following the numbers on each figure represented we come first to No. 1, the tall Khudayár, the son of an Akhun or Shiah priest of Nagyr, a country ruled by the old and wise Tham or Raja Zafar Ali Khan, whose two sons, Alidád Khan in 1866, and Habib ulla Khan in 1886, instructed me in the Khajuná language, which is spoken alike in gentle but brave Nagyr and in its hereditary rival country, the impious and savage Hunza "Hun-land," represented by figure 6, Matavalli, the ex-kidnapper whom I took to England, trained to some Muhammadan piety, and sent to Kerbalá a year ago. No. 2 was an excellent man, an Uzbek visitor from Koláb, one Najmuddin, a poet and theologian, who gave me an account of his country. Nos. 3 and 4 are pilgrims from Nagyr to the distant Shiah shrine in Syria of the martyrdom of Husain at Kerbelá; No. 5 is a Chitráli soldier, whilst No. 7 is a distinguished Arabic Scholar from Gabriál, from whom much of my information was derived regarding a peaceful and learned home, now, alas! threatened by European approach, which my travels in 1866 and 1872, and my sympathetic intercourse with the tribes of the Hindu Kush, have unfortunately facilitated. The Jalkóti, Dareyli, and others, who are referred to in the course of the present narrative, will either figure on other illustrations or must be "taken as read." No. 8 is the Sunni Moulvi Habibulla, a Tájik of Bukhara and a Hakîm (physician). No. 9 is my old retainer, Ghulám Muhammad, a Shiah of Gilgit, a Shîn Dard (highest caste), who was prevented by me from cutting down his mother, which he was attempting to do in order "to save her the pain of parting from him." 10. Ibrahim Khan, a Shiah, Rôno (highest official caste) of *Nagyr*, pilgrim to Kerbelá. 11. Sultan Ali Yashkun (2nd Shîn caste) Shiah, of Nagyr, pilgrim to Kerbelá. The word "Yashkun" is, perhaps, connected with "Yuechi."

The languages spoken by these men are: Khajuná by the Hunza-Nagyr men; Arnyiá by the Chitráli; Turki by the Uzbek from Koláb; Shiná by the Gilgiti; Pakhtu and Shuthun, a dialect of Shiná, by the Gabriáli. The people of *Hunza* are dreaded robbers and kidnappers; they, together with the people of Nagyr, speak a language, Khajuná, which philologists have not yet been able to classify, but which I believe to be a remnant of a pre-historic language. They are great wine-drinkers and most licentious. They are nominally Muláis, a heresy within the Shiah schism from the orthodox Sunni Muhammadan faith, but they really only worship their Chief or Raja, commonly called "Thàm." The present ruler's name is Mohammad Khan. They are at constant feud with the people of *Nagyr*, who have some civilization, and are *now* devoted Shiahs (whence the number of pilgrims, four, from one village). They are generally fair, and taller than the people of Hunza, who are described as dark skeletons. The Nagyris have fine embroideries, and are said to be accomplished musicians. Their forts confront those of Hunza on the other side of the same river. The people of *Badakhshán* used to deal largely in kidnapped slaves. A refugee, Shahzada Hasan, from the former royal line (which claims descent from Alexander the Great), who has been turned out by the Afghan faction, was then at Gilgit with a number of retainers on fine Badakhshi horses, awaiting the fortunes of war, or, perhaps, the support of the British. He was a younger brother of Jehandár Shah, who used to infest the Koláb road, after being turned out by a relative, Mahmûd Shah, with the help of the Amir of Kabul. *Koláb* is about eleven marches from *Faizabád*, the capital of Badakhshán. The Chitráli is from Shogòt, the residence of Adam Khor (man-eater), brother of Aman-ul-Mulk, of Chitrál, who used to sell his Shiah subjects regularly into slavery and to kidnap Bashgeli Kafirs. The man from *Gabriál* was attracted to Lahore by the fame of the Oriental College, Lahore, as were also several others in this group; and there can be no doubt that this institution may still serve as a nucleus for sending pioneers of our civilization throughout Central Asia. Gabriál is a town in Kandiá, or Kiliá, which is a secluded Dard country, keeping itself aloof from tribal wars. *Gilgit* and its representative have been described in my "Dardistan," to which refer, published in parts between 1866 and 1877.

I POLO IN HUNZA-NAGYR.

ALTHOUGH our first practical knowledge of "Polo" was derived from the Manipuri game as played at Calcutta, it is not Manipur, but Hunza and Nagyr, that maintain the original rules of the ancient "Chaughán-bazi," so famous in Persian history. The account given by J. Moray Brown for the "Badminton Library" of the introduction of Polo into England (Longmans, Green & Co., 1891), seems to me to be at variance with the facts within my knowledge, for it was introduced into England in 1867, not 1869, by one who had played the Tibetan game as brought to Lahore by me in 1866, after a tour in Middle and Little Tibet. Since then it has become acclimatized not only in England, but also in Europe. The Tibet game, however, does not reach the perfection of the Nagyr game, although it seems to be superior to that of Manipur. Nor is Polo the only game in Hunza-Nagyr. "Shooting whilst galloping" at a gourd filled with ashes over a wooden scaffold rivals the wonderful performances of "archery on horseback," in which the people of Hunza and Nagyr (not "Nagar," or the common Hindi word for "town," as the telegram has it) are so proficient. Nor are European accompaniments wanting to these Central Asian games; for prizes are awarded, people bet freely in Hunza as they do here, they drink as freely, listen to music, and witness the dancing of lady charmers, the Dayál, who, in Hunza, are supposed to be sorceresses, without whom great festivities lose their main attraction. The people are such keen sportsmen that it is not uncommon for the Tham, or ruler, to confiscate the house of the unskilful hunter who has allowed a Markhôr (Ibex) that he might have shot to escape him. Indeed, this even happens when a number of Markhôrs are shut up in an enclosure, "*tsá*," as a preserve for hunting. The following literally translated dialogue regarding Polo and its rules tells an attentive reader more "between the lines" than pages of instructions:—

POLÓ=Bolá.—The Raja has ordered many people: To-morrow Polo I will play. To the musicians give notice they will play.

Hast thou given notice, O (thou)?

Yes, I have given notice, O Nazúr; let me be thy offering (sacrifice).

Well, we will come out, that otherwise it will become (too) hot.

The Raja has gone out for Polo; go ye, O (ye); the riders will start.

Now divided will be, O ye! (2) goals nine nine (games) we will do (play). Tola-half (=4 Rupees) a big sheep bet we will do.

Now bet we have made. To the Raja the *ball* give, O ye, *striking* (whilst galloping) he will take.

O ye, efforts (search) make, young men, to a man disgrace is death; you your own *party* abandon not; The Raja has taken the *ball to strike;* play up, O ye musicians!

Now descend (from your horses) O ye; Tham has come out (victorious); now again the day after to-morrow, he (from fatigue) *recovering Poló* we will strike (play).

Rules:—The musical instruments of Polo; the ground for the game; the riders; the goals; 9, 9 games let be (nine games won); the riders nine one side; nine one (the other) side; when this has become (the case) the drum (Tsagàr) they will strike.

First the Tham takes the ball (out into the Maidan to strike whilst galloping at full speed).

The Tham's *side* upper part will take.

The rest will strike from the lower part (of the ground).

Those above the goal when becoming will take to the lower part.

Those below the goal when becoming to above taking the ball will send it flying.

Thus being (or becoming) whose goal when becoming, the ball will be sent flying and the musicians will play.

Whose nine goals when has become, they issue (victorious).

No. 1. Dareyli.

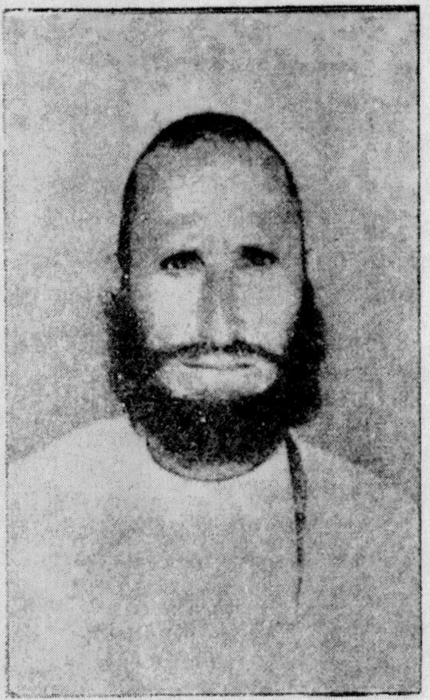

No. 2. Gabriáli.

No. 3. Hunza man.

No. 4. Nagyri.

II. THE KOHISTÁN OF THE INDUS, INCLUDING GABRIÁL.

Account of Mir Abdulla.

THE real native place of Mir Abdulla is in the territory of Nandiyar; but his uncle migrated to, and settled in, Gabriál. The Mir narrates:—

"In the country of Kunar there is a place called *Pusht*, where lives a Mulla who is famous for his learning and sanctity. I lived for a long time as his pupil, studying Logic, Philosophy, and Muhammadan Law, the subjects in which the Mulla was particularly proficient. When my absence from my native place became too long, I received several letters and messages from my parents, asking me to give up my studies and return home. At last I acceded to their pressing demands and came to my native village. There I stayed for a long time with my parents; but as I was always desirous to pursue my studies, I was meditating on my return to Pusht, or to go down to India.

In the meantime I met one Abdulquddūs of Kohistan, who was returning from India. He told me that a Dár-ul-u'lûm (House of Sciences) had been opened at Lahore, the capital of the Punjab, where every branch of learning was taught, and that it was superintended by Dr. L., who being himself a proficient scholar of Arabic and Persian, was a patron of learning and a warm supporter of students from foreign countries. I was accompanied by two pupils of mine, named Sher Muhammad and Burhánuddin; and I started together with them from my native village. We passed through the territory of *Dir*, which is governed by Nawab Rahmatulla Khan. The Qazi of that place was an old acquaintance of mine, and he persuaded me to stop my journey, and promised to introduce me to the Nawab, and procure for me a lucrative and honourable post. I declined his offer, and continued my journey. The next territory we entered in was that of Nawab *Tore Mian Khan*, who reigns over eight or nine hundred people. After staying there some days we reached *Kanan Ghárin*, which was governed jointly by Nawabs Fazl Ahmad and Bayazid Khan. After two days' march we came to *Chakesur*, which was under a petty chief named Suhe Khan. Here we were told that there are two roads to India from this place—one, which is the shorter, is infested with robbers; and the other, the longer one, is safe; but we were too impatient to waste our time, and decided at once to go by the shorter way, and proceeded on our journey. We met, as we were told, two robbers on the road, who insisted on our surrendering to them all our baggage. But we made up our minds to make a stand, though we were very imperfectly armed, having only one "tamancha" among three persons. In the conflict which ensued, one of the robbers fell, and the other escaped; but Burhanuddin, one of our party, was also severely wounded, and we passed the night on the banks of a neighbouring stream, and reached next day *Ganagar Sirkol Jatkol*, where we halted for eight or nine days. In this place the sun is seen only three or four times a year, when all the dogs of the village, thinking him an intruding stranger, begin to bark at him. Burhanuddin, having recovered there, went back to his home, and I, with the other companion, proceeded to the Punjab, and passing through the territory of a chief, named *Shálkhan*, entered the British dominions. On arriving at Lahore we were told that Dr. L. was not there, and my companion, too impatient to wait, went down to Rampur, and I stayed at Lahore." He then gave an account of—

THE KOHISTÁN (OR MOUNTAINOUS COUNTRY).

(A DIFFERENT COUNTRY FROM ONE OF THE SAME NAME NEAR KABUL.)

Boundaries.—It is bounded on the north by *Chitrál*, *Yasin*, and *Hunza*, on the east by *Chilas*, *Kashmir*, and a part of *Hazara;* on the south by *Yaghistán* (or wild country) ; on the west by *Swat* and *Yaghistán.*

It is surrounded by three mountainous ranges running parallel to each other, dividing the country into two parts (the northern part is called *Gabriál*). The Indus flows down through the country, and has a very narrow bed here, which is hemmed in by the mountains.

The northern part, which is called Gabriál, has only two remarkable villages—*Kandyá*, on the western side of the river, and *Siwa* on the eastern; and the southern part contains many towns and villages :—

On the eastern side of the river,—		On the western side of the river,—	
Town.	Name of influential Malak (Landowner).	Town.	Name of influential Malak.
(1) Ladai ...	... Machú.	(5) Batera	
(2) Kolai ...	Shah Said.	(6) Patan (8,000 pop.)	Qudrat Ali.
(3) Palas (9,000 pop.) ...	Lachur.	(7) Chakarga	
(4) Marín ...	Karm Khán.	(8) Ranotia	

That part of *Yaghistán* which bounds Kohistan on the west is divided into (1) *Thakot*, which is governed by Shalkhán, and (2) *Dishán*, which is under Ram Khan; and that part of Yaghistán which bounds it on the south is divided into three valleys,—

(1) Alahi, governed by Arsalan Khan.
(2) Nandiyar, „ Zafar Khan.
(3) Tikráí, „ Ghaffar Khan (has also two cannons).

Between the southern part of Kohistan and Alahi, in the eastern corner, there is a plain, of a circular form, surrounded on all sides by mountains. This plain is always covered with grass, and streams of clear and fresh water run through it. Both the grass and the water of this vast meadow are remarkable for their nourishing and digestive qualities. This plain is called "*Chaur*," and is debatable ground between the Kohistanis of Ladai, Kolai, and Palas, and the Afghans of Alahi.

People.—The people of this country are not allied to the Afghans, as their language shows, but have the same erect bearing and beautiful features

Language.—Their language is altogether different from that of their neighbours, the Afghans, as will be shown by the following comparison :—

KOHISTANI.	PUSHTO THE AFGHAN LANGUAGE).
1. To-morrow night to Lahore I will go. *Douche rate Lahore bajanwa.*	1. To-morrow night to Lahore I will go. *Saba shapa ba Lahore shazam.*
2. Thou silent be. *Tohe chut guda.*	2. Thou silent be. *Tah chup shai.*
3. Prepare, ye young men. *Jubti masha.*	3. Prepared be, O young men. *Saubhal she zalmú.*

There is a song very current in Kohistan which begins,—

Palas kulal mariga, Patane jirga hotiga, Johle johal madado propár asáli = "In Palas a potter was killed, in Patan the jirga (or tribal assembly) sat." "The corrupted (Jirga of Malaks) took a bribe, and retaliation was ignored." The Afghans are called Pathans.

Religion.—They have been converted to Islám since four or five generations, and they have forsaken their old religion so completely that no tinge of it now remains; and when a Kohistani is told that they are "nau-Muslims," that is, "new Muhammadans," he becomes angry.

Muslim learning, and the building of mosques have become common in Kohistan, and now we find twenty or thirty learned mullas in every considerable town, besides hundreds of students, studying in mosques.

Dress.—Their national dress consists of a woollen hat, brimmed like that of Europeans, and a loose woollen tunic having a long چاکی along the right breast, so that one can easily get out the right hand to wield one's arms in a fight. Their trousers are also made of wool and are very tight. In the summer they wear a kind of leathern shoes borrowed from the Afghans, but in the winter they wear a kind of boots made of grass (the straw of rice) reaching to the knees. They call it "pájola."

Till very lately their only arms were a small "khanjar" (dagger), bows and arrows; but they have borrowed the use of guns and long swords from the Afghans.

The dress of their women consists of a loose woollen head-dress with silken fringes, a woollen tunic and blue or black trousers of cotton cloth, which they call "*shakara.*" Generally their women work with their husbands in the corn-fields, and do not live confined to their houses.

Government.—They have no chiefs like the Afghans, but influential Malaks lead them to battle, who are paid no tribute, salary, etc.

When an enemy enters their country they whistle so sharply that the sound is heard for miles; then the whole tribe assembles in one place for the defence of their country, with their respective Malaks at their heads.

Mode of Living, and other Social Customs.—In winter they live in the valleys, in houses made of wood and stones; but in summer they leave their houses in the valleys for those on the peaks of mountains, and the mass of the population spends the summer in the cooler region; but those who cultivate the land live the whole day in the valley, and when night comes go up to their houses on the heights. Their food is the bread of wheat, and milk furnished by their herds of cattle (gaómesh, cows, goats, and sheep), which is their sole property. There are no regular Bazárs even in the large villages; but the arrival of a merchant from India is generally hailed throughout the country. The woollen cloth which they use generally is manufactured by them.

Marriage.—Very lately there was a custom amongst them that the young man was allowed to court any girl he wished; but now, from their contact with the Afghans, the system of "betrothal" at a very early age is introduced, and the boy does not go till his marriage to that part of the village in which the girl betrothed to him lives. The Kohistanis say that they have learned three things from the Afghans :—

(1) The use of leathern shoes,
(2) The use of long swords and guns,
(3) The system of betrothal.

III. A ROUGH SKETCH OF KHATLÁN (KOLÁB) AND ADJOINING COUNTRIES.*

By MAULVI NAJMUDDIN, a Theologian and Poet from Koláb.

NAMES OF MANZILS (STATIONS) FROM KOLAB TO THE PUNJAB.

كولاب	(1)	Kolab.
صياد	(2)	Sayad. Situated on this side of the Amoo, and belongs to Badakhshan.
ين قلع	(3)	Yan-Qalá.
چاهياب	(4)	Chahyáb. Governed then (18 years ago) by Sultan Azdahar, son of Yusuf Ali Khán.
دشت سبز	(5)	Dashti-sabz. A halting-place.
رستاق	(6)	Rustáq. Governed then by Ismail Khán, son of Yusuf Ali Khán.
قزل دره	(7)	Kizil Dara.
ال كاشان	(8)	Elkáshán. The Himalaya begins.
اتن جلب	(9)	Átin Jalab. Here the river *Kokcha* † is crossed.
دشت سفيد	(10)	Dasht-e-sufed.
فيض اباد	(11)	Faizabad. Capital of Badakhshan; governed then by Jahandár Shah; is situated on the river Kokchá.
رباط	(11)	Rubát.
دشت فراخ	(12)	Dashti Farákh.
وردوج	(13)	Wardúj. Contains a mine of sulphur.
	(14) (15)	Names are forgotten.
زيباق	(16)	Zibáq. Peopled by *Shi'as* (or rather Muláis).
ده گول	(17)	Deh Gôl. The frontier village of Badakhshán; only a kind of inn.

* Burns, in his travels to Bukhárá, points out the locality of the province of Koláb in the south of the Amu (Oxus), and calls it by the name of Gawalan, which I think is a corruption of Khatlan; but Najmuddin asserts with certainty that it is situated on the northern bank and is a part of Ma-vara-un-nahr (the country on that side of the river) (Transoxiana). Najmuddin is No. 2 of the group at the beginning of this paper.

† This river is formed by three tributaries (1) coming from Sarghalan (has a mine of rubies); (2) from Wardúj (sulphur mines); (3) يمغان Yamghan (iron mine). It flows through the territory of Badakhshan, and joins the Amu.

منگر (18) Sanghar. A halting-place.
چترال (19) Chitrál. Governed then by Aman-ul-mulk (as now).
مرغال (20) Sarghál.
رباطك (21) Rubatak.
دير (22) Dír. Governed then by Ghazan Khán.
سوات (23) Swat.
پشاور (24) Peshawar.

That part of the country lying at the foot of the Hindu Kush mountains, which is bounded on the north by Kokand and Karatigan, on the east by Durwaz, on the south by Badakhshan and the Amu, on the west by Sherabad and Hissar (belonging to Bukhara) is called *Khatlan* ختلان KOLÁB, a considerable town containing a population of about ten thousand, is situated at the distance of five miles from the northern bank of the Amu, and is the capital of the province. The other towns of note are *Mumin-abad* مومن اباد, Daulatabad دولتاباد, Khawaling خوالنگ, Baljawan بلجوان, and Sarchashmá سرچشمه.

The country, being situated at the foot of mountains, and being watered by numerous streams, is highly fertile. The most important products are rice, wheat, barley, kharpazá, etc.; and the people generally are agricultural.

There is a mine of salt in the mountains of خواجه مومن *Khawaja Mumin*; and the salt produced resembles the Lahori salt, though it is not so pure and shining, and is very cheap.

Cattle breeding is carried on on a great scale, and the wealth of a man is estimated by the number of cattle he possesses. There is a kind of goat in this country which yields a very soft kind of wool (called Tibit); and the people of Kolah prepare from it hoses and a kind of turban, called *Shamali* (from shamal, the northern wind, from which it gives shelter).

Religion.—Generally the whole of the population belongs to the Sunni sect (according to the Hanafi rite).

Tribes.—The population of the country is divided into *Laqai*, *Battash*, and *Tajiks*. The Laqais live in movable tents (khargah) like the Kirghiz, and lead a roving life, and are soldiers and thieves by profession. The Battashes live in villages, which are generally clusters of *kappás* (thatched cottages), and are a peaceful and agricultural people. The Tajiks live in the towns, and are mostly artisans.

Language.—Turki is spoken in the villages and a very corrupt form of Persian in the towns. Most of the words are so twisted and distorted that a Persian cannot understand the people of the country without effort.

Government.—The country is really a province of Bukhárá; but a native of Kolab, descended from the Kapchaqs by the father's and from the Laqais by the mother's side, became independent of Bukhará. After his death, his four sons, Sayer Khan, Sara Khan, Qamshin Khan, Umra Khan, fought with one another for the crown; and Sara Khan, having defeated the other three, came to be the Chief of the province, but was defeated by an army from Bukhará and escaped to Kabul.

When Najmuddin left his country, it was governed by a servant of the court of Bukhárá.

The houses are generally built of mud, cut into smooth and symmetrical walls, and are plastered by a kind of lime called *guch.* Burnt bricks are very rare, and only the palace of the governor is made partially of them. The walls are roofed by thatch made of "damish" (reeds), which grow abundantly on the banks of the Amoo.

The *dress* consists of long, flowing choghás (stuffed with cotton) and woollen turbans. The Khatlanis wear a kind of full boot which they call *chamush,* but lately a kind of shoe is introduced from Russia, and is called *nughai.*

The country is connected with Yarkand by two roads, one running through Kokand and the other through the Pamir.

The above and following accounts were in answer to questions by Dr. Leitner, whose independent researches regarding Kandiá in 1866–72 were thus corroborated in 1881, and again in 1886, when the photographs which serve as the basis of our illustrations were taken.

IV. THE LANGUAGE, CUSTOMS, SONGS, AND PROVERBS OF GABRIÁL.

Position.—A town in *Kandiá,* a part of Yaghistan (the independent, or wild, country) situated beyond the river Indus (Hawā-sinn), which separates it from *Chilás.* The country of *Kandiá* extends along both sides of the *Kheri Ghá,* a tributary of the Indus, and is separated from *Tangir* by a chain of mountains.

The town of *Gabriál* is situated three days' march from *Jalkôt,* in a north-west direction, and is one day's march from *Patan,* in a northerly direc tion. *Patan* is the chief city of Southern Kandiá.

Inhabitants.— The whole tract of Kandiá can send out 20,000 fighting men. They are divided into the following castes :—

(1) Shîn, the highest, who now pretend to be Quraishes, the Arabs ot the tribe to which the Prophet Muhammad belonged. (Harif Ullá, the Gabriáli, and Ghulam Mohammad, of Gilgit, *call themselves Quraishes.*)

(2) Yashkun, who now call themselves Mughals, are inferior to the Shîn. A Yashkun man cannot marry a *Shîn* woman. Ahmad Shah, the Jalkoti belonged to this caste.

3 { (3) Doeúzgar, carpenters.
(4) Jolá, weavers.
(5) Akhár, blacksmiths.
(6) Dôm, musicians.
(7) Kámìn, lowest class.

} (3)–(5): In reality these people constitute no distinct castes, but all belong to a third, the Kamìn, caste.

The people of *Northern Kandiá* (Gabriál) are called *Bunzárí,* and of the southern part (*i.e.,* Patan) *Maní,* as the Chilasis are called *Boté.* A foreigner is called *Rarávi,* and fellow-countryman, *Muqámi.*

Religion.—The Gabriális, as well as all the people of *Chilás, Patan,* and *Palas,* are Sunnis, and are very intolerant to the *Shias,* who are kid-napped and kept in slavery (Ghulam Mohammad, the Gilgiti, has been for many years a slave in Chilás, as Ahmad Shah reports). The Gabriális were converted to Muhammadanism by a saint named *Bâbâji*, whose shrine is in Gabriál, and is one of the most frequented places by pilgrims. The Gabriális say that this saint lived six or seven generations ago. Mir Abdulla (who is really of Afghanistan, but now lives in Gabriál,) says tha' the Gabriális were converted to Islám about 150 years ago. Lately, this religion has made great progress among the people of Kandiá generally. Every little village has a mosque, and in most of the towns there are numerous mosques with schools attached to them, which are generally crowded by students from every caste. In Gabriál, the Mullahs or priests are, for the most part, of the Shîn caste, but men of every caste are zealous in giving education to their sons. Their education is limited to Muhammadan law (of the Hanifite school), and Arabian logic and philosophy. Very little attention is paid to Arabic or Persian general literature and caligraphy, that great Oriental art; so little, indeed, that Harifullah and Mir Abdulla, who are scholars of a very high standard, are wholly ignorant of any of the caligraphic forms, and their handwriting is scarcely better than that of the lowest primary class boys in the schools of the Punjab.

The most accomplished scholar in Kandiá is the high priest and chief of Patan, named Hazrat Ali, who is a Shîn.

The people generally are peaceful, and have a fair complexion and erect bearing. Their social and moral status has lately been raised very high. Robbery and adultery are almost unknown, and the usual punishment for these crimes is death. Divorce is seldom practised; polygamy is not rare among the rich men (wadán), but is seldom found among the common people.

Government.—Every village or town is governed by a Council of elders, chosen from among every tribe or "taífa." The most influential man among these elders for the time being is considered as the chief of the Council. These elders are either Shîns or Yashkun. No Kamin can be elected an elder, though he may become a Mullá, but a Mulla-kamìn also cannot be admitted to the Council.

The reigning Council of Gabriál consists of 12 persons, of whom 9 are Shins and 3 Yashkuns. Patshé Khân is the present chief of the Council. The post of Chief of the Council is not hereditary, but the wisest and the most influential of the elders is elected to that post. Justice is administered by the Mullahs without the interference of the Council, whose operation is limited to inter-tribal feuds.

Customs and Manners.—Hockey on horseback, which is called "lughât" in Gabriál, is played on holidays; and the place where they meet for the sport is called "lughât-kárin-jha."

Guns are called "nâli" in Gabriál, and are manufactured in the town by blacksmiths.

Dancing is not practised generally, as in the other Shin countries. Only "Doms" dance and sing, as this is their profession; they play on the "surúi" (pipe), rabáb (harp), and shaṇdo (drum).

The "purdá" system, or "veiling" women, is prevalent among the gentry, but it is only lately that the system was introduced into this country

When a son is born, a musket is fired off, and the father of the new-born son gives an ox as a present to the people, to be slaughtered for a general festival.

Infanticide is wholly unknown.

MARRIAGE.—The father of the boy does not go himself, as in Gilgit, to the father of the girl, but sends a man with 5 or 6 rupees, which he offers as a present. If the present is accepted, the betrothal (lóli) is arranged. As far as the woman is concerned the "lóli" is inviolable. The usual sum of dowry paid in cash is 80 rupees.

A bride is called "zhiyán," and the bridegroom "zhiyán lo."

LANGUAGE.—On account of the want of intercourse between the tribes the language of Kohistan is broken into numerous dialects; thus the structure of the dialects spoken in Kandiá, *i.e.*, in Gabriál and Patan, differs from that of the language spoken in Chilás and Palus, *i.e.*, in the countries situated on this side of the Indus. Harifullah, a Gabriáli, did not understand any language except his own; but Ahmad Shah, an inhabitant of Jalkôt (situated in the southern part of Chilás), understood Gabriáli, as he had been there for a time. Ghulam Mohammad, our Gilgiti man, who had been captured in an excursion, and had lived as a slave in Chilás, also thoroughly understood Jalkóti.

The language of Kohistan (as Chilás, Kandiá, etc., are also called) is divided into two dialects, called *Shíná* and *Shúthun* respectively. In the countries situated on that side of the Indus, that is in Kandiá, Shúthun is spoken.

The following pages are devoted to *Ballads*, *Proverbs*, *Riddles*, and *Dialogues* in the Shúthun dialect.

Songs=Gíla. Meshón gíla=men's songs; Gharón gíla=female songs.

1. AN ELEGY.

Fifteen years ago a battle was fought between *Arslán Khan* of *Kali*, and *Qamar Ali Khan* of *Pálus*, in which 300 men were killed on both sides. *Phaju*, on whose death the elegy is written by his sister, was one of the killed. The inhabitants of Palus are called "Sikhs," in reproach.

i.

Rugé níle, jimátyán-kachh-dúkánt,
In a green place, next a mosque, in a sitting (resting) place,
Chá chápár gála mazé, shahzada marégil
In a surrounded fort within, the prince was killed
Rugé níle, jimátyán kachh, dúkánt
In a green place, next a mosque, in a resting place
Sheú wále, bathrí, sóh viráti walégil.
Bring the bier, lay it down, (so that) that heirless one may be brought to his home.

ii.

Rúge níle, wo Shérkot shar hogaé,
In the green place, that Sherkot, where the halting-places of guests
Diri Sikáno qatle karégil.
Are deserted, the Sikhs (infidels, that is the Pálusis) slaughter committed (did).

Rúge níle, Shérkot, barí bigá hojowo,
In the green place, in Sherkot, a great fight happened to be,
Kali Khel, Phajú dasgír marégil.
O Kalikhel (a tribe of Kohistan) Phajú is captured and killed.

TRANSLATION.

1. In a green place, next the mosque, in a place of rest.
Within an enclosure the prince was killed.
In a green place, next a mosque, in a spot of rest,
Bring the bier and lay it down, to bring him home who has no heir.

2. In the green place, that Sherkôt, where the halting-place of guests
Is deserted, the Sikhs committed slaughter.
In the green place, in Sherkot, a great fight took place,
Oh, Kalikhel tribe, Phajú was captured and killed.

2. The following song is a chârbait, or quatrain, composed by Qamrán, a Gabriali poet. The song treats of the love between Saif-ul-mulk, a prince of Rúm, and Shahparì (the Fairy-queen).

The first line of a *charbait* is called *Sarnâmâh*, and the remaining poem is divided into stanzas or "Khhạṛáo," consisting each of four lines. At the end of every stanza the burden of the song is repeated :

SARNAMAH.—*Ma húga musfar, mi safár hugde Hindustan wain*
I became a stranger, my travel became towards Hindustan.
Mí duâ' salám, duâ' salámi ahl Kohistan waiṇ
My prayer-compliments, prayer-compliments, to the inhabitants of Kohistan (may go forth).
Malá Malúkh thû, O Badrái tou iuê haragilua
I myself am Malukh (name of the Prince Saif-ul-mulk), O Badra, thou didst lose me.

BURDEN.—*Hái, Malá Malúkh thû, O Badrái, ché Malúkh tiṇ táó bar zithu*
Woe, I am Malukh, O Badra, now thy Malukh from thy sorrow has lost his senses.

i.

STANZAS.—1. *Mala Malukh thu, O Badrai, Malúkh tiṇ, tâó thú dazélo*
I myself am Malukh, O Badra, thy Malukh burnt has been from thy heat.

2. *Hyó nieṇ nidhéto qarârê, Malúkh Badré wátbe thú harzélo*
In the heart there is no ease, which Malukh after Badra has lost.

3. *Be tí áṇs yârâúñ, mah pai-mukhé á'ṇs soh wéloṇ*
Ours, yours, was friendship, I beardless at that time

4. *Gini kirí thi, hâê hâê, mi Azli qalam zikzithu*
Why dost thou . . woe ! woe ! the pen of Eternity wrote so.

BURDEN.—5. *Hái, Malá Malúkh thu, O Badrai, Ché Malukh tiṇ táó harzi thu.*
Woe, I am Malukh, O Badra, etc., etc.

ii.

1. *Gini kiri the, hae hae, mi azló mazé likh taqdir thú*
   Why dost thou . . woe, woe! in Eternity did Fate write so.
2. *Darwázoṇ mazá galáchhe dhuî Mato tiṇ daráṇ faqîr thu*
   On thy gate I lit fire (like Jôgís), I a boy was the beggar of thy door.
3. *To hikmat biu báz-shâî thi kishéu lúṇgo maza zanzîr thu*
   By thy stratagem thou takest the eagle a prisoner in the chain of thy black locks.
4. *Kisheu lúngá, narai narai, panar múṇla bé the zetdu*
   Black locks, in strings, on thy bright face are twined.
5. *Hae Mala Malukh thu.* . . .
   Woe, I am Malukh, etc. . . .

iii.

1. *Kisheu lúngá narai narai, panar múṇ la âwizâṇ thu*
   Black locks in strings on thy bright face are hanging.
2. *Mi laṛmûṇ mazá karáé, tiu makhchúe gi mi armâṇ thu*
   In my body is the knife, thine is this deed which was my desire.
3. *A'khir dhar hénti nímgaré shoṇ fáni na, malá rawâṇ thu*
   At length will remain unfinished this waning (world), I now depart.
4. *Hyó mi kir súrai súrai, Jandun giná thu, ma mari thu*
   My heart didst thou pierce in holes, where is my life, I am dead.
5. *Hae Hae.* . . .
   Woe, I am Malukh, etc

iv.

1. *Hyó mi kir súrai súrai térubir, teṇ shon nidzah ghiu*
   My heart didst thou pierce throughout, by this thy spear.
2. *Málạ thu muṛé, ti dalbaráṇ, lailo bá mi jandzah ghiu*
   I am thy dead boy, thy lover, O dearest, go off from my bier.
3. *Khún tiu gḥaṛ hoga, ghi tulá nibháé ansi khévah ghiu*
   My blood is on thy neck, alas! thou didst not sit with me, being engaged in thy toilet.
4. *Khévah kirethi zhare tin soh khiyál mudá chaizbithú*
   Thy toilet do now, now that thy remembrance of me is slackened by Time.

MATAL (Masl = Proverbs).

PROVERBS.—(1) *Zánda chapélo razan bhiyáṇt.*
One who is struck by all, fears even a rope.

(2) *Zoroṇ waé nhálé k hurá zhiká.*
Looking towards (the length of) the sheet, extend your feet.

(3) *Háte ché rachhélú darwáze aṛat kara.*
Elephant if you keep, make your door wide.

(4) *Karotál ghutágir, láwán na hol kir.*
The Lion attacks, the Jackal makes water.

(5) *Qá mil tillu gún kaánt, báz mil tillu máséu khánt.*
With crow went, ate dung; with eagle went, ate flesh.
i.e. In the company of the crow you will learn to eat dung and in that of the eagle, you will eat flesh.

(6) *Tangá gatam karé rupaé balyún.*
A penny, for collecting went, lost rupee.

(7) *Ain tale kanwalé déthé, mazé hár shárá tún.*
Big mouth flattery does, inwardly (in mind) breaks bones.

(8) *Dúní lawáno karú márch.*
Two Jackals a lion kill.

(9) *Dhon mazé ek bakri budi agalu, búton bakron ethi.*
In a flock, if a contagious disease to one goat come, it comes to all goats.

(10) *Gún khuch tánt son, ghúno chái hont.*
Dung is spread out however much, bad smell so much more becomes.

(11) *Zhá zhui dárú.*
Brother's remedy is brother.

(12) *Tálain uthi, kozá dishál, tiu dú bondi.*
A sieve rose, to pot said, "You have two holes."

(13) *Zar bádshah tamam hoton, hiyá bandgár shilát.*
Money of the king is spent, heart of the treasurer pains.

ISHOLÁ (Question).

RIDDLES.—(1) *Shún ghélá chíz thun, che nahálánt tasi wáin pashánt amá?*
Such what thing is, which they see towards it, they see themselves in it?

Answer: Mirror. Shún áhan thi. = Such *mirror* is.

(2) *Shún ghelá chíz thún che surat záné thi, tilhánt nai?*
Such what thing is, whose figure serpent-like is, does not move?

Answer: Rope. Shún rás thi. = Such rope is.

(3) *Shún ghelá chíz thún, angár dheráni gellú, dhúan darya bau nikánt?*
Such what thing is, fire is applied to dry grass, the river of smoke flows from it.

Answer: Hookah.

(4) *Shún ghélá chíz thún, che mut surté waré nahále? hasánt, khuron we nahále ront?*
Such what thing is, who seeing towards other body laughs, seeing towards feet, weeps?

Answer: Peacock.

SHÚTHUN.

WORDS AND DIALOGUES.

Words.

God, ***Khávand.***
fairy, ***khápeṛé.***
demon, ***div.***
female demon, ***baldi.***
paradise, ***janat.***
fire, ***angár.***
earth, ***uzmuk.***
water, ***wi.***
heaven, ***asmán.***
moon, ***yúṇ.***
star, ***tará.***
darkness, ***tamdí.***
shadow, ***chhoṇl.***
day, ***des.***
light, ***láwar.***
night, ***rál.***
midday, ***mazardi.***
midnight, ***áṛ-rál.***
evening, ***nosháṇ.***
to-day, ***ázuk des.***
yesterday, ***bayaluk des.***
to-morrow, ***rályaṇk des.***
heat, ***taó, tát.***
cold, ***hewán.***
flame, ***lám.***
smoke, ***dhúáṇ.***
thunder, ***hagá-dazi-gé.***
lightning, ***mili.***
rain, ***ájo.***
drop, ***ájo-tipo.***
rainbow, ***bijonṛ.***
snow, ***hiṇ yúṇ.***
ice, ***kambuk.***
hail, ***mékh.***
dew, ***palús.***
earthquake, ***bhúnál.***
dust, ***udhún.***
pebbles, ***lakh-bato.***
sand, ***sighál.***
mud, ***chichál.***
plain, ***maidán, meráh.***
valley, ***dará.***
mount, ***khdu.***
foot of mountain, ***múndh.***

river, ***sín.***
wooden bridge, ***siú.***
rivulet, ***uchhu.***
streamlet, ***kháṛ.***
avalanche, ***hiṇál.***
lake, ***dhám.***
pond, ***dhamkalú.***
confluence, ***milil.***
banks, ***sin-kai.***
yonder bank, ***pír sinkai.***
this bank, ***ár sinkai.***
a well, ***kohi.***
country, ***watau.***
village, ***gáṇ.***

---

place, ***zhai.***
army, ***kauár.***
leader, ***kauár sardár.***
lumberdár, ***malak.***
tax-gatherer, ***jám kai.***
policeman, ***zeitú.***
cannon, ***tof.***
gun, ***náli.***
sword, ***tarwál.***
dagger, ***kardi.***
lance, ***naizá, shel.***
powder, ***nálán daru.***
ball, ***goli.***
ditches, ***kahe.***
wár, ***kali.***
thief, ***lú.***
sentinel, ***ráth.***
guard, ***chár.***
guide, ***pan-pasháṇtuk.***
coward, ***khiá to.***
traitor, ***fatandár.***
bribe, ***baṛi.***
prisoner, ***bandi.***
slave, ***dim.***
master, ***maulá.***
servant, ***naukar.***
drum, ***shaudo.***
sheath, ***káti.***
grip, ***kauzá***

bottom of sheath, ***kundi.***
hatchet, ***chhdi.***
file, ***sodn.***
smoothing iron, ***ramb:***
scythe, ***liṇzh.***
tongs, ***ochhúṇ.***
razor, ***chhúr.***
mirror, ***áhin.***
plough, ***hól.***
oar, ***phiyá.***
yoke, ***úṇ.***
ladle, ***tagú.***
kneading roller, ***chhagór.***
kettle, ***chati.***
little kettle, ***chedin.***
stone kettle, ***botá-bháṇ.***
pan, ***to.***
coal, ***phúthe.***
key, ***kunji.***
lion, ***khará.***
shawl, ***shiyúṇ.***
bedding, ***bathár.***
lock, ***sáṛ.***
bolt, ***hul.***
vineyard, ***dhángá.***
stable, ***ghozai.***
„ for cattle, ***gáṇ zai.***
„ for sheep, ***bakroṇ-ghuzál.***
water mill, ***yáṇzh.***
iron peg, ***kili.***
bullet-bag, ***koti.***
powder-flask, ***darú kothi.***
iron and flint, ***tiz.***
tinder, ***khú.***
bow, ***shde.***
arrow, ***káṇb.***
quiver, ***káṇb bhaṇ.***
ship, ***jaház.***
boat, ***heṛi.***

---

century, ***shol kála.***
year, ***kála.***
half-year, ***aṛa-kála.***

three months, *sha-yúṇ.*
week, *sát-dés.*
spring, *basáṇ.*
summer, *barish.*
autumn, *sharal.*

LUNAR MUHAMMADAI MONTHS.

Khudá tálá yúṇ, Rajab.
Shahqadar, Shaaban.
Rozoṇ yúṇ, Ramazan.
Lukut (smaller) eed yúṇ, Shawal.
Kháli yúṇ, Zi Qáad.
Gháiṇ eed yúṇ, Zi Haj.
Hasan Husain yúṇ, Muharram.
Chár bheyáṇ (four sisters), four months of Rabiulawwal: Rabi 2, Jamadi 1, Jamadi 2.

---

man, *máṇsho.*
male, *mésh.*
woman, *gharoṇ.*
new-born child, *chinot.*
girl, *mati.*
virgin, *bikra-mati.*
bachelor, *cháur.*
old man, *zárá.*
old woman, *zíri.*
puberty, *zuáni.*
life, *zhigi.*
death, *máreg.*
sickness, *ráṇs.*
sick, *najúr.*
health, *mith ráhat.*
relation, *zhává.*
brotherhood, *sak zhá.*
friend, *yár.*
aunt, *máfi.*
father, *abá.*
paternal uncle, *pichá.*
mother, *yá.*
brother, *zhá.*
sister, *bhiyúṇ.*
son, *púsh.*
daughter, *dhí.*
daughter's husband, *zamá zhú.*
grandson, *pázho.*
granddaughter, *pozhi.*
nephew, *zhá-lichh.*
husband, *baryú.*
wife's brother, *sháóri.*
wife's mother, *ichosh.*
wife's father, *shor.*
pregnancy, *ghaleiṇ.*
nurse, *razáî mahal.*
priest, *moláṇ.*
mosque, *jamáat.*
pupil, *shágaṛ.*
sportsman, *dháuzír.*
goldwasher, *keryáṇ.*
peasant, *déqán.*
horse-stealer, *gálwáṇ.*
robber, *lú.*
brick-baker, *ustá kár.*
butcher, *qasábi.*
shepherd, *payál.*
cowherd, *go-chár.*
groom, *kharbal.*

---

body, *surté adúmá.*
skin, *chám.*
bones, *hár.*
marrow, *métho.*
flesh, *maséṇ.*
fat, *miyún.*
blood, *rát.*
veins, *rage.*
head, *shish.*
occiput, *shisháṇ-kokar.*
brain, *metho.*
curls, *chaṇdú.*
tresses, *pétú.*
forehead, *tál.*
eyes, *aṇchhi.*
eyebrow, *ruzi.*
eyelids, *papdiṇ.*
pupil, *machhá.*
tears, *áṇchhe.*
ears, *kaná.*
hearing, *shúoṇ.*
cheeks, *hargel.*
chin, *dái.*
nose, *nathúr.*
nostrils, *shúli.*
odour, *gháṇ.*
sneezing, *zhitá.*
upper lip, *bul-dhút.*
nether lip, *múṇ-dhút.*
mouth, *áiṇ.*
taste, *khoṇd.*
licking, *chara.*
sucking, *chúshoṇ.*
beard, *dái-bál.*
moustaches, *phuṇge.*
teeth, *daná.*
tongue, *zib.*
jaw, *tálú.*
throat, *marri.*
neck, *shák.*
shoulder, *phyá.*
back, *dah.*
fore-arm, *mutá.*
palm, *hát-zil.*
nails, *nakhá.*
thumb, *aṇgú.*
middle finger, *muzwál aṇgúi.*
breast, *heṇ li.*
lungs, *phap.*
liver, *shúr.*
kidneys, *juká.*
breath, *dhéṇs.*
coughing, *kháṇg.*
spleen, *shiyáṇ.*
belly, *vari.*
side, *ṣhigát.*
ribs, *pash.*
thighs, *sethi.*
knee, *kútá.*
feet, *khurá.*
sole, *sháṇdá.*

---

anger, *rush.*
aversion, *achháq.*
boastful, *amá-tikú.*
cheating, *ṭhag.*
courage, *hyo-kura.*
cowardice, *bhiyáto.*

---

blind, *shéo.*

deaf, *borá.*
dumb, *cháo.*
dwarf, *khátoṇ.*
giant, *zhigo.*
hunch-back, *dakoro.*
stammering, *hup-hup.*
one-eyed, *ek-áchhá.*

---

bed, *shi-úṇ.*
broom, *láhúli.*
canal, *yáh.*
fort, *kalá.*
house, *báo.*
ladder, *párchaṇgi.*
street, *durro.*
water-jug, *dhomb-lú.*
wall, *kúṛ.*
window, *bá-úṇ.*

---

guest, *maláshi.*
host, *malásh-khais.*
breakfast, *vépli.*
midday meal, *ashari-goli.*
luncheon, *mazardiṇ-goli.*
evening meal, *bilalú-ki-goli.*
sour dough, *kham birá.*
light, *lawár.*

I, *má.*
thou, *tú.*
he, *úṇ.*
we, *améṇ.*
you, *tus.*
they, *áiṇ.*

---

great, *ghéroṇ.*
small, *lakho.*
much, *che.*
beautiful, *sugá.*
ugly, *adash.*
clean, *sáf.*
dirty, *mulgán.*
deep, *khatoṇ.*
rich, *poyandá.*
poor, *kám todṇ.*
miserly, *sakh.*

---

oath, *súgáu.*

Dialogues.

What is your name? *tíṇ ná gi thú?*
Where do you come from? *tú guláṇ ethú?*
Where do you go to? *tú guláṇ byáṇ thú?*
When did you come? *tú kal ethú?*
Come quickly, *zino é.*
Go slowly, *suple bká.*
Beat him now, *as uskéṇ koteḥ.*
Kill him afterwards, *as hilék pásrih máreh.*
How is the road between this and there? *ungái shálgái har páṇ goshe the?*
Very bad and dangerous, *chai kharáb thi, chai gi aṇ thi.*
Very easy; a plain, and nothing to fear, *chai hasán thi; bodi maiadn kingi bhil nithi.*
Is there any water on the road? *paú mazé wi thú ya na thú* (way-in water is or not is)?
Why should there not be any? *giné nithú?*
There is plenty, and good water, *cho thú, sains thú.*
The water is bad and salty, *achhak thú, lúsuláe milál thú.*
There is a big river on the road, which you will not be able to cross, *pánda mazé, ghdi síu thi, pir-khingi* (on that side) *ni biháṇt.*
Why? Is there no bridge? *ginah? siú nithú?*
There was a rope bridge, but to-day it broke, *bilálá siú áṇs, áz sher thi.*
Can it be not repaired? *sáṇdhat nai ẽṇ?*
There are no men for two days' march all round. There are neither twigs nor ropes to be got. How am I to do? *shásh taraf se másh nithu, doṇ diṇ so mazaló-mazé, gishi sandhyi?*
How can he come; he has gone about some business, *sóh gishé ẽshòto, soh kámi béjthú.*
Go! be silent. Bring him at once, or else I shall be very angry, *bóh! chubbó; má khapá hothiú, zino bádi á.*
What do you want? *tú gi lukhát?*
I do not want anything except to drink and eat, *má kiṇgeh ni lukhant, kháṇ púr lukhánt.*
I have nothing; what can I give you? *minge kingé nithú, má gi dáwá?*
First of all bring cold water, *buttó mú tḥo tú mitḥa wi á.*

Afterwards bring milk, ghi, butter, *pailōṇ shír, ghil, shishaṇ.*

How many days will you stay here? *tú ondháṇ ketúk desi bhayáṇto?*

I will start to-morrow early, *má ráli béṇto.*

Get coolies (porters), *petwáre á.*

How many coolies do you want? *ketúk petwáre pakár thú?*

The road is full of stones, *páṇdá maẓe batáh chai vaṇte.*

Your loads are very heavy, *tiṇ aiṇ* (-this) *peté chai abur thiṇ.*

The coolies will not be able to carry them, *zaṇ petwaré búi ner haṇthé.*

I beg that you will make your loads a little lighter, and then you will arrive quicker, *mi arzi thi, as peté hilék achhrá; amén hálo chhil.*

Be patient; I will pay for all; I will give the rate to the coolies. If you act well I will reward you, *sabar karé; mōṇh buto mazdúri dashul; téṇ miṭh kám karlu, má tighé inám dashut.*

Get the horses ready, *ghúi tayár karáh.*

Put the saddle on, *ghúi tal káṭhi sambhál karé.*

Take the saddle and bridle off, *ghúi na maláni alú karé, háṇ káthé.*

Catch hold of this, *as dhái.*

Do not lose it, *as phat niré.*

Do not forget what I say, *miṇ bál* (my word) *né ushá.*

Hear! look! take care, *káno hin shúnd, anchhi náhli! fikar karé.*

Tie the horse to that tree, *gho as gái mél gáṇdá.*

Keep watch all night, *rál chokidári karáh.*

Are there many thieves here? *úndá lú ché thé?*

What is this noise? *shún awáz kasiṇ thúṇ?*

Who are you? *tú káṇ thúṇ?*

Get away from here, *uṇd gái báh.*

Shoot him the moment he comes near, *uṇgái ígálo, asiṇ tumakáh deh.*

This man is treacherous, *úṇ másh bepat thú.*

Don't let him go, *as másh úṇdú phat niyáréh.*

Bind him, imprison him, enchain him; put him into stocks, *as gaṇdáh; asiṇ háthe zanzír gáláh; as kundi galáh.*

I am going to sleep, *hú iṇ má sútá bijáṇtaé.*

Don't make a noise, *chozuk niyáreh.*

How many people are there in the village? *as gáṇó maz katú maṇsh thé?*

I have not counted them, *méṇ ishmár niyárchi.*

Is the soil fertile or sterile? *dol níl thé, gíh shishi thé?*

Is there much fruit? *mévá chai thé?*

Is there much grain in the village? *as watné maz án cho thú?*

How many taxes do you pay in the year? *ek kál maz ketúk masúl diyáṇt tus?*

Are you satisfied? *tú khush-hál thú?*

How is your health? *tú uṇdáṇ arám thú?*

I am in good health, *arám thú.*

Good temper, *tabyát sáf.*

Bad temper, *tabyát asak.*

God bless you, *khudáé tigé barakat dé.*

May God lengthen your life, *khudáe tiṇ umar chai kare.*

My name is Gharib Shah, *miṇ ná Gharíḅ Sháh thú.*

My age is twenty years, *mín umar bísh káláh thú.*

My mother is dead; my father is alive; *miṇ mháṇli marigai, miṇ mahálo zaná thú.*

How is the road, good or bad? *pán mit thi ghi achak thi?*

In one or two places it is good, in others bad, *ek dú zéé mit thiṇ, ek dú zéé achak thiṇ.*

How did you come from Chilas? *tú Chilasúṇ gishéi thú?*

I could not get a horse, I went on foot, *gho nyans, maton, khuron tal ethú.*

Are the mountains on the road high? *pán maze khúná úchat thé?*

When are you going back? *tú kaid bashotá?*

I am poor, *má gharíh thú.*

We kill all infidels, *bé bud kafrá marán̩ the.*

I have come to learn the language, *má zib chhitáiṇ éthú.*

What do I care about? *miṇ gi parwá thú?*

I make my prayers five times every day, *má har dés panjwaqtúṇ nimáz karáṇ thé.*

Where did you come from? *tu guláṇ ethú?*

Come into the house, *bá khuni é.*

Sit at your ease, *mitho bhai.*

Are you well? *tú mit thú?*

Are your children well? *tiu chinomati júṛ thé?*

Is your sister's son well? *tiu sazú júṛ the?*

Are you very ill? *tú cho náchaq* (sick) *thé?*

May God restore you to health! *khudá tálá tú joṛ kéré.*

Light the fire, *angár guyáh.*

Cook the food, *goli pazáh.*

Spread the bed, *bathári karé.*

It is very cold, *chai lúi thẹ.*

It is very hot, *chai tut thẹ.*

Put on your clothes, *zúr shá.*

Catch hold of the horse, *gho dhai.*

Look at that man, *pishas másh nahálá.*

Take care, *fikar karé.*

You will fall, *tú ullá shat.*

Take a good aim, *mithi nazir karé.*

I will give you help, *ma timál madat karéshat.*

I am hungry, bring food that I may eat, *má húshoshat, goli á, khéij.*

I am thirsty, bring water that I may drink, *má chúha húga, wi á, púmá.*

I am sleepy now, I will go to sleep, *migé nizh ige, nizh karáṇthú.*

What do you call this in your language? *tus shas chizi tai zib hin gimá manáth?*

How much is the produce of this land? *as zaimuz ketúk paidá húnt?*

Can you sing? *tige gila eṇthe?*

APPENDIX V.

Anthropological Observations on the following Dards and Kafirs in Dr. Leitner's service:

1. Abdul-Ghafûr, Kamôz Káfir.
2. Jamshêd, Katár Káfir.
3. Khudayár, Nagyr Dard, Yashkun.
4. Matavalli, Hunza Dard, Yashkun.
5. Ghulam Muhammad, Gilgit Dard, Shîn.
6. Mir Abdullah, Gabriál Dard, Shîn.
7. Ghulám, Astor Dard, Shîn.
8. Abdullah, Astor Dard, Shîn.
9. Ibrahim, Nagyr Dard, Rôno.
10. Sultan Ali, Nagyr Dard, Yashkun.
11. Khudadád, Nagyr Dard, Yashkun.
12. Hatamu, Nagyr Dard, Yashkun.

ETHNOLOGICAL.

(*See also Drawing* 1 *of Appendix IV.*)

A Gabriáli Student and Two Messengers (a Chitráli and a Yasini), from a Brother of the late Mihtar Aman-ul-Mulk, Ruler of Chitrál.

ANTHROPOLOGICAL.

Gilgiti (Ghulám Muhammad). Nagyri (Khudáyár). Hunza Man (Matavalli).

V.—ANTHROPOLOGICAL OBSERVATIONS ON DARDS AND KAFIRS IN DR. LEITNER'S SERVICE.

(*Measurements in Centimetres.*)

1. ABDUL GHAFÛR, KAFIR OF KAMÔZ, *about 24 or 25 years of age.*

Height, 168·5; hair, black; eyes, hazel; colour of face, ruddy; colour of body, very light brown; narrow forehead; high instep; big boned; length round the forehead, biggest circumference of head, 53·75; protruding and big ears; square face; long nose, slightly aquiline; good regular teeth; small beard; slight moustache and eyebrows; distance between eyebrows, ordinary; good chest; fine hand; well made nails. Weight, 10 st. 2¾ lbs.

2. KHUDAYÁR, YASHKUN NÁGYRI; *age* 24.

Height, 182; colour of body, light yellow brown; round the head, 52·5; teeth, good, regular; nose, very slightly aquiline; little growth on upper lip; none on cheeks; long, straight, coarse black hair; eyes, hazel; ears, not so protruding; better-proportioned forehead; small hand; good instep; foot bigger, in proportion, than hand (not so good as other's hand); 80 puls". Weight, 9 st. 10 lbs.

3. IBRAHÎM, RÔNO, NAGYRI; *age* 34.

Height, 162·3; round the head, 56·5; eyes, dark brown; big hands and feet; instep, good; colour, brown; good muscular foot; strong arms; hair, black; plentiful growth on upper lip; nose, aquiline; broad nostrils; full lips. Weight, 10 st. 12 lbs. (No. 10 on Drawing 1 of Appendix IV.)

4. MATAVALLI, YASHKUN OF HUNZA; *age* 30.*

Height, 164·0; very hairy, including hands; round the head, 54·0; head, pyramidal pointed; sinister countenance; very big hands and feet; thin lips; great moustache, coarser hair; more flat-soled than rest. Weight, 9 st. 8½ lbs. (*Full details in "Comparative Table."*)

5. SULTAN ALI, YASHKUN OF NAGYR; *age* 35.

Height, 165·25; round the head, 53·75; square head; retroussé, small nose; small mouth; red beard, plentiful; black hair; brown eyes; very big hands and feet, also instep. Weight, 9 st. 12 lbs. (No. 11 on Drawing 1 of Appendix IV.)

6. KHUDÁDAD OF NAGYR; *age* 30.

Height, 163·3; round the head, 54·4; stupid expression; big chest, ordinary hands and feet; low forehead; rising head; very muscular; eyes, brown; complexion, brown; thickish nose; very narrow forehead; underhung jaw; lots of hair. Weight, 9 st. 12 lbs. (No. 3 on Drawing 1 of Appendix IV.)

7. HATÁMU OF NAGYR; *age* 16.

Height, 162·1; round the head, 54·4 (broad head); low Grecian forehead; small nose; eyes, dark brown; light brown complexion; small hands and feet; regular, white teeth. Weight, 7 st. 13 lbs. (No. 4 of above Drawing.)

8. GHULAM MUHAMMAD, SHÎN OF GILGIT; *age* 38.*

Height, 161·0; round the head, 54; beard, prematurely grey; lost second incisor; small hands and feet; fair instep; brown eyes and complexion; nose, straight; ears all right. Weight, 8 st. 5 lbs.

* See also "Comparative Table" at the end of this Appendix, and the "Anthropological Photograph" facing this page. Read also page 1 of Appendix IV. "The Races of the Hindukush," opposite to Drawing 1 of that Appendix, on which look for Nos. 1, 6, and 9.

FURTHER MEASUREMENTS OF THE ABOVE MEN BY THE SCHWARZ SYSTEM.

(*See explanations of these numbers further on, page* 5.)

Numbers by Schwarz.	1. Abdul-Ghafûr, Kamôz Káfir.	2. Khudayar Yashkun, Nagyri.	3. Ibrahîm, Nagyri Róno.	4.* Matavalli, Hunza Yashkun.	5. Sultan Ali, Yashkun, Nagyri.	6. Khudadád Nagyri.	7. Hatamu Nagyri.	8. Ghulam Muhammad, Gilgiti Shîn.
28	30	26·7·5	29·2	31·5	25·5	28·5	24·7	29·5
29	15	24·7·5	14	13·5	14	11·75	31·1	15·5
30	14·5	13·5	14·5	13·6	13·7·5	14·2	12·7	14
31	10·2·5	8·7·5	9·5	9·6	8·7·5	9·2	8·1	9·1
32	3·7·5	3·5	3	3·7·5	3·25	3·3	3·8	3·9
34	3·9	4	4 6	4·1	3·6	3·6	3·4	3·5
35	5·5	4·7	4·7·5	5	4·1	5·5	4·5	4·8
36	14	11·2	11·7·5	11·25	11·2	11·2	11·1	10·2
37	18·7·5	20·2·5	20·6	20·8	19	20·75	19·2	18·5
39	46	44·7·5	48	44·5	44·5	48·6	41·5	39·6

* Matavalli, and a new man, Mîr Abdullah of Gabriál (column F of subjoined Comparative Table), were also measured at Lahore on the 23rd March, 1886, with the following results that may be added to the above measurements or may be compared with those in the "Comparative Table," respectively columns A and F, (*Matavalli* and *Mîr Abdullah*).

I. Head : Greatest breadth, A, 14·3—F, 14·1.

Greatest length from glabella to the back of the head, A, 18·8—F, 18·6.

Greatest length from root of nose to the back of the head, A, 19·6—F, 19·1.

Height of ear, A, 11·2—F, 11·9. Breadth of forehead, A, 10·6—F, 10·7.

Height of face (*a*), chin to edge of hair, A, 18·4—F, 19·1.

Height of face (*b*), root of nose to chin, A, 12·7—F, 12·1.

Middle face, root of nose to mouth, A, 8·1—F, 7·6.

Breadth of face, zygomatic arch, A, 13·8—F, 13·6.

Distance of the inner angles of eyes, A, 3·4—F, 3·4.

Distance of the outer angles of eyes, A, 9·2—F, 8·8.

Nose : Height, A, 5·1—F, 5·8 ; Length, A, 5·3—F, 5·9 ; Breadth, A, 3·9 —F, 3·5.

Mouth : Length, A, 5·4—F, 5·3.

Ear : Height, A, 6·1—F, 6·3 ; distance from ear-hole to root of nose, A, 12·1—F, 12·1.

Horizontal circumference of head, A, 55—F, 53.

II. Body : Entire height, A, 165·7 centim.—F, 166.

Greatest extension of arms, A, 166·5—F, 165. !!

Height : chin, A, 142—F, 143. Height to navel, A, 96·5—F, 99.

,, shoulder, A, 138—F, 138. ,, middle finger, A, 73—F, 71·5.

,, elbows, A, 104—F, 105. ,, patella, A, 45—F, 44·5.

,, wrist, A, 78—F, 80.

Height in sitting, to top of head (over the seat), A, 88—F, 85.

Breadth of shoulder, A, 43—F, 36.

Circumference of chest, A, 87—F, 81.

Hand : length middle finger, A, 8—F, 7·5 ; breadth, base of four fingers, A, 10—F, 7·5.

Foot : length, A, 26—F, 25·5 ; breadth, A, 11—F, 8·25.

Circumference of upper leg, A, 46—F, 42·5.

Circumference of calf, A, 34—F, 32.

DESCRIPTION OF JAMSHÊD, THE SIAH PÔSH KAFIR.

Jamshêd of Katár, the nephew of General Feramorz, the renowned Kafir General in the service of the late Amir Sher Alí of Kabul, was a confidential orderly both in the service of the Amir Sher Alí and in that of Yakúb Khan, whose cause he espoused against that of his father, in consequence of which, when his master was imprisoned, he fled to Rawalpindi, where he came to me. He had witnessed some of the most exciting scenes in modern Kabul history, had risen to the rank of Major, and had served with Prince Iskandar of Herát, whom he afterwards again met in London.

In 1872 I published from Jamshêd's dictation an account of the "Adventures of Jamshêd, a Siah Pôsh Kafir, and his wanderings with Amir Sher Alí," and also "a statement about slavery in Kabul, etc.," which contained the names of places and tribes previously unknown to Geographers and Ethnographers, as well as historical and political material, the value of which has been proved by subsequent events. I took him with me to England, not only on account of the interest which exists in certain scientific quarters as regards the "mysterious race" of which he was a member, but also in order to draw the attention of the Anti-slavery Society and of Government to the kidnapping of Kafirs—the supposed "poor relations" of the European—which is carried on by the Afghans.

His measurement was taken, according to the systems of both Broca and Schwarz (of the Novara expedition), by Dr. Beddoe, and the type appeared to approach nearest to that of the slavonized Macedonians of the Herzegovina, like one of whose inhabitants he looked, thus creating far less attention, especially when dressed *à l'européenne* in Europe, than he did at Lahore, where Lord Northbrook saw him. The Anti-slavery Society sent him to the Chiefs of Katár with a communication to the effect that Englishmen strongly disapproved of slavery, and that they should represent their case to the Panjab Government. A curious incident in connection with his presence in England may be mentioned. It was the 6th May, 1874, the day of the "Two Thousand"; the result of the Newmarket race was eagerly expected, when the *Globe* came out with the following titles placed on the posters: "Result of the 'Two Thousand.'" "An Interesting Race" (the latter was an article on the race of the Siah Pôsh Kafirs). The result may be imagined. Hundreds of Welshers plunged into an account of the Siah Pôsh Kafirs under the notion that they were going to have a great treat in a telegraphic description of a Newmarket race. I was informed that the wrath of the sporting roughs who besieged the office was awful when they found out their mistake. Poor Jamshêd was seen across the Panjab border by one of my Munshis, but returned some months later to Lahore, whence he found his way to Brussa, in Asia Minor. It is supposed that he took service in the Turkish Army, but he has not since been heard of. As I intend to publish an account of the Káfirs of Katár (now, I fear, all Nimchas, or half-Muhammadans), Gambir, etc., I reserve the interesting statements of Jamshêd to their proper Section in my "Káfiristán."

JAMSHÊD, THE SIAH PÔSH KAFIR,
BROUGHT TO ENGLAND BY PROF. LEITNER IN 1872.

JAMSHÊD.—A KATÁR KÁFIR; NEPHEW OF GENERAL FERAMORZ.

MEASUREMENTS OF HEAD (BY DR. JOHN BEDDOE).

		ENGLISH INCHES.	MILLIMETRES.
1.	Greatest length of head from glabella	6·8	172·7
2.	Length from tuber occip. to greatest convexity of frontal arch	6·7	170·2
3.	Length from tuber occip. to glabella	6·8	172·7
4.	Greatest length of head from smooth depression above glabella (ophryon)	6·75	171·4
5.	Greatest length of head from depression at root of nose	6·65	168·9
6.	Length from chin to vertex	9·1	231·1
7.	Least breadth between frontal crests	3·7	94
8.	Greatest breadth between zygomata	5·1	129·5
9.	Breadth from tragus to tragus	5·	127
10.	Greatest breadth of head ... ... yielding cranial index 86·7	5·9	149·8
11.	Breadth between greatest convexities of mastoid processes	5·3	134·6
12.	Greatest circumference of head	20·6	523·2
13.	Circumference at glabello-inial line	20·4	518·1
14.	Circumference at inion and frontal convexity ...	20·5	520·6
15.	Arc from nasal notch to inion (tuber occip.) ...	12·8	325·1
16.	Arc from one meatus to the other across top of head ...	14·4	365·7
17.	Arc from one meatus to the other over glabella ...	11·5	292·1
18.	Length of face (nasal notch to chin), giving facial index, 80·4	4·1	104·1
	Height from meatus to vertex	5·3	135·5
	Bigoniac breadth	4·1	103·5

The head, though strongly brachy-cephalic, is distinctly of Aryan type; high and round, but not at all acro-cephalic; the inion is placed very high.

JAMSHÊD—(*continued*).

THE FOLLOWING MEASUREMENTS ARE ACCORDING TO THE SYSTEM OF SCHWARZ, OF THE NOVARA EXPEDITION.

		CENTIMETRES.
28.	From the growth of hair to the incisura semilunaris sterni ...	25·
29.	From the inion to the Halswirbel (vertebra prominens) ...	14·45
30.	Direct diameter, from one meatus aud. ext. to the other ...	11·85
31.	Outer angle of the eye to the other	8·75
32.	Inner angle of the eye to the other	2·75
33.	Distance of the fixed points of the ear	4·05
34.	Breadth of the nose...	3·2
35.	Breadth of the mouth	5·
36.	Distance of the two angles of the lower jaw	10·35
37.	From incis. semil. sterni to the seventh vertebra	12·95
38.	From the axillary line over the mammæ to the other ..	26·4
39.	From sternum to columna vertebralis, straight across ...	19·3

JAMSHÉD.—SYSTEM OF SCHWARZ—(*continued*).

		CENTIMETRES.
40.	From one spina anterior superior ilii to the other	22·35
41.	From one troch. maj. to other	26·05
42.	Circumference of the neck	33·5
43.	From one tuberculum majus to the other...	37·
44.	From middle line of axillary line over the chest, above mammæ, to the other middle line	41·5
45.	Circumference of chest on the same level	88·25
46.	From nipple to nipple	19·25
47.	Between anterior spines of ilia	26·85
48.	From trochanter major to the spina anterior ilii of the same side	13·5
49.	From the most prominent part of the sternal articulation of the clavicular to above	43·4
50.	From same point to the navel	39·2
51.	From navel to upper edge of the symphysis ossium pubis ...	14·75
52.	From the 5th lumbar vertebra along the edge of the pelvis to the edge of the symphysis	43·
53.	From the 7th vertebra to the end of the os coccygis ...	60·35
54.	From one acromion to the other across the back	43·7
55.	From the acromion to the condyl. ext. humeri	32·25
56.	From ext. condyl. humeri to processus styloideus radii ...	25·
57.	From processus styloideus radii to metacarpal joint ...	10·2
58.	From the same joint to the top of the middle finger ...	9·8
59.	Circumference of the hand	21·4
60.	Greatest circumference of upper arm over the biceps ...	26·8
61.	Greatest circumference of forearm	24·5
62.	Smallest circumference of forearm	15·2
63.	From trochanter major to condyl. ext. femoris	34·35
64.		
65.		
66.		
67.		
68.	From condyl. ext. femoris to mal. ext.	38·6
69.	Circumference of knee joint	32·4
70.	Circumference of calf	36·4
71.	Smallest circumference of leg	21·3
72.	Length of the foot	23·3
73.	Circumference of instep	23·5
74.	Circumference of metatarsal joint	23·5
75.	From external malleolus to ground	8·1
76.	From condyl. intern. to malleolus int.	36·9
77.	Greatest circumference of thigh	48·5
78.	Smallest circumference of thigh	35·5
79.	Round the waist	68·4
80.	Height of man (English, 5' 3¾)	161·9
81.	Colour of hair, very dark reddish-brown.	
82.	Colour of eyes, hazel-grey.	
83.	Colour of face, yellowish-brown.	
84.	Colour of skin of body, lighter than above.	
85.	Weight,	
86.	Strength,	
87.	Pulsation, 80 (a little excited).	

APPENDIX VI.

A ROUGH ACCOUNT, COLLECTED IN 1886, OF ITINERARIES IN THE "NEUTRAL ZONE" BETWEEN CENTRAL ASIA AND INDIA. By RAJA KHUSHWAQTIA AND DR. G. W. LEITNER.

ROUTE I.

FROM GILGIT TO KABUL, viâ Dareyl, Tangir, Kandiá, Ujù, Torwál, Swat, Dir, Maidán, Jandūl, Bajaur, Muravarri, Pashàt, Kunèr, Jelalabad, Kabul.

GILGIT TO SHERKILA, 9 katsha (rough) kôs * ($1\frac{1}{2}$ miles), ruled by Isa Bahadur's son, Raja Akbar Khan, under Kashmīr, a faithful ally, contains 70 zemindars' (peasants') houses on the Yasin river.

SHERKILA TO PATÀRI (is uninhabited), over a ridge Pīr (17 katsha kôs) called Batrèt, which is a plateau on which the Dareylis graze their flocks in the spring.

PATÀRI TO YATSHŌT (12 katsha kôs), road stony and jungly. Yatshōt is a village of Dareyl of one hundred houses, occupied by zemindars who have cattle, sheep, goats, and *buffaloes* (which are not found in Badakhshan). The ground produces much white maize (from which bread is made), wheat, barley, grapes growing to a gigantic size, nuts, etc. There is excellent water, but it is very cold. The people are Sunnis, and speak Shiná (the dialect of Chilás). [The Shins appear to have been a Hindu tribe expelled from Kashmir territory and converted to a sort of Muhammadanism, both Shiah and Sunni. They are the highest caste in Dardistan; but, instead of the Brahminical veneration for the cow, they abhor everything connected with it—its flesh and milk—and only touch its calf at the end of a prong.] Yatshōt has two mosques, and Mullas who understand Arabic well. The Dareylis are very religious, and attentive to their ceremonial practices. The streamlet of Dareyl runs past it.

YATSHŌT TO MANIKÁL, 3 katsha kôs, a plain easy march through a prairie. Manikál has two forts, one of which has about 500 houses, and is called Dòrkans; and the other, Manikál proper, which has 300 houses and an old Mosque. Manikál is surrounded by forests. When the Kashmīr troops reached Manikál, the Dareylis, after fighting, burned down their old fort rather than surrender. There are many Mullas and disciples there, some coming from Peshawar, Swat, etc.

MANIKÁL TO SAMANGÁL, 3 katsha kôs, over an inhabited plain. The fort contains 800 houses. A great elder (Djashtero) called Kalashmīr resides there, whom all the Dareylis respect and follow, although there are many other Djashteros, like Muqaddams (elders, mayors), in Kashmir villages. He is wise and rich, possessing, perhaps, in addition to cattle,

* A kôs is a measurement of distance varying from 1 to $2\frac{1}{2}$ miles, and often depending on the speaker's impression due to hardships encountered or to other causes. "Katsha" and "pakka," for "rough, unfinished," and "thorough" respectively, are terms well known to Anglo-Indians. "Katsha" and "pakka" are generally spelt "kucha" and "pucka."

etc., 5 or 6 thousand tolas of gold; and he has one wife and two or three children. Persian is read there in addition to Arabic. There is also another fort containing 500 houses, also called Samangál, a few hundred yards from the first. In fact, Dareyl, although a small country, is thickly populated.

SAMANGÁL TO PÙGUTSH, a fort, with 500 houses, 2 katsha kôs—thence 1 katsha kôs to Gayál, a fort with 600 houses—all an easy road.

GAYÁL TO KÀMI, Fort Tangīr, over a high mountain called Kùbbekunn, very windy, and wooded. Water must be taken with one when starting from Gayál, as none is found before reaching Rîm, a small village of 20 houses, on the Tangīr side. The road for 8 kôs is difficult, being an ascent of 4 kôs on each side. From Rîm to Tangīr the road is good, water abundant, and habitations numerous. Kàmi fort has 1,000 houses of Gujars (a shepherd and cowherd tribe that is found following its peaceful occupation, either as settlers or nomads, in the most dangerous districts), and zemindars, who are tributaries to Yasin, paying taxes in gold and kind. There is a direct road from Tangir to Yasin, viâ Satil—6 kôs, plain, with many Gujars, paying their grazing tax in gold; thence over a small peak, Mayirẻy, to the plateau of Batrêt, 8 katsha kôs. (See second stage of this route.)

FROM BATRÊT TO RÀUSHAN, over a small mountain. Ràushan is a small fort of Yasin, whence there are roads to Yasin, Chitrál, Gilgit, etc. Gold is washed from the Indus, which is 3 katsha kôs from Kàmi. The Tangīris are braver than the Dareylis and equally religious, having many Mullas; but the country, although larger, is not so well populated as Dareyl, the people of which are also rather shepherds than hunters. The *Gabdr* are the ruling people in Tangīr, about 1,000 families, of which 500 are in Kàmi. They are the old proprietors of the country, and are all Shins who *now* have given up their old aversion to the cow, its flesh and milk.

KÀMI, over the mountain Tràk, called by the Pathans Chaudunno, which has no snow on the Tangīr side, but a snow-covered plateau 1½ kôs long on the Kandiá side. Then comes a green plain. To the foot of the mountain Tràk on the Tangīr side 11 kôs pakka (11 good kôs, or nearly 22 miles), over a tree-covered plain. Then over the Tràk pass and plateau, the road goes along a plain which extends for 17 kôs to GABRIÁL. There are a great many Gujars along the road. [The road to Yasin is through the Gujar-frequented district of Kuranjá, belonging to Tangīr. Multán is the Muqaddam of the Gujars, a brave man.]

GABRIÁL has only 40 houses, but the country of Gabriál generally is studded with habitations. The famous Mullah Habîbulla, a relative of Raja Khushwaqtia, is a most influential man among Kohistanis. His tribe is Mullakheyl, and all the Gujars of Kandiá are obedient to him. The Mullakheyl are Shîns, but Yashkuns also live there. Yashkuns are the peasantry of Dardistan, including Hunza, and supposed to be aborigines, though some derive the Yashkuns of Hunza from the white Yuechi, or Huns, and others give them a Western origin. They have always been Sunnis. (The Dareylis were formerly Shiahs.) (See detailed account of Gabriál by one of its Maulvis, Mir Abdullah, and of Kandiá or Kiliá, translated by Dr. G. W. Leitner.) The people of Kandiá are wealthy in flocks, ghi (=clarified butter, exported to Peshawur, 18 to 25 pakka seers for the rupee). It is subject to Yasin. They possess double or Indian rupees and mahmudshahis, some having 10 or 20 thousand rupees. The poorest have 10 to 12 cows, 100 sheep, etc. The greatest among the Gujars intermarry with Yasin chiefs. The Kohistanis are independent, but the Gujars pay a tribute to Yasin. The Samu or Samasi village is 2 kôs from Gabriál. From Gabriál, ½ kôs distant, is a mountain called by the same name, with an ascent of five to six pakka kôs, with excellent water; road only open in summer. A descent of 5 kôs brings one to *Ushu*, a big village of 600 houses inhabited by Bashkaris. (See special account by Dr. Leitner of Bashkar and its language.) The Swat river touches it. The Bashkaris pay a small tribute to Yasin, but are practically independent. They are generally on good terms with the Torwaliks, who were formerly their rulers. The languages of Torwal and Bashkar are different.

From Ushù to Torwál, 13 kôs, very bad, stony road, after Kalám (2 miles from Ushù). Torwál has 200 houses. They are not so rich as the people of Kandiá and Jalkôt.

From Torwál to Branihál, the frontier of Torwál, 12 to 13 kôs, a bad stony road, 600 houses and a Bazár in which there are 5 or 6 Hindu merchants. [The Hindu traders are not molested in Yaghistán ("the wild land" as Dardistán, the country between Kabul and Kashmir is often called), because no one is afraid of them; whereas if a Sahib (English man) came, people would be afraid.] There are many wealthy people in Branihál, which may be considered to be the capital of Torwál.

Branihál to Swat, a plain; at only 1½ kôs is Shagrám, composed of 3 villages, under the children of the Sayad (descendant of the prophet Muhammad), Pir Bâba. The three villages are inhabited by Sayads and contain 500 houses. Then to Tiráh (1 mile, a plain), where the Mîna- or Akhunkheyls live (300 houses).

Tiráh to Landéy, 1 kôs pakka, a Patán village, in which rice grows, beginning from Branihál; Landéy to Lalkún (a small village away from the big road to Hoti Murdan) 5 kôs, a plain. Thence Fazil banda, 12 kôs, a plain; thence to a mountain, Barkànn, 12 kôs, a plain, leaving the Swat for the Dīr territory. Jarughey (hamlet of Gujars) is the halting-place. From Jarughey into the Dara of Ushuréy, in Yaghistan proper; it is the home of the Khan of Dīr, and is inhabited by the Panda Kheyl tribe. Halt at Jàbar, a village 14 kôs from Jarughey, a fairly inhabited road. From Jàbar to Maidán (16 kôs) by the mountain Káir Dara, and passing the fort Bībiól (100 houses) a fort of the Khan of Dīr. The mountain is high. Maidán fort and Bazar, and Bandey fort (500 houses), Kumbàr 1 kôs distant, 1,000 houses, of Mians, and Bazar with many Hindus. Thence to Bandey Mayár, a great Bazár, and a renowned Ziáret (shrine), and Langar (almshouse) of Saukanó Miân, a village of Peshawar, are 2,000 or 3,000 houses, belonging to Jandūl. It is 14 kôs distant from Maidán, over an inhabited plain. Umr Khan, the ruler, has 240 excellent horsemen, 3,000 infantry, fights with Dīr, who has 500 inferior horses and numerous footmen, but not so brave as Jandúl. Terkanì is the name of the Jandúl ruler and tribe up to Jellalabad, and Irubsì that of Dīr, Swat, Buneyr, Samè, Pakli, etc. At 1½ kôs of Mayar is Miákil, a big town, of 5,000 houses and a Bazar. Miákil to (Bajaur) Badâm, are Kakazis, of the Mamùnd tribe, for 16 kôs a plain, 400 houses, Yágis (wild); Badàm to *Mureweri*, are 16 kôs, over a small mountain (Mohmands) in Yaghistan, has 1,000 houses. (At Nawagai is a Khan, Ajdar Khan, with 20 horsemen and 3,000 footmen.) At Khàr was another Khán, Dilawar Khan, who fled to Peshawar, his place having been conquered by Ajdar Khan; 100 houses. The place is surrounded by the Tuman-kheyl tribe. On the other side of the river, Kabul rule begins, and opposite is Chagar Sarai, leading to Katár, once a stronghold of Kafirs. Gambīr is subject to Kabul, the rest of the Siah Posh being independent; and another road leads to Petsh, which is Yági, or independent.

FROM MURAWERI TO PASHÙTT, 5 or 6 kôs pakka. Below Muraweri, 2 kôs, is Serkanni, where there are 200 Kabul troops. From Pashùtt cross stream on jhallas (inflated skins) to Jelalabad, 20 or 22 kôs; whence the road to Kabul is too well known to need even a passing reference.

Uninteresting as rough accounts of itineraries may be to the general reader, they are not without importance to the specialist. My material on the subject of routes to, and through, the Hindu-kush territories is considerable, though necessarily defective. It was mainly collected in 1866–72, when a portion of it was used by that leader of men, General Sir Charles MacGregor. I published a few "routes" at various intervals in the hope of stimulating inquiry, and of eliciting corrections or further information; but Indian official Departments, instead of co-operating, are uncommunicative of the partial, and therefore often misleading, knowledge which they possess, and, above all, jealous of non-official specialists. The First part of my work on Hunza has recently been printed by the Indian Foreign Office; where and when the Second will appear, is doubtful. I think the public have a right to know how matters stand in what was once called "the neutral zone," the region between the Russian and the British spheres of influence in Asia. At any rate, the learned Societies and International Oriental and other Congresses, that, on the strength of the material already published, have done me the honour at various times to apply with but very partial success, to Government on behalf of the elaboration of my material, shall not be deprived of it, though I can only submit it to them in its rough primitive state. The reader of *The Asiatic Quarterly Review* will, I hope, not be deterred by the dulness of "routes" from glancing at material which, in future articles, will include accounts, however rough, of the languages, the history and Governments, the customs, legends, and songs of, perhaps, the most interesting countries and races in Asia. The information, often collected under circumstances of danger, is based on personal knowledge, and on the accounts of natives of position in the countries to be dealt with.

G. W. L.

[Reprinted from *The Asiatic Quarterly Review*, April, 1891.]

ROUGH ACCOUNTS OF ITINERARIES THROUGH THE HINDUKUSH AND TO CENTRAL ASIA.

BY DR. G. W. LEITNER.

ROUTE II.

IN connection with my note in "Routes in Dardistan," I now propose to publish a series of accounts which have been supplied to me by native Indian or Central Asian travellers of position and trustworthiness, and which cannot fail, whatever their scientific or literary deficiencies, to be of topographical and ethnographical, if not of political, value. I commence with the account of a loyal native Chief, who has had opportunities of comparing Russian with British administration. The Chief first passes quickly from JELALABAD TO GANDAMAK, thence to Tazîn, Butkhák, Balahisár (where he left his sword with D... S...); he then proceeds from KABUL TO CHALIKÁR, a distance of 17 kôs over a plain); then stops at the *Salán* village, at the foot of the Hindukush, 11 kôs, and then goes on to say: "*Salán*: one road goes to the Hindukush and one to *Bajgá* (a halt) 14 kôs,* over a mountain into Afghan Turkistan. *Anderáb*, district of *Kundûz*, 17 kôs, plain; Anderáb to Bazderá; then Baghbán; then Robât (where there is a camp of Kabul troopers against Uzbak robbers), 14 k. in Haibak district to Haibak town; stayed at a small place of Tashkurghán, which has 6,000 houses, and is held by a Risála (troop) of the Amir; stayed at an intermediate cantonment established by Kabul; then to Mazari Sharif, 13 kôs (all belonging to Balkh). Daulatabad (300 houses); thence to the river Amu over a Rēg (sandy and dusty place) *in a buggy of two horses*, paid three double rupees,† took water with us (20 kôs). There are 100 men over the ferry for protection against raiding Turkomans. Sherdil Khan Loináb gave me a passport to visit the Ziárat (shrine) of Khaja Bahauddin Naqshbandi, at Bokhára. Went on ferry with 100 cattle and 50 men all day long, to the village of Talashkhán (500 h.) in Bokhára territory, where we rested in the evening. Next day by road to Sherabad, 7 kôs, plain (2,500 h.); then to Chinarî (600 houses), passing the *Khirga* Nishīn Khirghiz and Uzbak, "living in huts" (also Zemindars); Cheshma-i-Hafiz, 40 h., and a Serai for travellers. Then again on to the plain; made a halt among the Khirga-nishīn. Next day went on to the large city of Ghuzár (250,000 inhabitants, with villages, etc.). (Thence to Karshi to Bokhára); thence to Karabagh (700 houses); to town of Chiraghtshi in Shehrsabz (Ch. has 3,000 h.), whence it is four miles distant. Shehrsabz is

* Or about 20 miles. The reader should notice that such abbreviations as "14 kôs, plain" mean that "the distance is 14 kôs over generally a plain or easy ground"; "h" stands for houses.

† Or British-Indian Rupees.

a beautiful place of 6,000 houses. (The Bokhára army has a band in Russian style, and is drilled in a Russian way; it is better fed and clad than are the Afghans, but it is not so brave.) Thence to Kitáb, 3,000 houses, and Bokhára troops; did not stay there, but went to Takhta Karatsha, 10 kôs: thence to Kurghántippé Bazár; thence to *Samarcand*, a paradise (500,000 inhabitants, two rivers); there is a Hákim and General, the place belongs to the White Czar=the Ak Padishah. There were 12 regiments of infantry, and 8 of cavalry there. Then to Jám, 4 kôs (a large Russian force), 12 regiments of infantry, 4 of cavalry. I stayed with A.R. at Samarcand). There is a Russian cantonment between Jezakh and Samarcand, Kōr, Khoshgurū. ***The guns everywhere are directed towards Yasin, or India.*** I was nowhere molested in visiting Russian cantonments. Jezakh, Tamburabad, little Bokhara; Zamīn, Uratippa, a great town, and among 40,000 inhabitants there are 6 battalions and 8 regiments of infantry; Náu in Khojend district. Then Khojend, 800,000 inhabitants, great army; Mahràm, Besharih in Khokand, then to the city of Khokand; Karawultippa, 8 kôs, plain, Murghilán, a big city, 350,000 inhabitants with villages; Mintippé, 3,000 houses (or inhabitants?), Arabán; Ush, a large army (Kashghár is eleven days' march). Induján, big Russian army; 150,000 (inhabitants). Then to the Kokand river, Derya Sīr, crossing to Namangán, big city and army, thence returned to Induján, then to Asáka, 8 kôs plain, 9,000 inhabitants and army (1 cavalry, 4 infantry), then to Shahrikhán, 6 kôs, big city, 8,000 inhabitants or houses; then to Kawa, 5 kôs. Utshkurghán, 10 kôs, big city in Khokand: thence into a valley to a Langar, 17 kôs, plain, at night, where there are Khirghiz subjects to Khokand; over a mountain into Alai, 13 kôs, plain of Pamir, inhabited by Khirghiz, very cold; then to Chaghalmak, 15 kôs, plain, a small village, 100 houses of Khirghiz. District of Karateghin, which is subject to Bokhara (Alai being under the Russians); Chaghalmak to Zankù, 16 kôs, plain (horses are to be found everywhere for hire, according to distance by Farsang). (At Samarcand one mule's wheat load=two double rupees; a big sheep costs one rupee, and one and a half long-tailed sheep at Khokand, also one rupee. The fat of sheep is used instead of Ghi. Gold and notes abound more than silver. (Abdurrahman received 700 tungas=350 rupees per day, for self and eighty followers.) Silk Atlas one and a half yards is sold for one rupee. The Russian ladies are well dressed, and great respect is shown to them. The officers are very polite. There are free dispensaries, and schools in which Russian and the Korán are taught. (Haldi and black pepper from India is dear); there is no tyranny, and they are exactly like the English; the Russians live in bungalows. The Kázis and the man who beats the drum at night for Ramazan are paid by the Russians; sanitation is well attended to; all the troops are Europeans, except the Noghais, who are Tartars. I was much struck at Khojend by seeing the cavalry mounted according to the colour of the horses. (Gold is said to come from Kashgar and Khokand, but I have not seen the mine.) Camels abound and are eaten. Zankù to Kila-i Lab-i Ab (300 houses), 16 kôs, plain, to a village Shòkh d trà (300 houses).

It is a fine country; the people talk Persian, and are Sunnis (belongs to Bokhára).

KILA-I LAB-I AB, governed by a Bokhára Kardár, called Hákim Muhammad Nazir Beg, at a Fort Gharm to Shughdaréy, 12 kôs, plain, on horseback all along to Samarcand (300 h.), Shughdaréy to Fort Gharm, 3 k. (1,500 houses or inhabitants), Gharm to Childará, a village in Derwáz, plain, 17 k. packa (buggies do not go there), 150 h.; thence to Khawaling, Bazar, 1,000 h. (in the District of *Koláb*), 17 kôs, plain; carriages can go; thence to the city of Koláb 14 kôs, plain (Koláb is under Bokhára) (was formerly governed by Kartshîn Khan, a raider), whose brother Serakhan is at Kábul. Koláb, 6,000 houses, is a fine city, and there are six other cities belonging to it (Khawaling, Kungár, etc.); thence to Sar-i-Chashma, 10 kôs, plain; carriages can go (200 houses); thence to Baràk, 40 h. on the Amu 4 kôs, a warm place like Koláb generally; cross into Samptì (60 h.), in the district of *Rostáh*, belonging to Badakhshán (paid 4 annas for conveyance of five horses costing me 3 tolas in Koláb = 30 rupees); to Chayáp city, 2,000 houses (Jews are wealthy and not oppressed, and at Koláb there are Jews and Hindus, the latter with no families). Jews wear front curls, and have furs; women are handsome, but are dressed like Mussulman women; men, however, wear caps and narrow trousers, not turbans, as a rule, or wide trousers. The Jews in Turkestan are very clean. "*They have a learning like the Shastras of the Pandits.*" They lend money to the Khan of Bokhára. (The utensils are of china.)

Mare's milk is much consumed cooked with meat, and has a highly intoxicant effect. Chayàp to *Rosták*, 8 kôs, plain, 2 Afghan regiments of cavalry, 4 regiments of infantry (there are also some troops at Chayàp) 4,000 houses. Bazár well-frequented; springs; is a hot place. Atunjuláb, 12 kôs, plain, carriages can go (60 houses); Faizabád 16 kôs, great city and large Afghan force (3,500 houses?). I stayed at Bárak, 10 kôs; a nice place for illustrious strangers (100 houses); plenty of Zemindars, very easy, plain, full of fruit (apples, apricots, etc.); Chaugarán 9 kos, plain (200 houses); Tirgarán (60 houses, of MULÁIS, the strange sect regarding which elsewhere) 11 kôs, plain, with the exception of a small bad bit, over which horses, however, can go, called Rafâq = Parrì in Punjabi. From Tirgarán to Zerkhan in Zebák, 14 kôs, plain, but carriages cannot go. Zebák is a fine cool place. Its great Mulai, Sayed Abdurrahim, has fled to Arkari in Chitrál. Zerkhan has 500 Khassadars of Kabul (even the infantry there have horses), and 150 houses. Zerkhan to Shikashìm, small fort, 11 kôs, plain, 300 houses in villages all round; it is now well garrisoned with Kabulis (2 k. from Shikashìm are the ruby mines worked in winter near Gharàn on the road to Shignán). (In the time of Mir Shah rubies as large as candles were said to be got, lighting up the place.) "Lajvard" (Lapis lazuli) is got from Yumgan, a village in mountain above Jirm in Badakhshan. "Lajvard" is sold at a rupee of a Rupee size. (Gold streaks are often found in it.) Shikashìm to Kazi-deh, 10 kôs, plain (carriages could go) in Wakhan, which begins at Putr about half kôs from Shikashìm (another road from Shikashìm to Shignán in two days *viâ* Ghasann 10 kôs, plain, very cold; thence 12 kôs to a fort in Shignan. Kazi-deh has 40 houses. Kazi-deh to Pigisth 12 kôs, very plain, 15 houses of very wealthy people, all Mulais; Shoghör under Chitrál, 500 houses. Fort over the Khatinza, Nuqsan and Dura passes from Zeibák all under Chitrál; the first-named pass is open all the year round, but violent storms blow at the top.

PIGITSH TO FORT PANJAH, a plain 12 kôs; Ali Murdan Khan, its former ruler, is a refugee with Chitrál; 200 Afghan cavalry; there are 5 or 6 houses in the fort, and a number of villages round it (Zròng, a warm mineral spring, 40 houses; Kishm, 40 houses; Gatskhòn, 30 houses. Above Pigitsh are other villages. Khindàt, 50 houses; supplies are most plentiful).

From PANJAH TO ZÀNG (50 houses) 11 kôs, plain (artillery could go); ZÀNG TO SERHADD 12 katcha kôs, 200 houses, plain, cold, much wheat, cattle, etc.; *here the Pamir begins.* Thence to Ushàk, 14 k. plain, except a small elevation, very cold (here there is a road to Yarkand, and another to Hunza; the Wakhanis graze their cattle and flocks here in winter as there is abundant grass); USHÀK TO LANGÀR, 12 kôs, plain; the roads divide, of which the left one goes to Sarikol, and the right one to Hunza. Cattle are kept there in winter by the Serhadd people; Langàr to Baikará 8 kôs plain.

BARKARÁ TO BABAGUNDÌ, 12 kôs over the Irshád Pir (somewhat steep and snow-covered on the Wakhan side, but otherwise easy). Here there is a road on the other side to Babagundì (small town); place for Ghazan Khan's cattle (Dannkut). Babagundì is a famous shrine of Pir Irshád, where even the Mulai Ghazankhan gives cooking pots for travellers, and makes offerings; there are 5 or 6 houses of Zemindars, who look after the shrine. (Half a kôs beyond Babagundi the various roads to the Karumbar, Badakhshan, and one to Hunza join.)

BABAGUNDI TO RÍSHATT; small fort, 11 kôs; inhabited; 5 villagers' houses employed in agriculture. Ríshatt; for 4 kôs there is a plain road; then a difficult road, Ráship Jeráb, with precipices (6 kôs from Ríshatt), which can be destroyed, so as to make the approach from that side very hazardous; the road continues to Yubkatí, with scarcely much improvement, for 1½ kôs. There is a small town there, as generally on difficult defiles, or places than can be defended. Yubkatí to Gircha, 1 kôs katcha (10 houses); Gircha to Murkhon, 10 houses of Zemindars, 1 kôs; 2 katcha-kôs comes the Khaibar village of 4 houses, a defile defended by a small town, *with a door shutting the road* (*Der-band*); Khaibar, 4 kôs to Pàss; road over snow or glacier for 1½ kôs; below the glacier is the village of Pàss, 25 houses.

Pàss to Hussain, 20 houses; also a shrine 1½ kôs; fair road; also a deep natural tank (hauz) (where there is a place to keep cattle in winter) a few hundred yards from village. Beyond there is again one of the streaks of never-melting icefields, and dividing it from Ghulkin, a village of 60 houses (the gardens flourishing in the close vicinity of these icefields). Immediately near Ghulkin is Gulmùtti, 100 houses; thence for 10 kôs to Alti, a bad road over an elevation, Refáq, closed by one of the doors to which I have referred. The door is 1 kôs distant from Gulmùtti. Alti (150 houses), the residence of Salim Khan, father of Ghazanfar, who built Balti, where his son, the present ruler of Hunza, Ghazankhan, lives. Balti is ½ kôs from Alti, and above it. Balti has 1,000 houses, Zemindars Muláis; there are 50 Mosques, but no one reads prayers in them; people build them for the sake of glorification, not worship. They are used for dancing, drinking, etc. (the Raja used to dance himself on the Naurõz, and give presents to the Zemindars). Hunza *may* turn out 2,000 fighting men. Near it Fort Haiderabad (½ kôs), with 300 houses; close to it is another fort, Chumarsingh, with 100 houses; near it Dòrkhann Fort, with 200 houses (the inhabitants are more numerous than the wasted ground can support. People live largely on apricots, etc.; the land is generally sterile). ½ kôs from Dòrkhann is Gannish Fort, 600 houses, above the river which divides Hunza from Nagyr, where the Sumeir Fort confronts Gannish. There is also a small fort near Gannish, called Karál, with 50 houses. (Near Dòrkhann is also a similar small fort, the name of which I forget.) Coming back to Dòrkhann, and going from it straight in the Gilgit direction, is Aliabad Fort, with 600 houses, and close to it Hasanabad Fort, with 100 houses. There is also a "Derrband" between Hasanabad and Murtezabad, about a mile distant over a stream. Mürtezabad has 2 forts, one with 100, and the other with 50 houses.

FROM MURTEZABAD TO HIRÌ for two kôs; difficult ascent and descent. Hirì, a large village, with 800 houses of Zemindars *in* the fort (Shins live there); 2 kôs of bad road, excepting about 1 mile; to Mayôn, 50 houses. Four katcha kôs bring one without much difficulty, except over one ascent, over the Budalèss stream, violent in summer, where there is also a fort (a warm spring in a fort called Barr, 25 houses, occupied by 20 Sepoys of the Maharaja) to Chálta, in Gilgit territory, near Budalèss. There is a fort there, 150 houses, and 100 Sepoys. Over the Nulla, about one kôs above, is Chaprôt, 50 Sepoys and 60 houses; is a strong position (Natu Shah came to grief, with 1,000 men, between Budalèss and Mayôn). From Chálta, crossing the river and a small mountain, is a plateau to Nilt Fort, in Nagyr territory, 4 kôs from Chálta, and confronting Mayôn. From Chálta to Nomal, in Gilgit territory, with two Rifáqs each; near to these respective places for 11 kôs (kacha), 100 houses. There are 20 Sepoys in the Koti to guard the grain. The Zemindars now live outside the fort, which is merely used for the storage of grain. From Nomal to Gilgit 1 kôs, plain, which now contains 200 houses.

ROUTE III.

FROM ZEIBÁK TO CHITRÁL, over the Khatinza, a very high Pass, to Shoghor, or the other passes already mentioned. *Viâ* the Khatinza, which is always open, the road from Zeibák to Deh-i-gul, 1 kôs, 25 houses.

There the roads separate, one going over the Nuqsán, which is closed in winter, and the other one over the Khatinza, both joining at Kurubakh, a place ensconced by stones, and about 5 kôs either way from Deh-i-gul; from Kurubakh to Owîr, 20 houses, 3 kôs, easy road; from Owîr to Arkari, 80 houses, 5 kôs, easy road (Sháli, 10 houses, is one kôs from Arkari); Mõmi, 5 kôs farther on, 50 houses. From Arkari to Shoghor is 10 kôs katcha. (From Shoghor, 3 miles below, is Rondur, 5 or 6 houses; 4 kôs is another Shali, 20 houses, and thence over a plain by a village (the name of which I forget) 5 katcha kôs.

Below Shoghor the streams of Arkari and Lodko join, at Andakhti, two katcha kôs from Shoghor. The Rajah of Chitràl's son lives there (Bahram); another son, Murid, lived in Lodko district. There is little snowfall on the high Khatinza, but there is plenty on the easy Nuqsán. A third road, over a plain, also leads to Chitrál from Zeibák, namely, to Uskútul (3 kôs from Zeibák); thence to Singlich, 2½ kôs, maidán; thence to the great tank, lake, or Hauz, five miles long and 1½ miles broad, full of big fish. Thence over the Durra, infested by Kafirs, only a katcha kôs, easy ascent, when the snow melts (otherwise impassable), and an easy descent of one kôs to Shai Sidèn, at foot of pass (below which is, 2 kôs, Gobôr, where there is some cultivation in summer). (Birzin is a village of 40 houses, about 8 kôs distant from Gobôr.) Parabêg, 50 houses, 2 kôs; Parabêg to Kui, 70 houses, 1 katcha kôs; below Kui, ½ kôs, is Jìtur; below is a ziarat of Pir Shah Nasir Khosrō at Birgunnì, one kôs, a warm spring, 50 houses; Birgunnì to Drôshp, 2 katcha kôs, where Raja Imán-ul-Mulk's son, Murid, resides. Drôshp, 40 houses; one kôs further is Mogh, 20 houses; thence to Andákhti, 4 or 5 kôs. Over the Hauz is the Mandàl mountain towards the Siah Posh country. Ahmad Diwanè, 50 houses, is the first village of Kafirs, subject to Chitrál. Over Gabôr is the Ṣhuitsh Mountain, behind which is the Aptzai Fort of the Siah Posh Kafirs, 200 houses; these are the two places from which Kafirs descend to plunder caravans coming from Peshawar, and of whose approach they may have been warned from Chitrál, keeping clothes and weapons for themselves, and giving the horses, etc., to Chitrál. The Kafirs of Kamōz (2,000 houses) are subject to Chitrál; also Ludde (1,000 houses), Aptsai (200 houses), Shudgol Fort (150 houses).

Istagàz is subject (100 houses) to Chitrál; Mēr (40 houses) subject to Chitrál; Mundjèsh, 500 houses; Madugàll (500 houses and two forts), on a difficult road, is between Kamōz (1 kôs above it) and Kamtán (Ludde, Aptsai, Shudgol, Ahmad Diwané), 4 kos. These Madugallis are independent, and plunder caravans from Dīr or Zemindars. Sometimes they are bribed by the Chitrál Raja to keep quiet.

Dull as the above account may read, it is full of topographical, if not political, interest to whoever can read "between the lines"; and the telegrams and articles in *The Times* of the 23rd and 25th Sept., 1891, throw light on an unpleasant and hitherto concealed situation. Since 1866 I have, in vain, drawn the attention of the Indian Government to the Gilgit frontier. In 1886, or twenty years after my exploration, Colonel Lockhart's mission, no doubt, did service, as regards Chitrál; but Hunza and Nagyr have been mismanaged, owing to the incompetent manner in which my information has been used. I have recently, after three years' labour, much expense, and some danger, completed the first quarto volume of my work on Hunza, Nagyr, and a part of Yasin, the language of which has been a great puzzle, that has now been unravelled, giving a new departure to philology; and the Foreign Department of the Indian Government has presented me with 100 copies of my work, a compliment that is often paid to the honorary contributor of a paper to the ASIATIC QUARTERLY REVIEW.

APPENDIX VII.

A SECRET RELIGION IN THE HINDUKUSH [THE PAMIR REGION] AND IN THE LEBANON.

I.—THE MULÁIS OF THE HINDUKUSH.

A NUMBER of conjectures as to the origin of the word "Mulái," all of which are incorrect, have been made by eminent writers unacquainted with Arabic or the meaning of its theological history and terms. A few of these conjectures, however, go very near some fact or view connected with the "Muláis." The word may not mean "terrestrial gods," but there are no other, for practical purposes, in the creed of the "Muláis." It is certainly not a corruption of "Muláhid" or "heretic," if not "atheist," although this term has been specially applied to them by their enemies. It can have nothing whatever to do etymologically with "Muwáhidîn" or worshippers of "One" [God], though they, no doubt, call themselves so, *i.e.*, "Unitarians." There is this additional difficulty, moreover, introduced into the question, that no name can be conclusive as to the esoteric appellation of a sect that has been obliged to practise "Conformity" or "Pious fraud" or "concealment" of its religion, in order to escape persecution or wholesale massacre. The Shiahs,* whose belief, in the hereditary succession, through the descendants of A'li, of the *spiritual* "Imámat" or leadership or apostleship of the prophet Muhammad, rendered them overt or covert enemies of those Sunni rulers who held the *temporal* power or "the Khiláfat" (misspelt as "the Caliphate"), were, and are, allowed to practise "Taqqîa" (which I have rendered as "Conformity") outwardly and the more exaggerated or exclusive a particular A'liite or Shiite sect, the more careful had it to be. The Sunni and Shiah may both publicly confess "There is no God but God, and Muhammad is his prophet"; but

* It is superfluous to inform readers of this Review that the Persians are Shiah, and the Turks Sunni, Muhammadans. Most of the Indian Muhammadans are Sunnis.

the Shiah adds under his breath, "A'li is the Deputy (Governor) of God and the heir of the prophet of God." Now this word for "Deputy" is "*vali*," "to be close to," whether it be to God, a king, a priest, a master, or other position of eminence in Arabian belief, society, history, or intellectual creations.* "Maulá" or "Mulá" comes from the same root and is generally applied to a spiritual master, but, among the Shiahs, specially to their "LORD" A'li. Therefore, "Muláis" are the special followers of the "Lord A'li," just as the Jesuits claim to be a fraternity of special followers of "the Lord Jesus" When, then, the term "Mauláná" or our "Master or Lord" is specially used in the Druse Covenant of Initiation [see further on], there is not far to seek for the meaning of the appellation "Mulái," though it was left for me to find it out from the A'liite songs of the Muláis of the Hindukush. Whatever the innermost coterie of the "initiated" may practise or believe, a connecting link of the sect with some existing creed is necessary for their safety or respectability. Thus, the *Ismailians* might call themselves "*Sadiqis*" or "the righteous," in order to spread the belief of their being special adherents of the 6th Imám, (in the order of descent from A'li), the Imám Ja'far *Sádiq* (the righteous), without entering into the vexed question as to whether his son "*Ismáîl*" was the real "seventh" Imám or his other son, Mûsa (through whom the bulk of Shiahs look for their Mahdi or Messiah, the 12th Imám). Nor would any such special fervour in revering a particular phase or man be necessarily deemed to be heretical, even among Sunnis. I have often heard a Sunni, especially if he was a Persian scholar and the strange magic of that language had subdued him, admit the impeachment of having "a particular love

* Many words denoting proximity, become honorifics, such as "Sherif" (Shereef), "Hazrat," "Jenáb," etc. "Khalîfah" is one who succeeds, or follows, or is a deputy. Strictly speaking, this title refers to the Sultan of Turkey as the successor of the Prophet Muhammad in the temporal headship of the Sunnis, but even the successor of the heretical Mahdi in the Sudán calls himself "Khalifa."

for the house of A'li," and the numerous class of Sayads, who claim to be descendants of the Prophet, is respected, if not venerated, among Sunnis, who, in theory, oppose the "hereditary" claims of Shiahs.* The Máulais, therefore, of the Hindukush, being, consciously or not, a sub-sect of Shiahs, can make friends with the main body of Shiahs, and yet pretend to the Sunnis as being, in many respects, with them. Normally, the Mauláis would profess to be good Muhammadans of the Shiah persuasion, leaning, however, to the 7th Imám; if surrounded by, or in danger of, Sunnis, they would *outwardly* "conform" (which is all that the Sunnis require), and, at home, practise their own rites. The Khojas of Bombay, who had been converted from Hinduism, but whose very name is Ismailian, used to read the "Das-awtar" or "ten incarnations," in which "A'li" is made out to be the "Tenth Incarnation,"-thus rendering their step from Wishnu Hinduism to Shiah Muhammadanism an easy one. "All things to all men" is the dictum of the Muláis, without, thereby, sacrificing their own convictions. The more a Mulái knows, the more he acts on Disraeli's sneer that all sensible men are of *one* religion, but do not tell what that religion is. The less a Mulái knows, the more fanatically is he an A'liite, centreing however his faith on the living descendant of the 7th Imám. "Nothing is a crime that is not found out" may, or may not be, the theory among the Druses, or the practice all over the world; the fact remains that neither the Druses nor the Muláis, whatever their belief, are worse than their neighbours. Even the odious signification that attaches to the term "Assassin" has been a calumny against those misguided Ismailians who sought to rid the world of tyrants

* The "Sherifs" or "Shereefs," in a special, princely or official sense, are lineal descendants of Muhammad through his daughter Fatima who was married to A'li, and have, perhaps, even a higher claim to the respect of the Faithful, than ordinary descendants or "Sayads." The Grand Shereef of Mecca, the Shereefian dynasty of Morocco, the Shereef of Wazan, who also bears the title, like the Emperor of Marocco, of "Muláy," or "Maulái," show the great extent of the "House of A'li."

who had ordered the general massacre of the sect or who sacrificed one man in order to save a whole people.

In 1866 I discovered the languages and races of "Dardistan" and gave that name to the countries between Kashmir and Kabul, including Hunza in them. In 1886 I was again on a special mission regarding the language of Hunza-Nagyr and a part of Yasin. I had already pointed out in 1867 the importance which our good friend, His Highness Agha Khan of Bombay, the Head of the Khojas in that city, enjoyed in those, then nearly inaccessible, regions, as also in Wakhan, Zebak, Shignán, Raushan, Koláb and Derwáz, where the Muláis predominate and are governed by hereditary Pîrs or ancient sages of their own choice,* to whom they yield implicit obedience, as do also the covenanters with "Al-Hákim" among the "initiated" of the Druses. Of these Pîrs, Agha Khan is Chief, and any command by him would be obeyed in some of the most dangerous parts of the Hindukush. Advantage was only taken in 1886 of this hint, when Colonel Lockhart's mission was supplied with letters of recommendation by His Highness to the Mulais. My identification of their mysterious rites with those of the Druses connects the Lebanon with the Hindukush through the Ismailia sect, which under the name of the "Assassins" enjoyed such an unenviable notoriety during the Crusades and establishes a link among the nations of Richard Cœur de Lion,† of Palestine and of the Pamirs. The connection of Hunza with the Huns or Hunas and the relations between the "Old Man of the Mountain" and our own Richard may be the subject of a future article. At present, I will confine myself to translating from the Persian original a Pythian utterance out of the "Kelám-i-Pîr" or "the Word of the ancient Sage," which takes the place of the Korán among Mauláis,

* Among these Pîrs each Mulái chooses his own, of course, ***under*** the supreme headship of Agha Khan.

† Who has been accused of instigating the "Old Man of the Mountain" to send his emissaries to murder Conrad of Montferrat, titular King of Jerusalem. The Ismailian "Assassins" are also accused of an attempt to murder Prince Edward of England at Acre.

and of which the following is the first extract ever given from that hidden book. It was partly dictated to me and partly written out on the occasion of His Highness, the present Agha Khan, paying me a visit, by the leader of some Muláis, who had fled, first from Russian tyranny, and then from the still heavier Afghan oppression in the border-countries of Central Asia, my own Hunza man also being present on the occasion.* The extract was called the Mulái "Mukti" or "Salvation" Cry of the Muláis. It may be incidentally mentioned that Shah Abdurrahim in Zeibak was (and perhaps still is) the greatest Pîr in Central Asia. He controls Hunza, so far as that God-forsaken country can be controlled. In Wakhan, Khwaja Ibrahim Husain was the Mulái leader, and in Sarikul, Shahzada Makîn. Sayad Jafar Khan ruled what there is of the sect in Bokhara, Balkh, Kabul and Kunduz. "*The* Pîr" or "ancient sage," however, was the historical Shah Nasir Khosrô, who is styled "a missionary of H. H. Aga Khan's ancestor." He is said to have had the complete "Kelám-i-Pîr," a book of which I have for so many years in vain tried to get a copy, although assisted by my friend, the Mihtar Nizám-ul-Mulk of Yasin and Chitrál. The following extract from it, in one and the same breath, affirms and denies the special doctrine of metempsychosis and other notions opposed to the professed Muhammadanism of the Muláis:

The MUKTI or "SALVATION."

The Mulái "ÁQIL" or "intelligent" = "initiated" [the singular of the Druse "U'qalá" or "initiated"] first asks, in inelegant and enigmatical Persian:

"ALA! In what I say, can I remain *knowingly* an Á'qil?" or "initiated" or "I remain knowingly an Á'qil, although what I say

---

1. "Come, solve for me a difficult story [or conjecture]

* Whom I took to England and whose name, curiously enough, was "Mata*vali*," which is also a derivative of "vali."

Come, tell me the Light which the spirit from the world-shape [this world of Phenomena]

When it becomes [gets] beyond [of] this shape, where [is] its abode and station ? [place of descent = "manzil"]

Is its place [of existence] in plants or in the Higher Universe [the world above ?]

Or in the Lower Universe between water, dust and clay" [or stone] ? [the strata between the centre and the surface of the earth]

---

2. "If, *knowingly*, that secret, come and tell me : 'Light'

And, if not, away ! not *knowing*, without head-wandering, careless [care not]

Dear ones ! The spirit of the *knowing* when it departs from these chains,

Does it become [wend] towards the skies [heavens] ? Is that its Station obtaining ?*

Or why in the shape of man [anthropomorphic shape] is the Adamite created ?†

Nay (?) the perfect man [ko-burd] cultured perfect,‡ or 'the ruling man [if] perfect, develops perfect culture'

But they who are not wanted [the useless] are ignorant doubters"

---

3. "Let me tell its Commentary ; every one, Come ! in the ear make it acceptable.

The present is one stride [or state of a man]

When they put him outside the body

They bind him in chains ; he becomes with cow or ass entering

Another time his place [of staying] is the [world of] plants. They hold him [there]

* Also, "Does it rise in the direction of heavens, or is its descent in vegetation ?" [taking "Hásil" = obtaining for "Mehásil" = vegetation], re-production (?)

† Also, "Or in the form of Man how does it again rotate into being born an Adamite ?" or, "Why is man created in the form of a human being ?"

‡ Also, "Nay, but the perfect man, the seemly, the all-perfect wins the prize."

He will remain inside these chains for three years [many a year] [under] that vain curse" [this is a vain word]

---

4. AL LÁY! Helper of Chosroes!* Such secrets to men why recklessly impart? [it only makes them impudent] Not will say ever this the *A'qil* [or "the initiated one."]

[The wise do not mention their religion; if they do, they only make the unwise impudent.]

So, after all, we have not been told the process or secret of after-life, whether ascending into air, descending into earth, renewing human life or migrating into animal, plant or stone. In fact, we are made to understand that our inquiry is folly and that its answer, whether true or not, is also folly. Yet are we allowed to conjecture the belief of "the initiated" in transmigration.

As for the Muláis "being all things to all men" in matters of religion—Sunnis with Sunnis and Shiahs with Shiahs—this is, as already stated, a mere amplification of the Shiah doctrine of *Taqqîah* or concealment in times of danger, to which I have specially referred in my "Dardistan."

The leaning of the Muláis is, of course, rather to poetical Shiism, with the chivalrous martyr A'li as its demigod or "next to God" in the A'lewia sect, than to prosaic and monotonous Sunniism, so that to strangers they seem to be Shiahs, as will be seen in an extract from a native Indian Diary† written some 20 years ago, and which, it may be

* These words are so badly written that they may also be read as, "O, thou that waitest not for wisdom."

† "Degol is the first village of Zebák . . . which is ruled by Shah Abdur-Rahim, a Sayad of the Shiah sect, worshipped by all the Shiahs of Kashkar, (Chitrál), Yarkand, and Khokand. They also worship Shah Bombáy, Shah Madkasan, who is learned, good-natured, and friendly to travellers. . . . The people give a tenth of their income to their preceptors; if one has ten children, he consecrates one to Shah Abdur-Rahim. . . . The inhabitants are strong and hardy; the women do not cover their faces from strangers. Although Shiahs, they have no mosques and repeat no prayers. Abdur-Rahim has one in his village, where *he* prays. Every

incidentally stated, still throws much light on the present conflicts in Dir, Bajaur and other petty States bordering on our frontier. No stranger is allowed to see the Kelám-i-Pîr, which takes the place of the Korán with Muláis, but in the most popular poem that is recited by them, the Imám-ul Zemán or Sahib-al-Zemán = the Imám or Lord of the Age (H. H. Aga Khan) is worshipped as the Monarch of this World, the visible incarnation of the Deity, offerings or a pilgrimage to whom dispenses a Mulái from prayer, fasting or a visit to the sacred shrines of Mecca or Madina, or rather the Shiah Kerbelá, the place of the martyrdom of Hasan and Husain, which Shiahs annually celebrate by what are inappropriately called "miracle plays," but which really are "elegies," and commemorative funeral recitations and processions. A person who has seen "the Lord of the Age" or who possesses some of the water in which he has washed his feet is an honoured guest in Mulái countries. The poem above alluded to is a parallel to the Druse "Contract" which will be considered further on, and begins with an invocation for "Help, oh Ali."

"Nobody will worship God, without worshipping Thee, Lord of the Age!
Jesus will descend from the fourth heaven to follow Thee, Lord of the Age!
Thy will alone will end the strife with Antichrist, Lord of the Age!
Thy beauty gives light to heaven, the sun and the moon, Lord of the Age!
May I be blessed by being under the dust of Thy feet, Lord of the Age!"

A Maulái is, if sincere, already dead to sin, and can, therefore, not commit any. He needs, therefore, no resur-

---

morning at *Chasht* (the middle hour between sunrise and noon) he sits in the assembly and distributes breads of wheat among the members, followed by the servants handing round tea in porcelain cups in which each one soaks his bread, and, after eating it, lifts his hand to bless the giver, a custom also followed by the nobles on entering the assembly. If Shah Abdur-Rahim addresses any of them, he rises from his seat and answers as if he were reading a *ruka't* at the time of praying, and then returns to his place, and sits on his knees, for to sit otherwise is reckoned a sin amongst these men." In other words, the only worship of the prayerless Muláis is to their Pîr, to whom they address the *ruka't* given by real Muhammadans in prayers to God [bowing, whilst standing, with hands resting on the knees].

rection or last Judgment day. Obedience to the Pír is his sole article of faith, and he holds his property, family and life at this Chief's disposal.

I must now conclude this introduction to a comparison of the creeds of the Druses and of the Muláis by quoting a few words from a rhapsody of A'li, repeated by the ordinary Mauláis till the pious frenzy is at white heat:

"Oh A'li, to God, to God, oh A'li, my sole aim, the only one, our Mula A'li; My desire, the only our Mula A'li; My passion only the beauty of A'li: My longing day and night for union with A'li; Higher and Higher A'li, oh A'li; A'li is the Killer of difficulties, oh A'li; He is the Commander of the Faithful, namely A'li; *That* one is the Imám of the steadfast in faith, namely A'li," and so on *ad infinitum* till we come to the natural connection between normal Shiism, its exaggeration into A'li worship, its mysterious interpretation of the self-sacrifice of Husain to save the world, and, finally, to all other aberrations of which Maulaism is one. The poem then goes into wild Turkish and Arabic measures, which exhausted my informant, Ghulam Haidar, who adds on behalf of himself, also in verse: "It is not proper that I should not answer the question which you ask me, but what am I to say? The answer from me is easy, but I see a difficulty in *your* way. Oh Ghulam Haidar" (thrice repeated). Then in prose. "In the night of Friday, the Muláí men (in Hunza), instead of worship and prayer. taking Guitars and Drums (Rabábs and Daffs) in their hands, play the above "Ghazals" on them. Then six old men, Akhunds (priests), having assembled, read (sing) them in the Mosque, when the men of the mass of the people gather and give ear to them:

'"Yá A'li, Yá A'li, Yá Imám-i-Zemán"'—
'"Oh Ali, Oh Ali, Oh Imám (and Lord) of the Age"'—

is the mention (Chorus) which they take on their tongues. From the beginning of the evening till the morning they thus show their zeal; the Raja then as a reward of thanks for that worship bestows (gold dust to the value of) four tilas on the priests and gives them a quantity of butter of the weight of four measures and one sheep or big calf and one maund of wheat in order to hold a feast."

II.—The Covenant of "the initiated" Druses.

The following is a rendering of the Covenant or Contract which the U'qalá or "the initiated" amongst the Druses are reciting in mysterious seclusion. It was overheard by my informant, an "uninitiated" Druse.* It formed, as it were, the evening prayer of his uncle and aunt. Although an educated and highly intelligent person, he was not aware of even its local interest, much less of its general historical and religious importance.

The Covenant = Al Mitháq:

"O Governor [Valî] of the Age,† may Allah's blessing and peace be upon him" (this phrase seems intended to delude

* The Druses are divided into "Juhelá" = "uninitiated," or the Laity, and "U'qalá" = the "initiated."

† It should be noticed that this apotheosis of "Al-Hákim," the mad Fatimite Khalifa of Cairo (A.D. 996-1020), who was the head and originator of the special Ismailian sect, which became subsequently known to the Crusaders under the name of the "Assassins"—a corruption of "Hashishin," or drinkers of Hashish (*Canabis Indica*)—commences with titles of governorship or Age which would seem (to the uninitiated) to be compatible with his subordination to the Deity, although, for practical purposes, Al-Hákim is the "ruler of this world," whether for good or for evil. He is, therefore, the Prince of this world, if not Apollyon, and the fact that the words "Valî" = a deputed governor or "Hákim" = a governor, may cause him to be confounded with either an ordinary ruler, or be merely ringing the changes on his own name of "Al-Hákim," it is clear, at any rate to the initiated, that the only Deity worth caring for is thereby meant, and that he began with the Khalifa Al-Hákim, who lives for ever. In the titles "Maula" and "Valî" there is also an allusion to A'li, who is "next to God," and from whom Al-Hákim was descended. The Mauláis or Muláis of the Hindukush use similar titles for their spiritual head, whether dead, or continuing in his lineal descendant, Agha Khan of Bombay. The "Kelám-i-Pîr," or "the Logos or word of the Pîr or ancient sage," mainly refers to the sayings attributed to the "Sheikh-ul-Jabl," or "Old Man of the Mountain." In Hunza itself, the Muláis equally address their practical Deity as "The Ancient of the Age," or "Pîr-uz-Zamán."

Muhammadans into the belief that the Druses have the same Allah or God, but it has an esoteric sense which will become apparent further on). "I put my confidence into 'our spiritual head the Lord' (literally 'OUR MAULA AL-HÁKIM') (here is one of the esoteric formulæ)—'the One, the Single, the Everlasting (Lord), the (serenely) Distinct from Duality and Number.' (This is a protest not only against the female form of the Deity, but also against the notion of a distinct good and evil principle, an Ahriman or Ormuz, whilst its Muhammadan form would seem to outsiders to be merely a protest against giving any 'companion to God.') The initiator and the to be 'initiated' then go on repeating together the following, the former using the 3rd, and the latter the 1st, person. 'I so and so' (here comes name of the initiated), 'son of such a one, CONFESS firmly the confession to which he (or I) respond from his [or my] soul, and bears testimony to it upon his spirit, whilst in a condition of soundness of his spirit and of his body, and with the (acceptance of the passing of the) lawfulness of the order, obeying without reluctance and under no violence: THAT he verily absolves (himself) from all Religions and Dogmas and Faiths and Convictions, all of them, in the various species of their contradictions, and that he does not acknowledge anything except the OBEDIENCE TO OUR MAULA AL-HÁKIM, may his mention be glorious! and this obedience it is the worship, and that he will not associate in his worship any (other) that is past or is present, or is to come, and that he has verily entrusted his spirit and his body, and whatever is to him and the whole of what he may possess to OUR MAULA AL-HÁKIM, and that he is satisfied to fulfil all His orders unto himself and against himself without any contradiction, and not refusing anything and not denying (refusing) anything of His actions, whether this injures him or rejoices him, and that he, should he ever revert (apostatize) from the religion of our Maula Al-Hákim which he has written upon his soul, and to which he has born testimony unto his spirit, that HE SHALL BE BEREFT (free) of the Creator, who is worshipped and deprived of the benefits of all the sanctions (rules, laws), and that he shall be considered as deserving the punishment of God, the High, may His mention be glorious! And that he, if he acknowledges that there is not to him in Heaven and not in the Earth an Imám in existence *except our Maula Al-Hákim*" (this confession distinguishes the Druses of the Lebanon and the Muláis of the Hindukush from the orthodox Shiahs, who believe in the coming of the ever-present Mahdi, or the twelfth Imám, a view that had been fostered by us in the Sudán to our endless confusion by our inexcusable opposition to the Sultan of Turkey as the Khalifa of the Sunnis), "then will the mention of him (who only believes in Al-Hákim) become glorious, and he will be of the *Muwáhidín* (who profess the unity of God), who will (eventually) conquer." (This appellation is common to the Druses and to the Muláis, but is not admitted as being applicable to them by orthodox Shiahs or Sunnis. In retaliation they call the Sunni a dog, and the Shiah an ass.) "And (the above) has been written* in the month so and so of the year (chronology) of the I'd (festival) of our Maula Al-Hákim, whose nation be glorious, whose Empire be strengthened to Him alone." (The Maulái Chronology is said to begin with the *special* revelation of the Imám on the 17th Ramadán in the 559th year of the Hejira, at the castle of Alamût.)

The Special Recitation.

The following is repeated by Druses at the conclusion of their prayers: "May God's blessing be upon him who speaks (confesses) the Lord of goodness and benefits. May God bless the Ruler of the Guidances (Hidāyā); to him be profit and sufficiency. May God's blessing be on our Lord the Hādi" (the Guide or "Mehdi" means one who is guided aright by God = the coming Messiah of the Shiah world,) "the Imám, the greatest of the perfect light" (this is an allusion to the 7th Imám, Ismail, descendant of *the* light†

* The contract is thus repeated from a written document.

† Many Shiahs call A'li "the light" of God.

(Mohammed), "who is waiting for the refuge (salvation) of all living beings. On Him may be (our) trust, and from him (may be) the peace. May God bless him and them whatever passes of nights and of days and of months and of years, whenever flashes the dawn of morning or night remains in darkness may abundant peace and trust be for ever! *O Allah-humma!*" (the mystic Muhammadan remnant of Elohim = Lords, Gods) "provide us with *Thy* contentment" (this is a play of words implying that our best "daily bread" is God's contentment with us) "and with *Their* contentment" (this is either a Trinitarian or Polytheistic invocation to "Elohim") "and with *their* intercession and with *Thy* mercy and with *their* mercy in this world and in the next! O our Maula! and Lord of the Imám" (this is indeed significant as to the pretensions of Al-Hákim to the godhead, or to some dignity very near it).

Now comes an ancient curse with a modern application and an appeal to arms (whispered along the line of assembled Druses):

"Pray for the ornament of sons,

In the East the five* residing (compare also the Shiah Panjtan'† and the five main Shiah sects)‡

* There are *five* books of the *Sheikh-ul-A'ql*, "or old man of the intelligence," or of the "initiated," and also apparently a book of investigation and of the unity of the Godhead for the "initiated of the retirement" = "U'qala al Khalwat." There are *five* "Maulas" or Mulas of "the initiated," which I take to be the names of five books, namely: (1) the Mula of the A'ql, or Mind, or of the body-corporate of the "U'qalá" or "the initiated"; (2) the Mula of the Nafs, or Breath; (3) the Mula of the Zeman, or the Age; (4) the Mula of the Kalima, or the Word; (5) the Mula of Al-Hákim, or the founder of the sect. Numbers 3 and 4 are probably the Kelám-i-Pír and other dicta of the Mulais of the Hindukush, to which I have already referred.

This holy roll among extreme Shiahs has *five* names, namely, God, Ali, Fatima, Hasan, and Husain, which positively excludes the prophet Muhammad, but includes his son-in-law (Ali), his daughter, Fatima, and the martyred grandsons of Ali, namely Hasan and Husain. As a rule, however, the ordinary orthodox "Panjtan" among Shiahs (and even in some Sunni Mosque inscriptions) are: "Muhammad, Ali, Fatima, Hasan and Husain." "Panjtan" means "the five (holy) bodies."

‡ There are *five* main sects among the Shiahs, or, rather, "Adelias,"

They say: Father Abraham has appeared,
and they announce the good tidings to the worshippers of *One* (the Druses).

They say: With the sword has Father Abraham appeared;

A violence to his enemies
O brethren! Prepare earnestly for the campaign,
Visiting the House of Mecca.
The House of Mecca and the sacred places,
On them has destruction been ordained.
Oh people of the Berbers! Extermination is lawful.
With the sword shall ye be sacrificed.
The French are coming with stealth.
The 'A'ql' [or 'the body of the initiated'] will protect us with its sword.
Rejoice, people of China, in the hour of Thy arrival.
Welcome to thee, city of Arin (?), oh my Lady!" [Fatima ?].

A Druse wedding-song may also be quoted here: ("Allah, billáli, billáli.") *The Chorus:* "O God, with the pearls, with the pearls," "Sway on to me, oh my Gazelle!" *Song:* "Thou maid who combest her (the bride's) tresses, comb them gently, and give her no pain; for she is the daughter of nobles, accustomed to being a pet" [*delláli*]. *Chorus: Allah, billáli, billáli; wa tanaqqalí, yá Ghazáli!*

Another Song: "Sing the praises of the shore, oh daughters; sing the praises of the daughters of the shore; for we have passed by the pomegranate-tree bearing full fruit, and we have compared it with the cheeks of the daughters of the shore."

or advocates of "the rightful" and hereditary succession to the Apostleship of Muhammad, in opposition to the elective principle by the *consensus fidelium* of the Sunnis. The two sects that now concern us are the African Ismailians, and the Ismailians of the Lebanon and of the Hindukush. The number of Shiah sects is estimated variously from 3 to 72.

(b) THE KELÁM-I-PÎR AND ESOTERIC MUHAMMADANISM.

It is not my wish to satisfy idle curiosity by describing the contents of a book, concealed for nine hundred years, the greater portion of which accident has placed in my hands after years of unsuccessful search in inhospitable regions. The fragmentary information regarding it and the practices of its followers which I had collected, were contributed to publications, like this Review, of specialists for specialists or for genuine Students of Oriental learning. Nothing could be more distressing to me than the formation of a band of "esoteric Muhammadans," unacquainted with Arabic, which is the only key to the knowledge of Islám. The mastery of the original language of his holy Scripture is, still more emphatically, the *sine quâ non* condition of a teacher, be he Christian, Muhammadan, or other "possessor of a sacred book." Nor should anyone discuss another's faith without knowing its religious texts in the original as well as its present practice.

The term "esoteric" has been so misused in connection with Buddhism, the least mystic of religions, by persons unacquainted with Sanscrit, Pali and modern Buddhism, that it has become unsafe to adopt it as describing the "inner" meaning of any faith. Were Buddha alive, he would regret having made the path of salvation so easy by abolishing the various stages of Brahminical preparation, through a studious, practical and useful life, for the final retirement, meditation, and Nirvana. Yet there are mysterious practices in the Tantric worship of "the Wisdom of the Knowable," which Buddha alone brought to the masses that were to be emancipated from the Brahminical yoke. Even transparent Judaism has its Kabala, and the religion that brought God to Man has mysteries of grace and godliness, the real meaning of which is only known to the true Christian of one's own sect or school. Thus open, easy and simple

Muhammadanism has its two triumphant orthodoxies of Sunnis and Imamía Shiahs and 72 militant, or outwardly conforming, heterodoxies. Indeed, as long as words can be fought over, and even facts do not impress all alike, so long will the more or less proficient professors of a creed reach various degrees of "esoteric" knowledge.

It is the unknown merit of the religious system of the so-called Assassins of the Crusades to have discussed, dismissed and yet absorbed a number of faiths and philosophies. It adapted itself to various stages of knowledge among its proselytes from various creeds, whilst the circumstances of its birth, history and surroundings gave it a Muhammadan basis. *Non omnia scimus omnes* may be said by the most "initiated" Druse, Ismailian or "Mulái," the latter being the name by which I will, in future, designate all the ramifications of this remarkable system of Philosophy, Religion and Practical politics.

This system elaborates the principle that all truths, except ONE, are relative. It treats each man as it finds him, leading him through stages, complete in themselves, to the final secret. We, too, in a way admit that strong meat and drink are not the proper food for babes. We speak of professional training and of the professional spirit, of *esprit de corps*, terms which all have an "esoteric" sense, and imply preparation; indeed, every experience of life is an "initiation" which he, who has not undergone it, cannot "realize;" we, too, have medical and other works which the ordinary reader does not buy and which are, so far, "esoteric" to him, but we have not laid down in practice that he, who does not know, shall not teach or rule. This has been systematized, with a keen sense of proportion, by the Founders of the Ismailian sect. Fighting for its existence against rival Muhammadan bodies and in the conflicts of Christianity, Judaism, Magianism and various Philosophies, its emissaries applied the Pauline conduct of being "all things to all men" in order to gain converts.

After the establishment of mutual confidence, a Christian might be confronted with puzzling questions regarding the

Trinity, the Atonement, the Holy Communion, etc.—the Jew be called to explain an Universal God, yet exclusively beneficent to His people, or might be cross-examined on the miracles of Moses; a Zoroastrian, to whom much sympathy should be expressed, would be sounded as to his Magian belief; an idolater, if ignorant, could be easily shown the error of his ways and, if not, his pantheism might be checked by the evidences of materialistic or monotheistic doctrine; the orthodox Sunni would be required to explain the apparent inconsistencies of statements in the Korán, and the various sects of Shiahs would be confounded by doubts being thrown on this or that link of the hereditary succession of the apostleship of Muhammad; sceptics, philosophers, word-splitters, both orthodox and heterodox, would be followed into their last retrenchments by contradictory arguments, materialistic, idealistic, exegetical, as the case might be. With every creed, to use an Indian simile, the peeling of the onion was repeated, in which, after one leaf after the other of the onion is taken off in search of the onion, no onion is found and nothing is left. The enquirer would thus be ready for the reception of such new doctrine as might be taught him by the "Mulái"* preacher, or *Dái*, who then revealed himself one step beyond the mental and moral capacity of his intended convert, whilst sharing with the latter a basis of common belief. Now this required ability of no mean order, as also of great variety, so as to be adapted to all conditions of men to whom the *Dái* might address himself. Sex, age, profession, hereditary and acquired qualities, antecedents and attainments, all were taken into consideration. At the same time, in an age of violence, the missionaries of the new faith had to keep their work a profound secret and to insist on a covenant, identical with, or similar to, the one of

* I use the word "Mulái" to include not only the virtuous Druses with their self-denying "initiated" or "*U'qelá*" leaders, but also the Ismailians generally, whether religious or not, (as in impious Hunza) and of whatever degree of conformity or scepticism. As a rule, an ordinary Mulái will outwardly practise Sunni rites and hold Shiah doctrines.

the Druses, which I published in the last number of the *Asiatic Quarterly Review.* Even when confronted by Hinduism, the new creed could represent that Áli, the son-in-law of the prophet Muhammad, was the 10th incarnation of Vishnu, which is expected, as was the Paraclete and as are the Messiah and the "Mehdi" (many of those who adopted that title being secret followers of the Ismailian creed).* I have pointed out in my last article how the very name of 'Ali, his chivalrous character, his eloquence, his sad death and the martyrdom of his sons lent themselves to his more than apotheosis in minds already prepared by Magian doctrine and the spirit of opposition to the successful Sunni oppressor. I think that I can quote extracts, in support of this statement from the "Kelám-i-pír" or the "*Logos* of the Ancient," showing how the contributor to it (for I take

* In discussion, whenever expedient, with a Brahmin, or even Buddhist, the belief in a modified metempsychosis would form a bond of sympathy (see last A. Q. R.), whilst the survival "of the most adapted," rather than that of "the best,"—without, however, the loss of any individual or type,—would be connected with the notion of a certain fixed number of souls in evolution from "the beginning" and ever recurrent in living form. "The beginning," however, would be a mere term applying to this or that revealed condition, for behind what may be called "the terrestrial gods," behind Allah in whatever form, Deity or Deities, there was The BEING that existed without a beginning and whose first manifestation was the "Word" with its Replica as the type of the apostle and his fellow that ever succeeded itself throughout the generations of this world. If the visible Deity, preferring to show itself in human, rather than any other, form, is incorporated in the lineal descendant of the 7th Imám, it is, apparently, because humanity requires such an unbroken link in order to convert into certainty its hope of the deliverer, the Messiah, the Mahdi, the second [advent of] Jesus, who will similarly be the Deity in the shape of a man, reconciling the various expectations of all religions in one manifestation. That few, if any, Muláis, or even the most "initiated" Druses, should know *every* variety of their belief, is natural, not only in consequence of varying degrees of mental ability and of corresponding "initiation," but also because of varied historical or national surroundings, circumstances which underlie the guiding principle of all Mulái belief and practice. I venture to indicate, ***as purely my personal impression***, that this principle, which need not be further explained in this place, is the real secret of that faith. In my humble opinion, the *disjecta membra*, so to speak, of that faith form, if reconstituted, an embodiment of the religious thought of the World that seeks to reconcile all differences in one Philosophy and in one Policy.

the "Kelám-i-pîr" to be a collective name like "Homer"), the eminent mathematician, historian and poet, Shah Násir Khosrû, who was born in the year 355 A.H. = 969 A.D. was led, after a long life of purity and piety, of abstemiousness and study, to examine and reject one religion after the other and, finally, adopt the one with which we are now concerned and of which His Highness, Agha Sultan Muhammad Shah is the present hereditary spiritual head. His authority extends from the Lebanon to the Hindukush and wherever else there may be Ismailians, who either openly profess obedience to him, as do the Khojahs in Bombay; or who are his secret followers in various parts of the Muhammadan world in Asia and Africa.* The present

* In the interior of Arabia, Mr. W. B. Harris has come across a curious sect that may be connected with a section of the Kerámis or Keramátis, sects that gave much trouble in Syria in the 10th century, or, more probably, with an extreme and, probably, disavowed heterodox sub-sect of the Ismailians. It may be interesting to quote the correspondence that has taken place between us on the subject:

Tangier, *April* 5, 1893.

"During my journey through the Yemen last year I came across a sect of people calling themselves *Makarama*, of whom I was able to learn little, on account of their own reticence and the apparent want of interest of their Moslem neighbours. However, one of their number gave me a couple of lines of Arabic poetry, which translated, run:

"God is unknown—by day or by night.
Why trouble about him, there is no heaven and no hell."

All that I could find out about them in addition to this is that they hold an annual nightly feast with closed doors and lights in the windows, in which they are said to practise incest; and that they annually practise the form of driving a scapegoat into the mountains. The latter is clearly Judaic and the former custom savours of the Karmathians, but this seems improbable as the people are not Moslems. They are visited, it is said, by certain Indians who prize the charms written by these Yemenis. Beyond this I was able to discover nothing.

I have no valuable books of reference as to religions here, but if I remember aright there were Phœnician rites resembling this. Could it have anything to do with the Sabeans? I should be so grateful to you if you could let me know, when you have time, what you think about it. I can find no reference to them in any work on the Yemen. The name of the sect is, I suppose, of Persian origin. WALTER B. HARRIS.

[REPLY.] Vichy, *April* 14, 1893.

I, too, am not here within the reach of books of reference. I will, however, try to suggest what occurs to me on the spur of the moment in the hope young, but enlightened, Chief is, as his father and grand-father, likely to exert his influence for good.

---

that it may possibly be of some slight use in your enquiries. It is very important, first of all, to learn how "Makarama" is spelt by the Yemen people in the Arabic character, and especially whether the "k" is a "kef" or a "qaf" ق. Then the lines you quote should be sent to me in the original Arabic dialect and character (not the Maghrebi form, of course) and transliterated in Roman characters* *as you heard them*, for a good deal depends, *inter alia*, on the Arabic equivalents, used by "the Makarama" of "God," "heaven," and "hell." . . . The sentiment of the translation is the *Mulái* of Hunza, about whom I have written in the last *Asiatic Quarterly Review*. . . .

How do you know that the people are *not* Moslems? That their orthodox Muhammadan neighbours do not admit them to be such, is not conclusive, for I have heard rigid Sunnis even exclude Shiahs from that appellation. If you could remember the *exact* question which you put on that subject to your Mukarama friends and their precise reply, it might help to a conclusion.

Driving a scapegoat into the mountains is a common practice among the Afghans, who call themselves "Beni Israel" (not to be confounded with the *Jews* properly so called—their "Musáis" or "Yahûdis"). The other rites you speak of *were alleged* against the Karmathians and the Yazîdis *are* accused of them. Have you thought of the Yazîdis? The accusation of incestuous gatherings is, as you know, constantly brought by "the orthodox" against sectarians and I would not, in your place, give up the conjecture of a Karmathian origin of the "Makarama," before you have gone further into the matter. Please, therefore, to remember *all you can* about your friends and, if I can, I shall aid your enquiry to the best of my ability. I think you are right about the Phœnician rites and the Sabean conjecture.

I do not think that "Makarama" is of Persian origin. Is it possibly "*Mu*karama" or "*Mu*karrima"? If so, this would be an appropriate title for a specially "blessed" or enlightened sect. Why do you call them a "*sect*"? Are they also ethnographically distinct from their neighbours and what are their occupations? Could you get me a copy of one of their *charms*? Their being visited by certain Indians would rather show their Ismailian connexion than that they are not a heretical Muhammadan sect. Indeed, among the Ismailian sects mentioned by Makrizi as having spread in Yemen, among other countries, are "the *Kerámis*, *Karmátis*, Khárijis, etc.," "all of whom studied philosophy and chose what suited them." I really think these are your "Makaráma." G. W. LEITNER.

---

* I think "romanizing" the Oriental characters a great mistake, except "to make assurance doubly sure." The *Arabic* spelling would at once limit conjectures and lead to a solution.

The following is a short biographical sketch of this lineal descendant of the prophet Áli. His genealogy is incontestable and will, I hope, be included in my next paper.*

"H. H. Agha Sultan Muhammad Shah was born at Karachi on Nov. 2nd, 1877. It was soon seen that it would be necessary to give him a good education, and his father, H. H. the late Agha Ali Shah, early grounded him in the history of Persia and the writings of its great poets. But this education was certainly not sufficient in the present day, and Lady Ali Shah, after the death of her husband, very wisely carried out his wishes by placing his son under an English tutor, so that, whilst Persian was by no means neglected, a course of English reading was begun. Four years ago he stumbled over the spelling of monosyllables. The progress made now is really surprising; with natural talents he has found it easy to acquire a thorough English accent and converses freely with Englishmen. The histories of Persia, India and England, the series of the Rulers of India and the Queen's Prime Ministers, McCarthy's 'History of our Own Times' and the lives of eminent men that stock his library, mark a predilection for History and Biography. The subjects of conversation during a morning's ride are often the politics of the day or the turning points in the lives of illustrious men. But with this reading his other studies are not neglected. Algebra, Geometry, Arithmetic, elementary Astronomy, Chemistry and Mechanics. with English authors like Shakespeare, Macaulay, and Scott, form a part of his scholastic course.

"Unlike his father and grandfather, the Aga Sahib has little love for hunting, though he is seen regularly on the race-course and is well known in India as a patron of the turf. In the peculiarity of his position it will be difficult for him to

* We trust to be able to publish in our next issue the history of his family since 622 A.D. as also his photograph and those of his father and grandfather, the latter of whom rendered great services to our Government in Sind and Kandahar.—ED.

travel for some years, but his eyes are directed to Europe and he looks forward to the pleasure of witnessing at some future time an important debate in the House of Commons. From the fact that every mail brings English periodicals to his door, it will be seen that he closely follows everything that relates to English politics.

"With the work amongst the Khojahs and his other followers devolving upon him at so early an age his studies are, of course, liable to be interrupted, and it is hardly possible for him to devote himself to his books—Oriental and English—as much as he would wish to do. He is not yet married, nor does he seem inclined to marry early. A few years, however, must see him the father of a family, and there is little doubt that his children will be educated with all the advantages of the best ancient and modern education so as to make them worthy of their illustrious descent."

How far His Highness will be himself initiated into more than the practice and rites, public and private, of so much of his form of the Ismailian Faith as is necessary for the maintenance of his position and responsibilities towards his followers, depends on his attainments, mental vigour, and character. With greater theoretical power than even the Pope, who is not hereditary, his influence is personal and representative by the *consensus fidelium*. Nearly all of them are in the first, or second, degree, even their Pirs being generally in the 3rd or 4th, with a general leaning to a mystic divine A'li, not merely the historical A'li, whom their followers see incarnated in his present living descendant. Few, if any, of the leaders are in higher degrees, for they might be out of touch with the practical exigencies of their position in different countries and circumstances. Perhaps, among the Druses, there may be one professor in the highest stage of the "initiated"—the Ninth—but even then he would take his choice of Philosophies and find a microcosm of theory and practice in each. The result on mind and character would be ennobling, and he would die, if, indeed, an "initiated" can die, carrying away with him the secret of his faith, which he alone has been found worthy to discover. What that secret is, no amount of divulging will impart to any one who is not fit to receive it, though the infinite variety of its manifestations adapt it to every form of thought or life. That even Masonic pass-words may, for practical purposes and in spite of published books, be kept a secret, though possibly an open one, experience has shown, but the man does not yet exist who can, or will, apply the system, of which I have endeavoured to give a hint, to the Universal Federation of Religious Autonomies, which, in my humble opinion, the Ismailian doctrine was intended to found, little as its present followers may know of this use of the genuine ring of Truth, of which every religion, according to Lessing's *Nathan der Weise*, claims to have the exclusive possession. If this be not enough, I will, at the outset, give the advice that the old man in Lavengro with his dying breath gave to his disciple as the reward of a life-long devotion to learn the great secret—"LEARN ARABIC"—as a variation on his "Learn German." There is no royal road to learning or to salvation, and mental culture is impossible without the synthesis which the study of Classical languages—Oriental or European—still foster in this age of destructive analysis and of that scepticism which does not seek to re-construct.

Since writing above another accident has placed in my hands an evidently ancient manuscript in Persian verse, on the same or kindred subjects of Ismailian belief. The manuscript is duodecimo, about 200 pages in extent, and is written in exquisite miniature caligraphy. Its perusal may affect my decision as to the manner of dealing with the question, so far as the public is concerned; in the meanwhile, I am still in search of the name of its author, and of its date.

APPENDIX VIII.

ON THE

SCIENCES OF LANGUAGE AND OF ETHNOGRAPHY

WITH SPECIAL REFERENCE TO

The Language and Customs of the People of Hunza

BEING A REPORT OF AN EXTEMPORE ADDRESS

BY G. W. LEITNER, M.A., PH.D., LL.D., D.O.L., ETC.

Publications of the Oriental Institute, Woking.

LONDON
SWAN SONNENSCHEIN & CO.
PATERNOSTER SQUARE
1890

ON THE SCIENCES OF LANGUAGE AND OF ETHNOGRAPHY:

*With special reference to the Language and Customs of the People of Hunza.**

THE time has long passed since grammar and its rules could be treated in the way to which we were accustomed at school. Vitality has now to be breathed into the dry bones of conjugations and declensions, and no language can be taught, even for mere practical purposes, without connecting custom and history with so-called "rules." The influences of climate and of religion have to be considered, as well as the character of the people, if we wish to obtain a real hold on the language of our study. Do we desire to make language a speciality, the preparation of acquiring early in life two dissimilar languages, one analytic and the other synthetic, is absolutely necessary, because if that is not done, we shall always be hampered by the difficulty of dissociating the substance from the word which designates it. The human mind is extremely limited, and amongst the limits imposed upon it are those of, in early life, connecting an idea, fact, or process, with certain words; and unless two languages, at least, are learnt, and those two are as dissimilar as possible, one is always, more or less, the slave of routine in the perception and in the application of new facts and of new ideas, and in the adaptation of any matter of either theoretical or practical importance. It is a great advantage, for linguistic purposes, which are far more practically important than may be generally believed, that the study of the classical languages still holds the foremost place in this country; because, however necessary scientific "observation" may be, it cannot take the place of a cultured imagination. The stimulus of illustration and comparison, which, in the

* Being a report of an extempore address delivered before the Victoria Institute.

historical sense of the terms, is an absolutely necessary primary condition to mental advance, is derived from classical and literary pursuits. The study of two very similar languages, however, is not the same discipline to a beginner in linguistics; *e.g.*, to learn French and Italian is not of the same value as French and German, for the more dissimilar the languages the better.

Again, if you desire to elicit a language of which you know nothing, from a savage who cannot explain it and who does not understand your language, there are certain processes with which some linguists, no doubt, are familiar, and others commend themselves in practical experience; for instance, in pointing to an object which you wish to have, say, a fruit which you want to eat, you may not only obtain the name for it, but the gesture to obtain it, if you are surrounded by several savages whose language you do not know, may also induce one of the men to order another to get it for you,—I suppose on the principle that it is easy for one to command and for others to obey; but, be that as it may, this course, to the attentive observer, first obtains the name for the required thing and next elicits the imperative; you hear something with a kind of inflection which, once heard, cannot be mistaken for anything else than the imperative. Further, the *reply* to the imperative would either elicit "yes," or "no," or the indicative present. This process of inquiry does not apply to all languages, but it applies to a great many; and the attitude which you have to assume towards every language that you know nothing about, in the midst of strangers who speak it, is that, of course, of an entirely sympathetic student. You have, indeed, to apply to language the dictum which Buddhist Lamas apply to religion—never to think, much less to say, that your own religion (in this case your own language) is the best; *i.e.*, the form of expression in which you are in the habit of conveying your thoughts, is one so perfectly conventional, though rational in your case, that the greatest freedom from prejudice is as essential a consideration as the wish to acquire the language of others. In other words, in addition to the mere elementary acquisition of knowledge, you have to cultivate a sympathetic attitude; and here, again, is one of the proofs of a truth which my experience has taught me, that, however great knowledge may be, sympathy is greater, for sympathy enables us to fit the key which is given by knowledge. Gestures also elicit a response in dealing, for instance, with numerals, where we are facilitated by the fingers of the hand. Of course, one is occasionally stopped by a savage who cannot go, or is supposed not to be able to go, beyond two, or beyond five.

I take it that in the majority of cases of that kind, a good deal of our misconception with regard to the difficulty of the inquiry lies in ourselves—that ideas of multitude connected with the peculiar customs of the race that have yet to be ascertained, are at the bottom of the inability of that race to follow our numeration. For instance, we go up to ten, and in order to elicit a name for eleven, we say "one, ten;" if the man laughs, change the order, and say "ten, one;" the chances are that the savage will instinctively rejoin "ten *and* one," and we then get the conjunction. Putting the fingers of both hands together may mean "multitude," "alliance," or "enmity," according as the customs of the race are interpreted by that gesture.

I am reminded of this particular instance in my experience, because I referred to it in a discussion on an admirable paper on the Kafirs of the Hindukush by the eminent Dr. Bellew. If you do not take custom along with a "rule," and do not try to explain the so-called rule by either historical events or some custom of the race, you make language a matter entirely of memory, and as memory is one of the faculties that suffers most from advancing age, or from modes of living and various other circumstances, the moment that memory is impaired your linguistic knowledge must suffer—you, therefore, should make language a matter of judgment and of associations If you do not do that, however great your linguistic knowledge or scholarship, you must eventually fail in doing justice to the subject or to those with whom you are dealing.

The same principle applies as much to a highly-civilised language like Arabic, one of the most important languages in the way of expressing the multifarious processes of human thought and action, as to the remnant of the pre-historic Hunza language, which throws an unexpected light on the science of language.

Let us first take Arabic and the misconceptions of it by Arabic scholars. In 1859 I pointed out before the College of Preceptors, how it was necessary not only to discriminate between the Chapters in the Koran delivered at Mecca, and those given at Medina, but also to arrange the verses out of various Chapters in their real sequence. I believe we are now advancing towards a better understanding of this most remarkable book. But we still find in its translation such passages, for instance, as, "when in war women are captured, *take* those that are not married." The meaning is nothing so arbitary. The expression for "take" that we have there is *ankohu*—marry, *i.e.*, take in marriage or *nikáh*, as no alliance can be formed with even a willing captive taken in war, except through the process of *nikáh*, which is the religious marriage contract. Again, we have the passage, "Kill the infidels wherever you find them." There again is shown the want of sympathetic knowledge, which is distinct from the knowledge of our translators who render "qatilu" by "kill," when it merely means "fight" and refers to an impending engagement with enemies who were then attacking Muhammed's camp. Apart from accuracy of translation, a sympathetic attitude is also of practical importance. *E.g.*, had we gone into Oriental questions with more sympathy and, in consequence, more real knowledge, many of our frontier wars would have been avoided, and there is not the least doubt that in dealing with Oriental humanity, whether we had taken a firm or a conciliatory course, we should have been upon a track more likely to lead to success than by taking action based on insufficient knowledge or on preconceptions. For instance, in the *Times* there was a telegram from Suakim about the Mahdi, to the effect that El Senousi was opposing him successfully. I do not know who El Senousi is, but very many years ago I pointed out the great importance of the Senousi *sect* in Africa, and, unless the deceased founder of that name has now arisen, whether it is a man of that name or the now well-known sect that is mentioned, one cannot say from the telegram. The sender of the message states that as sure as the El Senousi rises to importance there will be a danger to Egypt and to Islam. It is Christian-like to think well of Islam, and to try to protect it. This very few Christians do, and it shows a kind feeling towards a sister-faith, but I am not sure that the writer accurately knew what Islam is; though there can be no doubt that the rise of fanatical sects, like the Senousi, which is largely due to the feeling of resistance created by the encroachments of so-called European civilisation, is opposed to orthodox Muhammedanism. Be that as it may, I have also turned to "the further correspondence on the affairs of Egypt" which a friend gave me, and, really, I now know rather less about Egypt than I did before. For instance, I find (and I am specially referring to the blue-book in my hand) that letters of the greatest importance from the Mahdi are treated in the following flippant manner: "This is nothing more or less than an unauthenticated copy of a letter sent by the deceased Mahdi to General Gordon!" Is this not enough to deserve attentive inquiry? General Gordon would, probably, not have agreed with the writer of this contemptuous remark, which is doubly out of place when we are also told that the Mahdi was sending Gordon certain verses and passages from the Korán, illustrative of his position, which are eliminated by the translator as unnecessary, of no importance, and of very little interest! Now, considering that this gentleman knew Arabic, I think I am right when I add that with a little more sympathy he would have known more, and had he known more he would have quoted those passages, for it is most necessary for us to know on what precise authority of the Korán or of tradition this so-called Mahdi based his claim, and knowledge of this kind would give us the opportunity of dealing with the matter. Again, on the question of Her Majesty's title of "Kaisar-i-hind," which, after great difficulty, I succeeded in carrying into general adoption in India, the previous translators of "Empress" had suggested some title which would either have been unintelligible or which would have given Her Majesty a disrespectful appellation, whilst none would have created that awe and respect which, I suppose, the translation of the Imperial title was intended to inspire. Even the subsequent official adopter of this title, Sir W. Muir, advocated it on grounds which would have rendered it inapplicable to India. With the National Anthem similarly, we had a translation by a Persian into Hindustani, which was supported by a number of Oriental scholars in this country, who either did not study it, or who dealt with the matter entirely from a theoretical point of view, and what was the result? The result was—that for "God Save the Queen," a passage was put which was either blasphemous, or which, in popular Muhammedan acceptance, might mean, "God grant that Her Majesty may again marry!" whereas one of the glories of Her Majesty among her Hindu subjects is that she is a true "Satti" or Suttee, viz., a righteous widow, who ever honours the memory of her terrestrial and spiritual husband—neither of those views being intended by the translator, or by that very large and responsible body of men who supported him, and that still larger and emphatically loyal body that intended to give the translation of the National Anthem as a gift to India at a cost of several thousand pounds, when for a hundred rupees a dozen accurate and respectful versions were elicited by me in India itself.

I therefore submit that in speaking of the sciences of language and ethnography, we have, or ought to have, passed, long ago, the standpoint of treating them separately; they must be treated together, and, as I said at the beginning, taking, *e.g.*, Arabic, with its thirty-six broken plurals (quite enough to break anybody's memory), you will never be able to learn it unless you thoroughly realise the life of the Arab, as he gets out of his tent in the morning, milks his female camel, &c., and unless you follow him through his daily ride or occupations. Then you will understand how it is, especially if you have travelled in Arabia, that camels that appear at a distance on the horizon, affect the eye differently from camels when they come near, and are seen as they follow one another in a row, and those again different from the camels as they gather round the tent or encampment; and therefore it is that in the different perceptions to the eye under the influence of natural phenomena, these multifarious plurals are of the greatest importance in examining the customs of the people. Then will the discovery of the right plural be a matter of enjoyment, leading one on to another discovery, and to work all the better; whereas, with the grammatical routine that we still pursue, I wonder, when we reach to middle or old age, after following the literary profession, that we are not more dull or confused than we are at present. When one abstract idea follows the other, as in our phraseology, it is not like one scene following another in a new country which is full of stimulus, but the course which we adopt of abstract generalisations, without analysing them and bringing them back to their concrete constituents, is almost a process of stultification.

Coming now to one of the most primitive, and certainly one of the remnants of pre-historic languages, that of Hunza, which I had the opportunity of examining twenty-three years ago, while Gilgit was in a state of warfare, and where I had to learn the language, so to speak, with a pencil in one hand and a weapon in the other, and surrounded by people who were waiting for an opportunity to kill me, I found, that on reverting to it three years ago, the language had already undergone a process of assimilation to the surrounding dialects, owing to the advance of so-called civilisation, which in that case, and which in the case of most of these tribes, means the introduction of drunkenness and disease, in this instance of cholera, for we know what has been the condition of those countries which lie in the triangle between Cashmere, Kabul, and Badakhshan, and to which I first gave the name of Dardistan in 1866.

Now, what does this language show us? There the ordinary methods proved entirely at fault. If one pointed to an object, quite apart from the ordinary difficulties of misapprehension, the man appealed to, for instance, might say "your finger," if a finger were the thing of which he thought you wanted the name. If not satisfied with the name given in response, and you turned to somebody else, another name was obtained; and if you turned to a third person, you got a third name.

What was the reason for these differences? It was this, that the language had not emerged from the state in which it is impossible to have such a word as "head," as distinguished from "my head," or "thy head," or "his head"; for instance, *ak* is "my name," and *ik* is "his name." Take away the pronominal sign, and you are left with *k*, which means nothing. *Aus* is "my wife," and *gus* "thy wife." The *s* alone has no meaning, and, in some cases, it seemed impossible to arrive at putting anything down correctly; but so it is in the initial stage of a language. In the Hunza language under discussion, that stage is important to us as members of the Aryan group, as the dissociation of the pronoun, verb, adverb and conjunction from the act or substance only occurs when the language emerges beyond the stage when the groping, as it were, of the human child between the *meum* and *tuum*, the first and second persons, approaches the clear perception of the outer world, the "*suum*," the third person. Now, during the twenty years referred to "his" (house), "his" (name), and "his" (head) are beginning to take the place of "house," "name," "head," generally, in not quite a decided manner, but still they are taking their place. When I subsequently talked to the Hunzas, and tried to find a reason for that "idiom," if one may use the term, it seemed very clear and convincing when they said, "How is it possible for 'a wife' to exist unless she is somebody's wife?" "You cannot say, for instance, if you dissociate the one from the other, 'her wife,' or 'his husband.' 'Head,' by itself, does not exist; it must be somebody's head." When, again, you dissociate the sound which stands for the action or substance from the pronoun, you come, in a certain group of words, to another range of thought connected with the primary family relation, and showing the existence of that particularly ancient form of endogamy, in which all the elder females are the mothers and all the elder men are the fathers of the tribe. For instance, take a word like "mother;" "m" would mean the female principle, "o" would be the self, and the *ther* would mean "the tribe;" in other words, "mother" would mean: "the female that bore me and that belongs to my tribe." Now, fanciful as this may appear to us, it is the simple fact as regards the Hunza language, which, when put the test of analysis, will throw an incredible light on the history of Aryan words. For instance, taking Sanskrit as a typical language, you will, I believe, find how the early relations grew, and you will get beyond the root into the parts of which the root is made up; each of which has a meaning, not in one or two instances, but in most. I am not going to read you the volume which I am preparing for the Indian Government, and which is only the first part of the analysis with regard to this language, and only a very small portion indeed of the material that I collected in 1866, 1872, and 1884 regarding that important part of the world, Dardistan, which is now being drawn within the range of practical Indian politics—a region situated between the Hindukush and Kaghan (lat. 37° N. and long. 73° E to lat. 35° N. and long. 74·3° E.) and comprising monarchies and republics, including a small republic of eleven houses—a region which contains the solution of numerous linguistic and ethnographical problems, the cradle of the Aryan race, inhabited by the most varied tribes, from which region I brought the first Hunza and the first Káfir that ever visited England, and of which region one of its bigger Chiefs, owing to my sympathy with the people, invested me with a kind of titular governorship. In that comparatively small area the questions that are to be solved are great, and it is even now in some parts, perhaps, as hazardous a journey as, say, through the dark continent. Whether you get to the ancient Robber's Seat of Hunza, where the right of plundering is hereditary, or into the recesses of Kafiristan or the fastnesses of Pakhtu settlers; whether you proceed to the republics of Darel, Tangir or Chilás, or proceed to the community where women are sometimes at the head of affairs, and which is neither worse nor better than others, an amount of information, especially ethnographic, is within one's reach which makes Dardistan a region that would reward a number of explorers. I may say, in my own instance, if my life is spared for ten years longer, all I could do would be to bring out the mere material in my possession in a rough form, leaving the theories thereon to be elaborated by others. My difficulties were great, but my reward has been in a mass of material, for the elaboration of which International, Oriental, and other Congresses and learned societies have petitioned Government since 1866. My official duties have hitherto prevented my addressing myself to the congenial task of elaborating the material in conjunction with others. In 1886, I was, however, put for a few months on special duty in connexion with the Hunza language, at the very time that Colonel Lockhart was traversing a portion of Dardistan. But I think you will be more interested if, beyond personal observations, I tell you something about that little country of Hunza itself, which in many respects differs from those surrounding it, not only in regard to its peculiar language, which I have mentioned, but in other respects also. Unfortunately, it is also unlike the surrounding districts, in being characterised by customs the absence of some of which would be desirable. The Hunzas are nominal Muhammedans, and they use their mosques for drinking and dancing assemblies. Women are as free as air. There is little restriction in the relation of the sexes, and the management of the State, in theory, is attributed to fairies. No war is undertaken unless the fairy (whom, by the way, one is not allowed to see) gives the command by beating the sacred drum. The witches, who get into an ecstatic state, are the journalists, historians, and prophetesses of the tribe. They tell you what goes on in the surrounding valleys. They represent, as it were, the local *Times;* they tell you the past glories, such as they are, of raids and murders by their tribe; and when the *Tham* or ruler, who is supposed to be heaven-born (there being some mystery about the origin of his dynasty), does wrong, the only one who will dare to tell him the truth is the Dayal, or the witch who prophesies the future, and takes the opportunity of telling the Rajah that, unless he behaves in a manner worthy of his origin, he will come to grief! This is not a common form of popular representation to be met with, say, in India. Grimm's fairy-tales sometimes seem to be translated into practice in Hunza-land, which offers material for discussion alike to those who search for the Huns and to those who search for the very different Honas.

Then with regard to religion, as I said before, though nominally Muhammedan, they are really deniers of all the important precepts of true Muhammedanism, which is opposed to drunkenness, introduces a real brotherhood, and enjoins great cleanliness as absolutely necessary before the spiritual purification by prayer can take place. The people are mostly Muláis, but inferior in piety (?) to those of Zébak, Shignán, Wakhan, and other places. Now, what is that sect? It is represented by His Highness Prince Aga Khan, of Bombay, a person who is not half aware of his importance in those regions, where, till very recently, men were murdered as soon as looked at. One who acknowledges him or has brought some of the water with which he has washed his feet, would always be able to pass through those regions perfectly unharmed! I found my disguise as a Bokhara Mullah in 1866 to be quite useless, as a protection at Gilgit, whence men were kidnapped to be exchanged for a good hunting dog, but in Hunza they used to fill prisoners with gunpowder, and blow them up for general amusement. His Highness, who is much given to horse-racing, confines his spiritual administration to the collection of taxes throughout Central Asia from his followers or believers, and the believers themselves represent what is still left of the doctrine of the Sheik-ul-Jabl or the Ancient of the Mountain, the head of the so-called Assassins, a connexion of the Mahdi, if he was the Mahdi, or the supposed Mahdi in the Soudan. I consider he was not the Mahdi as foretold in Muhammedan tradition; but, be that as it may, the 7th Imám of the Shiahs has given rise to the sects both of the Druses in the Lebanon and to the Hunzas on the Pamir. They are the existing Ismailians, who, centuries ago, under the influence of *Hashish*, the Indian hemp, committed crimes throughout Christendom, and were the terror of Knight-Templars, as "Hashîshîn," corrupted into "Assassins."

Now, I have been fortunate enough, owing to my friendship with the head of their tribe, to obtain some portions of the Kelám-i-pîr volume, which takes the place, really, of the Korán, and of which I have got a portion here. I thought it might not be unworthy of your society to bring this to your knowledge, as a very interesting remnant which throws, *inter alia*, considerable light not only on their doctrine, but also on the Crusades. By a similar favour, I have had the opportunity of hearing the Mitháq, or covenant of the Druses, and that covenant of the Druses is a kind of prayer they offer up to God, not only in connexion with the Old Man of the Mountain, the head of the assassins who began about 1022, but also with those mysterious rites which also take place in what I may call the fairy-land of Hunza. With regard to the covenants, or one of them, which the "U'qelá" or the "initiated" or "wise," as distinguished from the "Juhelá" or "ignorant" "laity," among the Druses, offer up every night, this was used by a so-called educated Druse, one who had been converted to Protestantism,—a very good thing; but, as often happens, with that denationalisation which renders his conversion useless as a means for the promotion of any religion, as there are no indigenous elements for its growth. Such a convert is often unable to obtain a knowledge of the practices of his still unconverted countrymen, as nobody can be looked upon with greater distrust than that native of a country who has unlearnt to think in his own language, and who cannot acquire a foreign language with its associations, which are part of the history of that language; he does not become an Englishman with English associations, but ceases to be a good native with his own indigenous associations. Therefore, in my humble opinion, of all the unfortunate specimens of mankind, the most degraded are those who, under the guise of being Europeanised and, therefore, reformers, have themselves the greatest necessity for reform. Their mind has become completely unhinged, thereby showing us that if we Europeans wish to do good among Orientals we can do so best by living good lives in the midst of professors of other religions, this being also in accordance with the 13th edict of Asoka.

This Druse covenant makes the mad Fatimite ruler of Egypt, Hákim, the "Lord of the Universe." As I said before, the present "Lord of the Universe" for the Hunzas is the lineal descendant of the 7th Imám, a resident of Bombay, one to whom the Muláis make pilgrimages, instead of going to Mecca or to Kerbelá. You may imagine that, even as regards the Druses, there must be something higher than *their* "Lord of the Universe;" but, such as he is, it is with him that this covenant is made. Reverting to his living colleague, the Indian "Lord," it may be stated that there are men scattered throughout India of whose influence we have only the faintest conception. I pointed out in 1866 that if any one wanted to follow successfully my footsteps is Dardistan, he would have to get recommendations from His Highness Aga Khan of Bombay, and I am glad to say that Col. Lockhart has taken advantage of that recommendation. The Druse "Lord of the Universe" is regarded as one with whom nothing can be compared. The Druses are to render him the most implicit obedience, and to carry out his behests at the loss of everything, good name, wealth, and life, with the view of obtaining the favour of one who may be taken to be God; but the sentence is so constructed as to make him, if not God, only second to God; in other words, only just a discrimination between God as the distant ruler of the Universe and, perhaps, some lineal descendant of Hákim, or rather, Hákim himself as an ever-living being, as the ruler of *this* world. This and some other prayers, with some songs, one amongst which breathes the greatest hatred to Muhammedanism, and speaks of the destruction of Mecca as something to look forward to, seem to be deserving of study. There are also references in them to rites.

connected with Abraham. A full translation of these documents, compared with invocations in portions of the Korán, would, indeed, reward the attention of the student.

I will now again revert from the Druses of the Lebanon to the Mulάis in the Himalayas. I obtained the poem in my hand from the head of that sect, and the wording is such that it denies whilst affirming the immortality and transmigration of souls. It says, "It is no use telling the ignorant multitude what your faith is." That is very much like what Lord Beaconsfield said—that all thinking men were of one religion, but they would not tell of what religion!—a wrong sentiment, but one that is embodied in the above poem. "Tell them," continues the poem in effect, "if they want to know, in an answer of wisdom to a question of folly: 'if your life has been bad you will descend into the stone, the vegetable, or the animal; if your life has been good you will return as a better man. The chain of life is undivided. The animal that is sacrificed proceeds to a higher life.' You cannot discriminate and yet deny individual life, and apportion that air, stone, or plant, to the animal and to man, but you ought to be punished for saying this to others!" And on this principle, at any rate, the Druses also act or acted, that that is no crime which is not found out; and a good many people, I am sorry to say, elsewhere, think much the same; whereas in Hunza they have gone beyond that stage, and care extremely little about their crimes being found out. The Mitháq and other religious utterances of the Druses and the Kelám-i-Pír of the Hunzas, if published together, with certain new information which we have regarding the Crusade of Richard Cœur-de-Lion, would, I think, were time given and the matter elaborated, indeed deserve the attention of the readers of the "Transactions." It also seems strange that where such customs exist there should be a prize for virtue, but there is one in Hunza for wives who have remained faithful to their husbands, something like the French prize for *rosières*.

Formerly Suttee was practised, but Suttee had rather the meaning of Sáthi or companion, as both husband and wife went to the funeral pyre. Prizes are similarly given to wives who have not quarrelled for, say, a certain number of years with their husbands. The most curious custom which seems to permeate these countries is to foster relationship in nursing, where a nurse and all her relations come not only within the prohibited degrees, which is against the spirit of Muhammedanism, but also create the only real bond of true attachment that I have seen in Dardistan, where other relatives seemed always engaged in murdering one another.

Nearly all the chiefs in Dardistan give their children to persons of low degree to nurse, and these and the children of the nurse become attached to them throughout life and are their only friends. But this foster-relationship is also taken in order to get rid of the consequences, say, of crime; for instance, in the case of adultery, or supposed adultery, the suspected person who declares that he enters into the relationship of a son to the woman with whom he is suspected, after a certain penalty, is really accepted in that position, and the trust is in no case betrayed. It is the only kind of forgiveness which is given in Dardistan generally to that sort of transgression; but, further than that, drinking milk with some one, or appointing some one as foster-father, which is done by crossing two vases of milk, creates the same relationship, except amongst the noble caste of Shins, who were expelled by the Brahmins from India or Kashmir, and who hold the cow in abhorence as one of their religious dogmas, whereas, in other ways, they are really Brahmins, among whom we find Hinduism peeping out through the thin crust of Muhammedanism.

The subject of caste, by the way, is also one which is generally misunderstood, and which, if developed on Christian lines, would give us the perfection of human society, and solve many of the problems with which we are dealing in Europe in more advanced civilisations. I have just read with concern some remarks against caste by Sir John Petheram, who has been in India some three or four years. I think that before people speak on subjects of such intricacy, they should take the position of students of the question, learn at least one of the classical and one of the vernacular languages of India, and then alone assume the role of teachers whilst continuing to be learners; even in regard to such subjects of infant-marriage and the prohibition of widow remarriage, there is a side of the question which has not yet been put sufficientlv before the British public. Infant-marriage, when properly carried out in the higher castes, is an adoption of the girl into the family where she and the husband grow up together and join in prayer in common, which is necessary for their respective salvation; there is much to learn in the way of tenderness, charity, and love, from some of the households in India, where we find a community constituted on the noblest principles of "the joint family," with an admirable and economical subdivision of labour, which enables them to live for a mere trifle, and yet so to prepare their food that in every dish you can see the tender care of the woman who prepares it for the good of the husband and of the household.

Then, as to the widow re-marriage, it has not been sufficiently pointed out to the British public that spiritual marriage renders the re-marriage of the Hindu widow impossible, because she is necessary for the spiritual salvation of the husband, and because as the representative of his property she may be called on to be the head of the family, for many of them *are* at the head of the family, and their position, therefore, renders it simply impossible for them to re-marry. These are matters that we should treat with respect, especially if we seek to adapt them to the spirit of the age. There are also differences amongst Muhammedans as great as there are between a Christian who tries to follow the Sermon on the Mount and a nominal Christian. Science and religion, according to a Muhammedan saying, are twins, and if I understand the object of this Society, it is in order to make this twinship (if I may be allowed to use the expression) more real that your labours have been initiated, and that, under Providence, they have been carried to the successful results that have followed them both here and abroad.